Brooklands
Books

AF324688

SUZUKI S.J

Gold Portfolio

1971-1997

Compiled by
R.M.Clarke

ISBN 1 85520 4703

BROOKLANDS BOOKS LTD.
P.O. BOX 146, COBHAM,
SURREY, KT11 1LG. UK

A-SZSJGP

Printed in Hong Kong

Brooklands
Books

MOTORING

BROOKLANDS ROAD TEST SERIES

Abarth Gold Portfolio 1950-1971
AC Ace & Aceca 1953-1983
Alfa Romeo Giulietta Gold Portfolio 1954-1965
Alfa Romeo Giulia Coupés 1963-1976
Alfa Romeo Giulia Coupés Gold Port. 1963-1976
Alfa Romeo Spider 1966-1990
Alfa Romeo Spider Gold Portfolio 1966-1991
Alfa Romeo Alfasud 1972-1984
Alfa Romeo Alfetta Gold Portfolio 1972-1987
Alfa Romeo Alfetta GTV6 1980-1986
Allard Gold Portfolio 1937-1959
Alvis Gold Portfolio 1919-1967
AMX & Javelin Muscle Portfolio 1968-1974
Armstrong Siddeley Gold Portfolio 1945-1960
Aston Martin Gold Portfolio 1948-1971
Aston Martin Gold Portfolio 1972-1985
Aston Martin Gold Portfolio 1985-1995
Audi Quattro Gold Portfolio 1980-1991
Austin A30 & A35 1951-1962
Austin Healey 100 & 100/6 Gold Portfolio 1952-1959
Austin Healey 3000 Gold Portfolio 1959-1967
Austin Healey Sprite Gold Portfolio 1958-1971
BMW 6 & 8 Cyl. Cars Limited Edition 1935-1960
BMW 1600 Collection No.1 1966-1981
BMW 2002 Gold Portfolio 1968-1976
BMW 6 Cylinder Coupés & Saloons Gold P. 1969-1976
BMW 316, 318, 320 (4 cyl.) Gold Port. 1975-1990
BMW 320, 323, 325 (6 cyl.) Gold Port. 1977-1990
BMW M Series Gold Portfolio 1976-1997
BMW 5 Series Gold Portfolio 1981-1987
BMW 6 Series Gold Portfolio 1976-1989
Bricklin Gold Portfolio 1974-1975
Bristol Cars Gold Portfolio 1946-1992
Buick Automobiles 1947-1960
Buick Muscle Cars 1965-1970
Cadillac Allanté 1986-1993
Cadillac Automobiles 1949-1959
Cadillac Automobiles 1960-1969
Checker Limited Edition
Chevrolet 1955-1957
Impala & SS Muscle Portfolio 1958-1972
Corvair Performance Portfolio 1959-1969
El Camino & SS Muscle Portfolio 1959-1987
Chevy II & Nova SS Muscle Portfolio 1962-1974
Chevelle & SS Muscle Portfolio 1964-1972
Caprice Limited Edition 1965-1976
Chevrolet Muscle Cars 1966-1971
Chevy Blazer 1969-1981
Camaro Muscle Portfolio 1967-1973
Chevrolet Camaro & Z-28 1973-1981
High Performance Camaros 1982-1988
Chevrolet Corvette Gold Portfolio 1953-1962
Chevrolet Corvette Sting Ray Gold Port. 1963-1967
Chevrolet Corvette 1968-1977
High Performance Corvettes 1983-1989
Chrysler 300 Gold Portfolio 1955-1970
Imperial Limited Edition 1955-1970
Valiant 1960-1962
Citroen Traction Avant Gold Portfolio 1934-1957
Citroen 2CV Gold Portfolio 1948-1989
Citroen DS & ID 1955-1975
Citroen DS & ID Gold Portfolio 1955-1975
Citroen SM 1970-1975
Cobras & Replicas 1962-1983
Shelby Cobra Gold Portfolio 1962-1969
Cobras & Cobra Replicas Gold Portfolio 1962-1989
Crosley & Crosley Specials Limited Edition
Cunningham Automobiles 1951-1955
Daimler SP250 Sports & V-8 250 Saloon Gold P. 1959-1969
Datsun Roadsters 1962-1971
Datsun 240Z & 260Z Gold Portfolio 1970-1978
Datsun 280Z & ZX 1975-1983
DeLorean Gold Portfolio 1977-1995
De Soto Limited Edition 1952-1960
Charger Muscle Cars 1966-1974
Dodge Muscle Cars 1967-1970
Dodge Viper Muscle Portfolio 1990-1998
ERA Gold Portfolio 1934-1994
Excalibur Collection No.1 1952-1981
Facel Vega 1954-1964
Ferrari Limited Edition 1947-1957
Ferrari Limited Edition 1958-1963
Ferrari Dino 1965-1974
Ferrari Dino 308 & Mondial Gold Portfolio 1974-1985
Ferrari 328 348 Mondial Gold Portfolio 1986-1994
Fiat 500 Gold Portfolio 1936-1972
Fiat 600 & 850 Gold Portfolio 1955-1972
Fiat Pininfarina 124 & 2000 Spider 1968-1985
Fiat X1/9 Gold Portfolio 1973-1989
Fiat Abarth Performance Portfolio 1972-1987
Ford Consul, Zephyr, Zodiac Mk. I & II 1950-1962
Ford Zephyr, Zodiac, Executive Mk. III & IV 1962-1971
Ford Cortina 1600E & GT 1967-1970
High Performance Capris Gold Portfolio 1969-1987
Capri Muscle Portfolio 1974-1987
High Performance Fiestas 1979-1991
High Performance Escorts Mk. I 1968-1974
High Performance Escorts Mk. II 1975-1980
High Performance Escorts 1980-1985
High Performance Escorts 1985-1990
High Perf. Sierras & Merkurs Gold Portfolio 1983-1990
Ford Automobiles 1949-1959
Ford Fairlane Performance Portfolio 1955-1970
Ford Ranchero Performance Portfolio 1957-1979
Edsel Limited Edition 1957-1960
Falcon Performance Portfolio 1960-1970
Ford Galaxie & LTD Limited Edition 1960-1973
Ford Thunderbird 1955-1957
Ford Thunderbird 1958-1963
Ford GT40 Gold Portfolio 1964-1987
Ford Torino Limited Edition 1968-1974
Ford Bronco 1966-1977
Ford Bronco 1978-1988
Goggomobil Limited Edition
Holden 1948-1962
Honda CRX 1983-1987
Hudson Limited Edition 1946-1957
International Scout Gold Portfolio 1961-1980
Isetta Gold Portfolio 1953-1964

ISO & Bizzarrini Gold Portfolio 1962-1974
Jaguar and SS Gold Portfolio
Jaguar C-Type & D-Type Gold Portfolio 1951-1960
Jaguar XK120, 140, 150 Gold Portfolio 1948-1960
Jaguar Mk. VII, VIII, IX, X, 420 Gold Port. 1950-1970
Jaguar Mk. 1 & Mk. 2 Gold Portfolio 1959-1969
Jaguar E-Type Gold Portfolio 1961-1971
Jaguar E-Type V-12 1971-1975
Jaguar S-Type & 420 Limited Edition
Jaguar XJ12, XJ5.3, V12 Gold Portfolio 1972-1990
Jaguar XJ6 Series I & II Gold Portfolio 1968-1979
Jaguar XJ6 Series III Perf. Portfolio 1979-1986
Jaguar XJ6 Gold Portfolio 1986-1994
Jaguar XJS Gold Portfolio 1975-1988
Jaguar XJS Gold Portfolio 1988-1995
Jaguar XK8 Limited Edition
Jeep CJ5 & CJ6 1960-1976
Jeep CJ5 & CJ7 1976-1986
Jensen Interceptor Gold Portfolio 1966-1986
Jensen Healey 1972-1976
Kaiser - Frazer Limited Edition 1946-1955
Lagonda Gold Portfolio 1919-1964
Lancia Aurelia & Flaminia Gold Portfolio 1950-1970
Lancia Fulvia Gold Portfolio 1963-1976
Lancia Beta Gold Portfolio 1972-1984
Lancia Delta Gold Portfolio 1979-1994
Lancia Stratos 1972-1985
Land Rover Series I 1948-1958
Land Rover Series II & IIa 1958-1971
Land Rover 90 110 Defender Gold Portfolio 1983-1994
Land Rover Discovery 1989-1994
Land Rover Story Part One 1948-1971
Fifty Years of Selling Land Rover
Lincoln Gold Portfolio 1949-1960
Lincoln Continental 1961-1969
Lincoln Continental 1969-1976
Lotus Sports Racers Gold Portfolio 1953-1965
Lotus Seven Gold Portfolio 1957-1973
Lotus Caterham Seven Gold Portfolio 1974-1995
Lotus Elan Gold Portfolio 1962-1974
Lotus Elan Collection No. 2 1963-1972
Lotus Elan & SE 1989-1992
Lotus Europa Gold Portfolio 1966-1975
Lotus Elite & Eclat 1974-1982
Lotus Turbo Esprit 1980-1986
Marcos Coupés & Spyders Gold Portfolio 1960-1997
Maserati 1965-1970
Matra Limited Edition 1965-1983
Mazda Miata MX-5 Performance Portfolio 1989-1996
Mazda RX-7 Gold Portfolio 1978-1991
McLaren F1 Sportscar Limited Edition
Mercedes 190 & 300 SL 1954-1963
Mercedes G-Wagen 1981-1994
Mercedes S & 600 1965-1972
Mercedes S Class 1972-1979
Mercedes 230 • 250 • 280SL Gold Portfolio 1963-1971
Mercedes SLs & SLCs Gold Portfolio 1971-1989
Mercedes SLs Performance Portfolio 1989-1994
Mercury Limited Edition 1947-59
Mercury Comet & Cyclone Limited Edition 1960-1970
Mercury Muscle Cars 1966-1971
Cougar Limited Edition 1967-1973
Messerschmitt Gold Portfolio 1954-1964
MG Mini Marque Portfolio 1929-1939
MG TA & TC Gold Portfolio 1936-1949
MG TD & TF Gold Portfolio 1949-1955
MGA & Twin Cam Gold Portfolio 1955-1962
MG Midget Gold Portfolio 1961-1979
MGB Roadsters 1962-1980
MGB MGC & V8 Gold Portfolio 1962-1980
MGB GT 1965-1980
MGC & MGB GT V8 Limited Edition
MG Y-Type & Magnette ZA/ZB Limited Edition
Mini Gold Portfolio 1959-1969
Mini Gold Portfolio 1969-1980
Mini Gold Portfolio 1981-1997
High Performance Minis Gold Portfolio 1960-1973
Mini Cooper Gold Portfolio 1961-1971
Mini Moke Gold Portfolio 1964-1994
Morgan Three-Wheeler Gold Portfolio 1910-1952
Morgan Plus 4 & Four 4 Gold Portfolio 1936-1967
Morgan Cars Gold Portfolio 1968-1989
Morris Minor Collection No. 1 1948-1980
Shelby Mustang Muscle Portfolio 1965-1970
High Performance Mustang IIs 1974-1978
High Performance Mustangs 1982-1988
Nash & Nash-Healey Limited Edition 1949-1957
Nash-Austin Metropolitan Gold Portfolio 1954-1962
Oldsmobile Automobiles 1955-1963
Oldsmobile Muscle Portfolio 1964-1971
Cutlass & 4-4-2 Muscle Portfolio 1964-1974
Oldsmobile Toronado 1966-1978
Opel GT Gold Portfolio 1968-1973
Opel Manta Limited Edition 1970-1975
Packard Gold Portfolio 1946-1958
Pantera Gold Portfolio 1970-1989
Panther Gold Portfolio 1972-1990
Barracuda Muscle Portfolio 1964-1974
Pontiac Tempest & GTO 1961-1965
GTO Muscle Portfolio 1964-1974
Firebird & Trans-Am Muscle Portfolio 1967-1972
Firebird & Trans-Am Muscle Portfolio 1973-1981
High Performance Firebirds 1982-1988
Pontiac Limited Edition 1949-60
Pontiac Fiero 1984-1988
Porsche 356 Gold Portfolio 1953-1965
Porsche 912 Limited Edition
Porsche 911 1965-1969
Porsche 911 1970-1972
Porsche 911 1973-1977
Porsche 911 SC & Turbo Gold Portfolio 1978-1983
Porsche 911 Carrera & Turbo Gold Port. 1984-1989
Porsche 911 Gold Portfolio 1990-1997
Porsche 924 Gold Portfolio 1975-1988
Porsche 928 Performance Portfolio 1977-1994
Porsche 944 Gold Portfolio 1981-1991
Porsche 968 Limited Edition
Range Rover Gold Portfolio 1970-1985
Range Rover Gold Portfolio 1986-1995
Reliant Scimitar 1964-1986
Renault Alpine Gold Portfolio 1958-1994
Riley Gold Portfolio 1924-1939
R.R. Silver Cloud & Bentley 'S' Series Gold P. 1955-1965

Rolls Royce Silver Shadow Gold Portfolio 1965-1980
Rolls Royce & Bentley Gold Portfolio 1980-1989
Rolls Royce & Bentley Limited Edition 1990-1997
Rover P4 1949-1959
Rover 3 & 3.5 Litre Gold Portfolio 1958-1973
Rover 2000 & 2200 1963-1977
Rover 3500 & Vitesse 1976-1986
Saab Sonett Collection No.1 1966-1974
Saab Turbo 1976-1983
Studebaker Gold Portfolio 1947-1966
Studebaker Hawks & Larks 1956-1963
Suzuki SJ Gold Portfolio 1971-1997
Vitara, Sidekick & Geo Tracker Perf. Port. 1988-1997
Avanti 1962-1990
Sunbeam Tiger & Alpine Gold Portfolio 1959-1967
Toyota Land Cruiser Gold Portfolio 1956-1987
Toyota Land Cruiser 1988-1997
Toyota MR2 Gold Portfolio 1984-1997
Triumph Dolomite Sprint Limited Edition
Triumph TR2 & TR3 Gold Portfolio 1952-1961
Triumph TR4, TR5, TR250 1961-1968
Triumph TR6 Gold Portfolio 1969-1976
Triumph TR7 & TR8 Gold Portfolio 1975-1982
Triumph Herald 1959-1971
Triumph Vitesse 1962-1971
Triumph Spitfire Gold Portfolio 1962-1980
Triumph 2000, 2.5, 2500 1963-1977
Triumph GT6 Gold Portfolio 1966-1974
Triumph Stag Gold Portfolio 1970-1977
TVR Gold Portfolio 1959-1986
TVR Performance Portfolio 1986-1994
VW Beetle Gold Portfolio 1935-1967
VW Beetle Gold Portfolio 1968-1991
VW Beetle Collection No.1 1970-1982
VW Karmann Ghia 1955-1982
VW Bus, Camper, Van 1954-1967
VW Bus, Camper, Van 1968-1979
VW Bus, Camper, Van 1979-1989
VW Scirocco 1974-1981
VW Golf GTI 1976-1986
Volvo PV444 & PV544 1945-1965
Volvo Amazon-120 Gold Portfolio 1956-1970
Volvo 1800 Gold Portfolio 1960-1973
Volvo 140 & 160 Series Gold Portfolio 1966-1975
Forty Years of Selling Volvo
Westfield Limited Edition

BROOKLANDS *ROAD & TRACK* SERIES

Road & Track on Alfa Romeo 1964-1970
Road & Track on Alfa Romeo 1971-1976
Road & Track on Alfa Romeo 1977-1989
Road & Track on Aston Martin 1962-1990
R & T on Auburn Cord and Duesenburg 1952-84
Road & Track on Audi & Auto Union 1952-1980
Road & Track on Audi & Auto Union 1980-1986
Road & Track on Austin Healey 1953-1970
Road & Track on BMW Cars 1966-1974
Road & Track on BMW Cars 1975-1978
Road & Track on BMW Cars 1979-1983
R & T on Cobra, Shelby & Ford GT40 1962-1992
Road & Track on Corvette 1953-1967
Road & Track on Corvette 1968-1982
Road & Track on Corvette 1982-1986
Road & Track on Corvette 1986-1990
Road & Track on Ferrari 1975-1981
Road & Track on Ferrari 1981-1984
Road & Track on Ferrari 1984-1988
Road & Track on Fiat Sports Cars 1968-1987
Road & Track on Jaguar 1950-1960
Road & Track on Jaguar 1961-1968
Road & Track on Jaguar 1968-1974
Road & Track on Jaguar 1974-1982
Road & Track on Jaguar 1983-1989
Road & Track on Lamborghini 1964-1985
Road & Track on Lotus 1972-1983
R & T on Mazda RX-7 & MX-5 Miata 1986-1991
Road & Track on Mercedes 1952-1962
Road & Track on Mercedes 1963-1970
Road & Track on Mercedes 1971-1979
Road & Track on Mercedes 1980-1987
Road & Track on MG Sports Cars 1949-1961
Road & Track on MG Sports Cars 1962-1980
R & T on Nissan 300-ZX & Turbo 1984-1989
Road & Track on Pontiac 1960-1983
Road & Track on Porsche 1951-1967
Road & Track on Porsche 1968-1971
Road & Track on Porsche 1972-1975
Road & Track on Porsche 1975-1978
Road & Track on Porsche 1979-1982
Road & Track on Porsche 1985-1988
R & T on Rolls Royce & Bentley 1950-1965
R & T on Rolls Royce & Bentley 1966-1984
Road & Track on Saab 1972-1992
R & T on Toyota Sports & GT Cars 1966-1984
R & T on Triumph Sports Cars 1953-1967
R & T on Triumph Sports Cars 1967-1974
R & T on Triumph Sports Cars 1974-1982
Road & Track on Volkswagen 1951-1968
Road & Track on Volkswagen 1968-1978
Road & Track on Volkswagen 1978-1985
Road & Track on Volvo 1957-1974
Road & Track on Volvo 1977-1994
R & T - Henry Manney at Large & Abroad
R & T - Peter Egan's "Side Glances"
R & T - Peter Egan "At Large"

BROOKLANDS *CAR AND DRIVER* SERIES

Car and Driver on BMW 1955-1977
Car and Driver on Corvette 1978-1982
Car and Driver on Corvette 1983-1988
C and D on Datsun Z 1600 & 2000 1966-1984
Car and Driver on Ferrari 1955-1962
Car and Driver on Ferrari 1963-1975
Car and Driver on Ferrari 1976-1983
Car and Driver on Mopar 1956-1967
Car and Driver on Mopar 1968-1975
Car and Driver on Mustang 1964-1972
Car and Driver on Pontiac 1961-1975
Car and Driver on Porsche 1955-1962
Car and Driver on Porsche 1963-1970
Car and Driver on Porsche 1970-1976
Car and Driver on Porsche 1977-1981
Car and Driver on Porsche 1982-1986
Car and Driver on Volvo 1955-1986

RACING

Le Mans - The Bentley & Alfa Years - 1923-1939
Le Mans - The Jaguar Years - 1949-1957
Le Mans - The Ferrari Years - 1958-1965
Le Mans - The Ford & Matra Years - 1966-1974
Le Mans - The Porsche Years - 1975-1982
Mille Miglia - The Alfa & Ferrari Years - 1927-1951
Mille Miglia - The Ferrari & Mercedes Years - 1952-57

A COMPREHENSIVE GUIDE

BMW 2002

BROOKLANDS *PRACTICAL CLASSICS* SERIES

PC on Austin A40 Restoration
PC on Land Rover Restoration
PC on Metalworking in Restoration
PC on Midget/Sprite Restoration
PC on MGB Restoration
PC on Sunbeam Rapier Restoration
PC on Triumph Herald/Vitesse
PC on Spitfire Restoration

BROOKLANDS *HOT ROD* 'MUSCLECAR & HI-PO ENGINES' SERIES

Chevy 265 & 283
Chevy 302 & 327
Chevy 348 & 409
Chevy 350 & 400
Chevy 396 & 427
Chevy 454 thru 512
Chrysler Hemi
Chrysler 273, 318, 340 & 360
Chrysler 361, 383, 400, 413, 426, 440
Ford 289, 302, Boss 302 & 351W
Ford 351C & Boss 351
Ford Big Block

BROOKLANDS RESTORATION SERIES

Auto Restoration Tips & Techniques
Basic Bodywork Tips & Techniques
BMW 2002 Restoration Guide
Classic Camaro Restoration
Chevrolet High Performance Tips & Techniques
Chevy Engine Swapping Tips & Techniques
Chevy-GMC Pickup Repair
Chrysler Engine Swapping Tips & Techniques
Engine Swapping Tips & Techniques
Ford Pickup Repair
Land Rover Restoration Tips & Techniques
MG 'T' Series Restoration Guide
MGA Restoration Guide
Mustang Restoration Tips & Techniques

MOTORCYCLING

BROOKLANDS ROAD TEST SERIES

AJS & Matchless Gold Portfolio 1945-1966
BMW Motorcycles Gold Portfolio 1950-1971
BMW Motorcycles Gold Portfolio 1971-1976
BSA Singles Gold Portfolio 1945-1963
BSA Singles Gold Portfolio 1964-1974
BSA Twins A7 & A10 Gold Portfolio 1946-1962
BSA Twins A50 & A65 Gold Portfolio 1962-1973
BSA A Triumph Triples Gold Portfolio 1968-1976
Ducati Gold Portfolio 1960-1973
Ducati Gold Portfolio 1974-1978
Ducati Gold Portfolio 1978-1982
Honda CB 750 Gold Portfolio 1969-1978
Laverda Gold Portfolio 1967-1977
Moto Guzzi Gold Portfolio 1949-1973
Norton Commando Gold Portfolio 1968-1977
Triumph Bonneville Gold Portfolio 1959-1983
Vincent Gold Portfolio 1945-1980

BROOKLANDS *CYCLE WORLD* SERIES

Cycle World on BMW 1974-1980
Cycle World on BMW 1981-1986
Cycle World on Ducati 1982-1991
Cycle World on Harley-Davidson 1962-1968
Cycle World on Harley-Davidson 1978-1983
Cycle World on Harley-Davidson 1983-1987
Cycle World on Harley-Davidson 1987-1990
Cycle World on Harley-Davidson 1990-1992
Cycle World on Honda 1962-1967
Cycle World on Honda 1968-1971
Cycle World on Honda 1971-1974
Cycle World on Husqvarna 1966-1976
Cycle World on Husqvarna 1977-1984
Cycle World on Kawasaki 1966-1971
Cycle World on Kawasaki Off-Road Bikes 1972-1979
Cycle World on Kawasaki Street Bikes 1972-1976
Cycle World on Norton 1962-1971
Cycle World on Suzuki 1962-1970
Cycle World on Suzuki Off-Road Bikes 1971-1976
Cycle World on Suzuki Street Bikes 1971-1976
Cycle World on Triumph 1967-1972
Cycle World on Yamaha 1962-1969
Cycle World on Yamaha Off-Road Bikes 1970-1974
Cycle World on Yamaha Street Bikes 1970-1974

MILITARY

BROOKLANDS MILITARY VEHICLES SERIES

Allied Military Vehicles No.2 1941-1946
Complete WW2 Military Jeep Manual
Dodge Military Vehicles No.1 1940-1945
Hail To The Jeep
Military & Civilian Amphibians 1940-1990
Off Road Jeeps: Civilian & Military 1944-1971
US Military Vehicles 1941-1945
US Army Military Vehicles WW2-TM9-2800
VW Kubelwagen Military Portfolio 1940-1990
WW2 Jeep Military Portfolio 1941-1945

26058

Brooklands
Books

CONTENTS

ACKNOWLEDGEMENTS

Recreational four-wheel drive vehicles, or sports-utilities, remain as popular as ever despite predictions a couple of years ago that the boom was over. Not a bit of it, as far as we can see - and even when the boom does end, the huge numbers of 4x4s out there will ensure that the subject remains of interest to enthusiasts for many years to come. In fact, it is enthusiast interest which has prompted us to search our archives and produce this latest volume, on one of the most popular of all sport-utilities, the Suzuki SJ.

As always, we are pleased to thank those magazines which have generously allowed us to reissue material they originally published. In the case of this book, our gratitude is extended to the publishers of *Autocar, Bushdriver, Car and Driver, Car South Africa, 4x4, 4 Wheel Drive, Four Wheeler, International Off-Roader, Motor, Motor Manual, Motor Trend, Off-Road, Off-Road Annual, Off-Road and Four-Wheel Drive, Overlander, Performance Tuning, PV4 Buyers' Guide Annual, Road and Track Buyers' Guide* and *Wheels*.

R.M. Clarke

Suzuki was a late entrant to the world of four-wheel drives. The company's first models were built at the beginning of the 1970's, and drew on proven micro-car technology to create a miniature 4x4 for markets in South-East Asia. To Western eyes, they appeared ludicrously underpowered and undersized, but before long it became apparent just how capable they really were. As the horizons of the Japanese car industry widened, so the little Suzukis began to appear in more and more Western countries - and wherever they appeared, they were a massive hit.

The real success story was that the SJ models, introduced in the early 1980s to replace the earlier LJs. To Western eyes, their cheeky appearance and fun-seeking nature gave them a very special appeal. On the road, their firm suspension and rather buzzy engines made them tiring to drive for long distances, but as chic urban runabouts with weekend off-road capabilities they were unbeatable.

Before long Suzuki found that they could not keep up with demand in Europe (where imports were of course restricted by the so-called "voluntary" agreements with Japanese manufactures). So an agreement was reached with Santana in Spain, who already had many years' experience assembling Land Rovers, and from the mid-1980's it was Spanish built Suzukis which were sold in European markets. Bigger engines and a fifth gear at the end of the decade were welcome if inevitable improvements, and there were even long-wheelbase derivatives to add to the SJ's versatility.

Limited editions and a vast array of accessories have all added to the appeal of these little 4x4s. Their off-road ability is not in doubt, and they have a long future in the enthusiast market. The articles in this book should persuade anyone who had doubts about the vehicles' charms that they really do have a lot to offer.

James Taylor

SUZUKI BRUTE

W E HADN'T ORIGINALLY intended to include the Suzuki Brute IV in this issue of *4wd Recreation Vehicles.* But it is a 4wd recreation vehicle, it is available to American buyers (at least in Southern California, Arizona and Nevada) and when the distributor offered to deliver one to us for test, how could we refuse? As we told each other, all magazines need a little comic relief and the Brute should at least be good for a few laughs. We were right, it was. And it was technically interesting as well.

First of all, what is it? The easiest description is to say that it's a miniature Jeep Universal. It's built on a 76-in. wheelbase, is 51 in. wide and only 117.9 in. long overall. So it is diminutive in all directions. It has absolutely typical 4wd design features—engine in the front, live axles on leaf springs at both ends—it's plain and it's rugged. It seems well put together and if you don't mind square corners, it's a cute little thing.

The engine is an aircooled 2-cylinder, 2-cycle of 360-cc (22-cu in.) displacement which puts out 32 horsepower at 6000 rpm. There is an oil tank under the hood and the oil is automatically mixed with gasoline from the tank for the 2-stroke engine. There's a 2-stage light on the dash to keep you in touch with the supply; when the center part glows, you've plenty of oil; when the whole thing comes on, the oil level is getting low. There's a 4-speed, all-synchromesh transmission and there is a high range and a low range set of gears in the transfer case.

Inside there are two bucket seats, the spare tire is bolted to the back of the passenger seat and the cargo area is covered with carpeting, as are the floorboards in front. In addition to the bare roadster, there is also a full fabric top with zip-up windows.

There's little optional equipment with the Brute. There are no free-running front hubs, no locking differentials and no fancy trim options. The standard tires are 6.00-16s and there is no overhanging sheet metal that would interfere with the optional wider tires of approximately the same diameter but you would need fenders with these to be street legal.

The basic west coast list price of the Brute IV is $2195 and in the same trim as our test model (soft top, electronic tachometer) it costs $2362.

Driving Impressions

Our test Brute had righthand drive, as do all the Brutes now being brought into the U.S., though a lefthand drive may be offered later. Personally, we don't mind righthand drive (both the editors are left handed) and except that it takes a while to get used to looking left instead of right for the rear view mirror, this created no problems. The small size of the Brute has something to do with this, of course, since you could still be in your own lane even if you forgot you were sitting on the wrong side of the car.

So you slip into the seat from the right side, fasten the fabric door with a turn-handle latch and there's a spring-loaded side bar that you can put up beside you. If the engine is cold you open the choke, then twist the key to activate the starter. Don't touch the accelerator until the engine is running or you will likely foul a plug. For a hot engine, just a twist of the key will do it.

The engine comes to life with all the familiar popping of a typical 2-stroke and soon settles down to idle with a noise something akin to a hard-working coffee percolator. It smooths out as you depress the accelerator but it is not a quiet engine under any circumstances and has a harsh note and lots of vibration even at an easy cruising speed.

The gearshift lever works smoothly but the H-pattern gate is very narrow, which results in an occasional visit to 4th gear when it was 2nd you wanted. The performance is very modest

4
WD
TEST
SUZUKI
ARCADIA—MONROVIA
Another New One
From
TRI-CITY MOTORS
MONROVIA
TRI-CITY MOTORS
TRI-CITY MOTORS

SUZUKI BRUTE

PRICES

Basic list, West Coast POE $2195

Standard equipment: 4wd, 32-hp engine, bucket seats, painted front bumper (no rear bumper).

Other prices for options are included in data below.

ENGINES

Standard engine: air cooled 2-cyl, 2-cycle
Bore x stroke, in 2.40x2.42
Displacement, cu in 360
Compression ratio 7.3:1
Bhp @ rpm . . . . 32 @ 6000
Torque @ rpm, lb-ft . . . . 27 @ 5000
Type fuel required . . . . regular
Air cleaner type . . . . dry

CHASSIS & BODY

Body/frame: ladder frame with separate steel body.

Brakes: 6.00x1.5-in. drums, front & rear.
Brake swept area 113
Power brakes . . . . .not available

Steering type . . . . ball & screw
Steering ratio 16.5:1
Turning circle, ft 28.8
Power steering . . . . .not available

Wheel size, std 16x4.0
Optional wheel size 15x8
Tire size, std 6pr 6.00x16
Optional tires: G70-15 (with optional wheels), $229.

Front axle capacity, lb . . . . .not available
Optional . . . . .none
Front spring rating, lb (at pad): not available.
Optional . . . . .none

Rear axle capacity . . . . .not available
Optional . . . . .none
Rear spring rating, lb (at pad): not available.
Optional . . . . .none
Additional suspension options: Bilstein competition shocks; front, $47; rear, $49.

ACCOMMODATION

Standard seats . . . . 2 buckets
Optional rear seat $40
Headroom, in 43
Pedal to seatback, max 33.5
Seat to ground 29.0
Heater & defroster . . . . .none
Tinted glass . . . . .not available
Air conditioning . . . . .not available
Load space (with seats in place), cu ft: 2.0.
With rear seat folded/removed 21.0

INSTRUMENTATION

Instruments: 80-mph speedometer, 99,999.9 mi. odometer, fuel level.
Warning lights: 2-stage oil level; electrical system.
Optional electronic tachometer $27

DRIVE TRAIN

Transfer case 2-speed
Transfer case ratio . . . . . .3.01 & 1.71:1
Free-running front hubs . . . .not available
Limited slip differential . . . .not available

Rear axle type . . . . . .semi-floating hypoid
Differential ratio 5.68:1
Final drive ratio 9.71:1
Optional final drive ratios . . . . . . .none

Standard transmission: all-synchro 4-spd manual.
Clutch dia., in 6.5
Transmission ratios: 4th 1.00:1
3rd 1.57:1
2nd 2.38:1
1st 3.96:1
Synchromesh . . . . .on all 4

Optional transmission . . . . .none

GENERAL

Curb weight, lb . . . . (mfgr) 1350

Maximum laden weight 2300
Payload rating 950

Wheelbase, in 76.0
Track, front/rear 43.0/43.3
Overall length 117.9
Height (top of windshield) 64.8
Width 51.0
Overhang, front/rear 19/20.5

Approach angle, degrees 34
Departure angle, degrees 38
Ramp breakover angle 28

Ground clearance at differential, in f/r: 10/10
At muffler 9.5
At transfer case 11.5
At fuel tank 11.3

Fuel tank capacity, U.S. gal 7.0
Optional .none

MAINTENANCE

Service intervals, normal use:
Oil change, mi . . . . .none
Filter change . . . . .none
Chassis lube 6000
Tuneup 6000
Warranty, months/miles 3/6000

OTHER OPTIONS

Towbar $135
Rollbar $55
Fabric top $140
Fender flares (required with optional tires): $20.
Gas can & spare tire mount $45
Trailer hitch $10
Carpeting (incl. cargo area) $35
Fiberglass top . . . .$298.

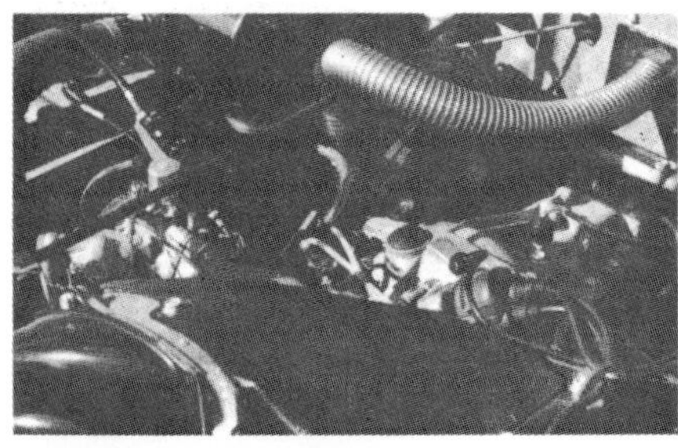

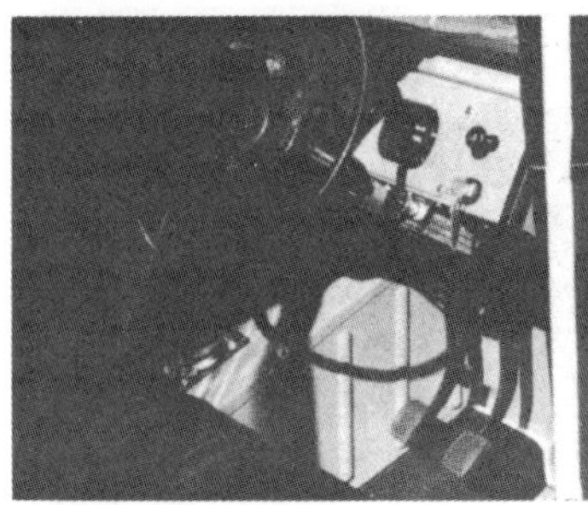

PERFORMANCE DATA

Note: all performance data taken with maximum rated payload on board.

Test model: Standard model with fabric top, carpeting, electronic tach. West Coast POE price, $2362.

DRY PAVEMENT

Acceleration, time to speed, sec:

0-30 mph	8.8
0-45 mph	27.6
0-60 mph	no way

Maximum speed in gears:

High range, 4th (4900 rpm)	48
3rd (6000)	38
2nd (6000)	26
1st (6000)	15
Low range, 4th (6000 rpm)	31
3rd (6000)	21
2nd (6000)	15
1st (6000)	9

Cruising speed at 3000 rpm 31

BRAKE TESTS

Pedal pressure to achieve 1/2-g deceleration rate from 60 mph: not taken.
Fade: Percentage increase in pedal pressure for 6 successive stops from 60 mph: not taken.
Overall brake rating . . . . fair

OFF PAVEMENT

Hillclimbing ability:

Climb test hill no. 1 (47% grade)	yes
Climb test hill no. 2 (56% grade)	yes
Climb test hill no. 3 (63% grade)	yes
Climb test hill no. 4 (69% grade)	no
Maneuverability	excellent
Turnaround capability	excellent

Comments: very harsh ride both on and off pavement.

GENERAL

Heater rating	none
Defroster effectiveness	none
Wiper coverage	fair

FUEL CONSUMPTION

Normal driving, mpg	28
Off-pavement, test conditions, mpg	16
Range, normal driving, mi	196
Range, off-pavement	112

by any standards above a golf cart and even little old ladies in blue Ramblers leave you in their wakes away from a stoplight. On the highway its top speed is an honest 48 mph (52 indicated) and that simply isn't sufficient to keep up with the normal flow. Slopes that would go unnoticed in most cars simply suck the Brute's breath away and on any long grade the speedometer begins a steady decline down the dial. The ride on a paved surface is as poor as we've ever encountered, the stiff springs, narrow track and short wheelbase allowing no irregularity to go unfelt.

Off the pavement, the Brute is more fun, providing you find it fun to bump and bounce along. The passenger has slightly less leg room than the driver (the seats are adjustable, somewhat, but only by moving bolts) and on a good fore-and-aft bump, the spare-tire bracket behind the seat will give you a thump in the back.

On our four test hills, the Brute IV made it up all but the steepest. On this hill it simply ran out of power, the engine giving up about two-thirds of the way up. Our deliberate, snail-like pace on these hills is admittedly a severe test and asks a lot of a small engine. By charging the hill, keeping the revs up in the power range and letting everything bounce, the Brute would undoubtedly have made it. But that isn't the test we established for climbing ability and the Brute goes down as failing on hill no. 4.

The ride off the pavement, while entertaining, is poor. Maybe the front to rear and side motion is part of the fun but when evaluating ride quality we have to say it was not as good as our poorest-riding pickup. And compared to something like a dune buggy—which has independent suspension—one is tempted to think the Brute's name is well chosen.

The traction of the Brute on our test hills was good. We were able to defeat it on a grassy bank, though, as the lack of limited slip differential allowed a front and a rear wheel to spin. We have tried other 4wds on this same bank and those with limited slip crawl up without trouble.

During an extended period of slow, low-range driving, we experienced a serious loss of power. No popping, no surging, just an engine weakness that led to our being defeated on hills we had previously climbed with impunity. As we were buried in the darkest depths of Saddleback Park this was a matter for some concern but we were able to creep on by selecting the gentlest grades and running in low-range 1st gear. Two-thirds of the way out, it came back to life and we deduced that we had fouled a plug. A set of spare spark plugs were noted in the glove compartment so these are apparently things you routinely carry in your Brute for such eventualities.

All in all, it's difficult to see a place for the Brute IV in the 4wd scheme of things. It isn't satisfactory as a dual-purpose vehicle because of its modest street performance and as a recreation vehicle it will carry neither enough gear for extended back-country travel nor get you there with the speed and comfort of a dune buggy. Neither is it so cheap as to fit into the inexpensive plaything class. It admittedly has a certain novelty and entertainment value but as practical transportation—either on-pavement or off—the Brute, in our opinion, doesn't have it.

SUZUKI BRUTE IV

ALTHOUGH YOU WILL not be the fastest driver among your PV4 friends in the Suzuki Brute IV, there will not be many places you can't go. It is almost the perfect replacement for the World War II Jeep, encompassing its drawbacks and advantages. It is underpowered and rides roughly, but it is maneuverable, handles easily and just keeps on going no matter what the terrain.

The Brute IV is small, measuring just about 10½-ft in overall length. It is 51 in. wide and the Wagon model is 63.6 in. high. The design is spartan and utilitarian, with no frills nor fancy extras. The suspension is basic with leaf springs on live axles both front and rear and is very rugged.

The engine in the present models is a 2-cylinder, 2-cycle water-cooled affair with 360 cc (22-cu-in.) and a net horsepower rating of 32 at 5500 rpm. There is an oil tank under the hood which automatically mixes the oil and gas for the 2-stroke engine, so as long as you keep the oil tank filled you don't have to worry about it. And there is a 2-stage warning light on the dash which keeps you informed of the status of the oil tank level. The transmission is a 4-speed manual all-synchromesh unit coupled to a 2-speed transfer case.

The interior is just as bare and basic as the exterior, with two bucket seats up front, floor-mounted shift levers for the transmission and transfer case, parcel tray and glove box. Our test model had the spare tire mounted on the tailgate outside, but in some the spare is carried inside just behind the passenger seat.

The list of optional equipment is abbreviated on the Brute IV, with no free-running front hubs, no limited slip differentials and very little of anything else. The Suzuki people appear to have much the same attitude as the builders of the Toyota Land Cruiser that the vehicle should be relatively complete from the start and it's difficult to disagree with such a philosophy.

TESTS & IMPRESSIONS

Our test Brute IV came to us in the back of a pickup truck and that's the way we returned it. We found this to be the most satisfactory arrangement for going more than 50 miles in the Suzuki, as optimum cruising speed is about 45 mph. We had the G78-15 tires on large spoked rims so that just sitting in the parking lot the Brute looked like a vehicle to be reckoned with. The earlier Suzukis which were imported into the U.S. all had right-hand drive, but they have now changed over to the American style so you sit in the normal position.

The starting operation is accompanied with the usual 2-cycle popping and rumbling, but it fires up very quickly and surely. Our test vehicle was the fabric top model and it sure was cozy for our over 6-ft tall staff members. With the two 6-footers who performed the test procedures inside it was reminiscent of two peas in a pod!

Motoring in the Brute IV is lots of fun. Plain old fashioned fun. You go very slowly, and the standard remark was that it was the only vehicle we had ever driven in which you could go flat out through all four gears and still be doing only 30 mph. As the Publisher remarked, you kind of have to have affection for a vehicle that allows you to drive at the optimum at all times.

On the pavement the ride is harsh and there is lots of noise and vibration. At the same time, our fabric top flapped a bit in the wind but strangely enough it wasn't as unpleasant as it reads. For the adventurous, it was like driving a real antique car. The lack of power is the most serious fault we could find, as it did get somewhat tiresome driving in the right lane all the time on the highway at a more or less steady 45 mph. However, around town, it was a good performer and very easy to maneuver in and out of traffic and into tight parking spaces.

Off the road the ride was even harsher. However, it is in the outback that the Brute comes into its own. You can amble

The Suzuki engine in all its splendor. This powerplant develops 32 net horsepower from its two cylinders.

Once you leave the highway and the traffic behind, you are into the natural element of the Suzuki Brute. We found that it would climb all of our test hills in 4wd low range without any problem and it was fun to drive off road.

1973 SUZUKI BRUTE IV

PRICES

Basic list, West Coast POE:

Brute IV $2495
Brute IV Wagon $2895

Standard equipment: 2-cyl inline engine, 4-spd manual transmission, 4wd, bucket seats

ENGINE

Standard .... 2-stroke, 2-cyl inline
Bore x stroke, in .... 2.40 x 2.42
Compression ratio 7.0:1
Net horsepower @ rpm ...... 32 @ 5500
Net torque @ rpm, lb-ft ..... 27 @ 6000
Type fuel required .... regular

DRIVE TRAIN

Standard transmission ..... 4-spd manual
Transmission ratios: 4th 1.00:1
3rd 1.53:1
2nd 2.39:1
1st 3.97:1
Synchromesh .... all forward gears

Rear axle type ...... semi-floating hypoid
Final drive ratio: 5.66:1
Overdrive .... n/a

Free-running front hubs .... not available
Limited slip differential .... not available
Transfer case 2-speed
Transfer case ratios .... 1.71 & 3.01:1

CHASSIS & BODY

Body/frame: ladder frame with separate steel body

Brakes (std): 6.0 x 1.5-in. drums, front & rear
Brake swept area, sq in 113
Swept area/ton (max load) 110
Power brakes .... not available

Steering type (std) .... ball & screw
Steering ratio 16.5:1
Turns, lock to lock 3.0
Power steering .... not available
Turning circle, ft 28.8

Wheel size (std) .... 6.0 x 16
Optional wheel sizes: .... 7.0 x 15
Tire size (std) 6.00-16 (6PR)
Optional tire sizes G78-15 (4PR)

SUSPENSION

Front suspension: live axle on leaf springs with tube shocks
Front axle capacity, lb .... not available
Optional .... none

Rear suspension: live axle on leaf springs with tube shocks
Rear axle capacity, lb ...... not available
Optional .... none

Additional suspension options: Bilstein competition shocks; front, $47; rear, $49

ACCOMMODATION

Standard seats: .... 2 buckets
Optional rear seat: $40

Headroom, in 36.0
Pedal to seatback, max 39.5
Steering wheel to seatback, max 21.0
Seat to ground 29.0
Floor to ground 15.0

Heater & defroster .... std
Tinted glass .... not available
Air conditioning .... not available

Unobstructed load space (length x width x height) in .... 38 x 31 x 40
Tailgate (width x height) .... 41 x 36

INSTRUMENTATION

Instruments: 80-mph speedometer, 99,999.9-mi. odometer, fuel level
Warning lights: 2-stage oil level; electrical system
Optional: electronic tachometer $27

MAINTENANCE

Service intervals, normal use, miles:

Oil change .... none
Filter change .... none
Chassis lube 6000
Minor tuneup 6000
Major tuneup 12,000
Warranty, months/miles 3/6000

GENERAL

Curb weight, lb (test model) 1560
GVW (max. laden weight) 2300
Optional GVWs .... none

Wheelbase, in 76.0
Track, front/rear 42.9/43.3
Overall length 125.8
Overall height 63.6
Overall width 51.0
Overhang, front/rear 25.0/20.0

Approach angle, degrees 36
Departure angle 42

Ground clearances (test model):

Front axle 8.5
Rear axle 10.0
Oil pan 20.0
Transfer case 16.5
Fuel tank 12.0
Exhaust system (lowest point) 8.5

Fuel tank capacity (U.S. gal) 7.0
Auxiliary tank .... none

OTHER OPTIONS

Towbar $135
Rollbar $55
Fabric top $140
Gas can & spare tire mount $45
Trailer hitch $10
Carpeting (incl. cargo area) $35

PERFORMANCE DATA

Test model: Brute IV, fabric top, G78-15 tires with wide wheels, rollbar, carpeting, gas can & tire mount.

West Coast list price $2915

ACCELERATION

Time to speed, sec:

0-30 mph 12.5
0-45 mph 33.6
0-60 mph .... not possible
Standing start, 1/4-mile, sec 30.3
Speed at end, mph 43

SPEED IN GEARS

High range, 4th (6000 rpm) 47
3rd (6000 rpm) 37
2nd (6000 rpm) 25
1st (6000 rpm) 15
Low range, 4th (6000 rpm) 32
3rd (6000 rpm) 20
2nd (6000 rpm) 15
1st (6000 rpm) 9

BRAKE TESTS

Pedal pressure required for 1/2-g deceleration rate from 45 mph, lb 38
Stopping distance from 50 mph, ft . 108.6
Fade: Percent increase in pedal pressure for 6 stops from 30 mph 10
Overall brake rating .... very good

INTERIOR NOISE

Idle in neutral, dBA 63
Maximum during acceleration 92
At steady 45-mph cruising speed 85

OFF PAVEMENT

Hillclimbing ability .... excellent
Maneuverability .... excellent
Turnaround capability .... excellent
Handling .... very good
Ride .... harsh

GENERAL

Heater rating .... good
Defroster effectiveness .... good
Wiper coverage .... fair

FUEL CONSUMPTION

Normal driving, mpg 28.5
Off pavement 19.5
Range, normal driving, miles 200
Range, off pavement 135

Coming down Hill No. 3 at our Saddleback Park test facility. The Suzuki Brute IV was as good a hillclimber as we have found in a 4-wheel-drive vehicle. The larger wheels and tires were quite efficient and we felt confident in it.

along over rocks, dirt, sand and just about anything else that looms ahead without too much fear of getting stuck or having to turn back. At our test hills at Saddleback Park we were pleased to find that the Suzuki would climb *anything*. We started out in 2-wheel-drive as usual and found that the lack of power was soon apparent. We did climb Hill No. 1, however. On Hill No. 2, a 56% grade, we were forced to shift into 4-wheel-drive. We tried the high range and found it only marginally better than 2-wheel-drive. Then we went on into the low range and we were ready for anything. We went up Hills 2, 3 and 4 without any trouble.

The information in our data panel for the Brute should be read closely as there are some changes from the normal. We were unable to do acceleration and braking tests in the 60-mph range which is normal as we were unable to get up to 60-mph. So the reader should be aware that the figures for the Suzuki cannot be directly related to those of other tested vehicles.

The Suzuki Brute IV was perhaps the most controversial vehicle we have tested at PV4. Some of our staff found it fun to drive and enjoyed all of its primitive features and lack of frills and comfort. Others were of the opinion that it was less than desirable. However, we feel that it can be a good vehicle for certain uses and purposes. It is not a good dual-purpose vehicle for the off-road enthusiast who does not live in or right next to his off-road area. For the average 4wd owner who drives 20 miles or more to get to the end of the pavement, the Suzuki admittedly leaves a lot to be desired. The highway performance is just not adequate. However, we also want to add that it is thrifty and economical and off the road it can be a lot of fun to bounce around in. One good solution seems to be loading it in the bed of a three-quarter-ton or larger pickup and piggybacking it to the end of the pavement.

The new Wagon model, which has a single piece steel body, is a great improvement in the area of weather-proofing, while the roadster version, with or without the fabric top (which is manufactured by Bestop, by the way) is sure lots of fun. The Brute-IV is certainly not everyone's cup of tea, but for the young at heart and adventurous types who don't have a lot of money to spend, it just may be the answer. ●

This is the instrument panel of the Suzuki Brute and it is rather spartan. Controls are all within driver's reach.

GO power from

the land of the . . .

"Rising Sun"

What else could you call a Suzuki Brute with a Datsun Engine?

Photos by Gene Layton

What do you do with a Suzuki Brute IV (that won't do over 50 mph on the highway) when you decide you want to do a little fooling around in sand competition? Well, you can either sell it and buy a CJ-5 or Land Cruiser with a full house small block Chevy, or you can do what Gene Layton did and go to work on your Suzuki.

Gene is the sales manager of Capitol Toyota, a dealer in Salem, Oregon. Capitol sold Suzuki's in 1972, which gave Gene his ideas. Gene bought his Suzuki Brute in December, 1972. After his first tryout at Sandlake, Oregon he decided more horsepower was needed if he was going to be competitive in sand racing. That's when he started his long search for the perfect powerplant to put some *go* in his Brute.

Although he works for a Toyota dealer, Gene crossed the street and came up with a 1200cc Datsun mill for his

Suzuki. His boss at Capitol didn't know what to think, but at least the engine was from the same country! The final creation was named the "Rising Sun."

Gene raced Jeeps for many years, then moved into a fuel injected Chevy sand rail. After that he went to a 5000-pound Blazer. After that variety of machinery, he decided that the Suzuki Brute might be a new and unique kind of sand runner. So far his creation has exceeded all his expectations.

The '72 Datsun 1200 was chosen because it was easy to install in his mini four wheeler. The matching Datsun 4-speed tranny was also used. Gene completely rebuilt the mill, adding a hi-performance camshaft and double valve springs from Cannon Industries in Culver City, California. The head was

Gene Layton calls his creation the "Rising Sun."

The modified 1200cc Datsun engine fits in the Brute with room to spare. Chrome topped engine now puts out about 120 horsepower.

From the front, the Suzuki Brute looks mean and all business.

milled and a set of tuned headers were also added by Cannon. Gene topped off the engine with a set of Dual Solex-Mikuni Carburetors from Interpart.

The next step was to take the vehicle and powerplant to Steve Reed, a very capable mechanic at Capitol Toyota, for installation of the engine and transmission. Steve moved the steering gearbox approximately 10 inches forward to clear the bellhousing, using a stainless steel shaft and an aircraft type U-joint. He then fabricated two "A" frame mounts for the sides of the engine and one rear tranny mount. A local Salem machine shop mated a Datsun yoke and Suzuki U-joint to connect the transmission to the Suzuki transfer case, which is a completely separate unit on its own crossmember. The clutch was a simple matter. They merely added a hydraulic master cylinder next to the brake cylinder, as the Datsun clutch is hydraulic. Throttle linkage was the same as the Suzuki, so that presented no problem. The voltage regulator had to be changed using a Datsun regulator, as the Suzuki has a magneto start and charge. The stock Datsun alternator fit perfectly.

The fuel line was also in the same location for both engines. A 1600 Pinto filter was used, as it is shorter than the Datsun filter and allowed more clearance at the frame.

A quarter-inch thick plate scatter shield was installed for safety and to meet competition requirements for racing.

A Toyota 1200 radiator was used by merely drilling four holes in the grille housing. Steve Reed also built and fabricated the roll cage for the Brute. A set of Toyota shocks with springs were installed at all four corners to stabilize the added load.

With all the mechanical work done, the Brute was given to Capitol Toyota's body shop manager, Ron Taylor, who gave it a black lacquer paint job. White cobweb lacing accents the hood.

Gene then contacted Dave Becket of Sand Tires Unlimited in Gardena, California, for a set of Superlight wheels and Padla-Trak Sand Tires, which were competition cut to complete the running gear. Gene also got help from the Stevens Equipment Company of Salem, who assisted in fabricating the .063-gauge aluminum dash and bumper, the housing for a full set of gauges and a Sun tachometer.

The Brute now tips the scales in racing form at a little over 1500 pounds and is presently putting out approximately 120 horsepower with an actual displacement of 1171cc's.

Gene has entered the mini four wheeler in three competition events in the H Competition Modified Class. So far he has captured three firsts and one top eliminator in hill climbs and one first place in the sand drags.

It just goes to show what a little ingenuity will do when you want something badly enough. If you want to get more information on the "Rising Sun," or to build your own, contact Gene direct: Gene Layton, 1006 Moneda Ave. North, Salem, Ore. 97303. He'll probably answer your letter. □

This is the view most competition gets as the Suzuki hauls the mail in the sand.

FOLLOWING their success with the LJ20 series, Suzuki have come up with a new four wheel drive model, the LJ50.

With typical Japanese thoroughness Suzuki have presented an immaculately designed marketing package, ideally suited to the economy-oriented state of the market. From the pre-release orders and the incredible amount of interest in the new model, especially from the rural regions, the Suzuki will undoubtedly be a success story.

The first shipment to arrive in Victoria reached the distributors, MW Motors in Melbourne, just prior to our closing date so all we could do was have a quick drive of the LJ50 one afternoon.

The new model comes in two basic versions, the LJ50 with quick detachable canvas top and the LJ50V, a hardtop version with an all steel cab.

The Suzukis are slightly smaller in dimensions than a jeep but they weigh a lot less. The engine is three cylinder, two-stroke design, water-cooled and displacing 539 cc. It is inclined about 45 degrees to fit under the bonnet and claimed figures are: 25 kW (33 hp) at 5500, with 57 Nm (24 lb/ft) of torque at 3500 revs.

FUN TWO THREE FOUR

Suzuki's little bush basher, hill climber and mud runner is not to be taken lightly. The two-stroke design, three-cylinder engine, four-wheel drive, LJ50 series could set new records for off-road vehicle sales.

FUN TWO THREE FOUR

Lubrication is the well proven Suzuki CCI injection system which has given Suzuki the reputation of being the most reliable two stroke engine in the motor cycle field. The smaller 360 LJ20 series certainly lived up to this reliability record. There is no reason why the new machine should not have a long and happy life.

With the CCI system oil is injected directly onto the crankshaft and the big ends of the rods at a controlled rate, depending on engine revs and load. At the same time oil is directed into the cylinders for top end lubrication.

The four-speed all synchro gear box is light and fast to use. It operates through a central transfer case and offers standard rear wheel drive, plus a high and low ratio four wheel drive.

Wheels are standard 6.00 x 16, the same as the bigger four wheel drive vehicles and this gives a ground clearance of 240 mm (9.5 ins).

The Suzuki has drum brakes all round with a fifth brake operating by hand on the centre drive shaft. There is a power take-off for operating winches and pumps and the winch assembly (capacity 500 kg), is available as an option.

But it is the finish of the Suzuki that will sell it. For $2799 for the soft-top and $2999 for the hardtop, the Suzukis are definitely in the price-to-beat department.

Add to that high back bucket seats, neat instrument panel with speedometer, fuel and temperature gauges, trendy lay-out and even a fan operated heater, plus a glove box that can be locked (a bonnet release is inside the glove compartment and by locking it the bonnet cannot be opened), all add up to a comfortable package.

Top: Engine is engineering sophistication at its best!
Above: Interior will not offend local cowboys or their girls and new 4WD will be seen on shopping trips.
Below: Light weight, manoeuvrability and excellent finish will sell new Suzuki model.

Big rear vision mirrors on the bonnet are ideal for city driving and while the engine must be revved initially at take-off the Suzuki sticks with traffic in similar vein to the medium size taxi-trucks. The speedo red lines at 80 km/h but extra revving will take it up a little further.

There is no doubt that the new concept of the four wheel drive will attract many newcomers to the Suzuki. It is a long way less in price than the big heavyweights among the four wheel drive set and while it will not do all they can, it offers a new set of uses and rules.

It will quite easily replace the farm ute, be ideal in many industrial situations, will fill the bill in certain government departments and also fit into many specialised tasks that have not really needed a big four-wheel drive before.

And the hardtop version will probably be seen around the city streets as well. The Victorian market for four wheel drives is not much more than 200 annually. MW motors expect to do better than that in the first four months. God knows how many they will sell in states like Western Australia and South Australia, where the four wheel drive Suzukis have had astounding success already. And with the economy in the mood it is, having people look for the best value for money, Suzuki couldn't have picked a better time to hit the scene. ●

Little S vs Little D

Four short months after its release Daihatsu's diminutive F10L had captured 14 percent. of the West Australian 4WD market. At the same time, in the Eastern States, the-year-old Suzuki LJ50 was accounting for nearly 23 percent of summer 4WD sales.

Yet they are both uncompromising, uncomfortable, largely off-road only vehicles that make a poor pretence of being caravan towers or round-Australia tourers. So why have they had such phenomenal sales success?

Perhaps Daihatsu director and F10L designer Masahiro Sugitani best summed it up when asked what the outstanding feature of *his* car was. "Driveability off-road," he replied unhesitatingly.

We proved the point during our exhaustive comparison test of the two vehicles. They put the fun back into off-roading. Whereas the bigger 4WDs are essentially workhorses, the littlies are a pleasure to drive. On fire-trails you find yourself consciously seeking the difficult way up rocky steps; at the beach tackling a 45-degree sand-dune becomes a challenge rather than a chore.

The two 4WDs also have a lot to offer the farmer. They may look like toys, but they aren't averse to hard slogging. Reliability and robust construction are built-in to their lightweight frames and lightweight price tags. And both machines will leave their bigger brothers gasping in really tricky terrain.

But which is better — the two-stroke 539cm^3 triple or the four-stroke 958cm^3 four? Can such dissimilar engines produce comparable results?

The answer is a qualified yes. As you might expect, each vehicle has its strong and weak points — and they don't necessarily coincide.

Paradoxically, it's the little Suzuki that makes the faster long-distance tourer and the Daihatsu which performs more competently in most off-road situations. The Daihatsu has a better power-to-weight ratio, but is less peppy at peak rpm. Where it shines is in rock-picking and ledge-climbing, which it can often accomplish at high range when the Suzuki is in low.

Like two illnesses, however, the essential difference between the pair lies not in effects but in causes. Whilst the design philosophies may be similar, the theoretical backgrounds are not.

Suzuki is the third largest motorcycle manufacturer in the world. Daihatsu builds trucks. Thus the LJ50 is a four-wheeled motorcycle; the F10L a subcompact truck.

The evidence for this is substantial. The Suzuki's engine is similar to the air-cooled 544 the company uses in one of its road bikes; the Daihatsu's a variant of the Compagna 1000 car engine, which is also used by John Deare Tractors of Canada. The Daihatsu's gearchange is lorry-like and notchy (it is a composite of truck clusters); the Suzuki's motorcycle-spongy. The Daihatsu is bigger in every respect than the Suzuki, and it's also 295kg heavier. In fact, the only exception to the rule is the wing mirror shape: oblong and truck-like for Suzuki; round and bike-like for Daihatsu.

Both vehicles have been around for longer than you might think. Suzuki's 4WD first arrived on the scene in 1970 (albeit not in Australia) with a 360 cm^3 air-cooled twin under the bonnet. Subsequently the vehicle got water-cooling (was anointed, you could say) and then an extra cylinder. It was in this form that it first appeared in Australia, in August '73.

The Daihatsu did not appear until August '75; Australia was its first export

Similar in concept and size, but oh-so-dissimilar in mechanical specification, these two low-budget 4WDs are setting the all-roads market alight. Overlander matched the machines against each other and harsh, unyielding Mother Earth:

target. But it had been designed in 1968. Why Daihatsu waited so long is anyone's guess.

(An interesting but little-known fact about Suzuki is that it actually produced its first motor vehicle in 1937 — and it was a four-wheeler (car). The motorcycles did not evolve until the early '50s. Since the company also developed a 758cm³ water-cooled three-cylinder car engine in 1965, it's a pretty safe bet that the triple-cylinder bike engines derived from it, and not vice versa).

Overlander tested the vehicles on a variety of trails &c. close to Sydney, as well as in the Myall Lakes region of the mid-northern NSW coast. We interspersed the dirt roading with a spell of city commuting in torrential rain. It was a comprehensive test package that included most of the conditions owners will experience — and some they won't! Here, firstly, is how they matched up on the beaten track:

On the road

Neither vehicle makes a good city commuter. Even in high range, first gear is so low that it does little more than move the car off the mark. Despite lots of noise (and smoke, in the case of the Suzuki), they accelerate as leisurely as a side-valve Morris Minor. Pick-up in top is little short of non-existent, although on the flat both 4WDs will throttle down to 40km/h and amble away.

On a positive note, cruising at 60km/h is a whole lot less strenous than at 60mph, and both four-wheelers are small enough to slot through miniscule gaps in the traffic. With the rear windows up, visibility is respectable, although the side panels do tend to obscure vision somewhat. Keeping your wing mirrors adjusted is a good idea if you want to float, rather than sink, in the motor mire. With the tops removed, of course, you get 359-degree vision: the spare tyres and thick windscreen pillars are the only detros.

Both vehicles brakes are superb, with the edge going to the Daihatsu in normal city traffic and to the Suzuki on the open road and after creek crossings. Our test Daihatsu snatched badly to the right after its brakes had been immersed, indicating that, once again, it is modelled more along the lines of a conventional 4WD than the Suzuki. Hamamatsu learnt how to water-proof drum brakes while evolving its dirt bike range.

The little S's handbrake is mounted under the glove-box, where it restricts passenger leg room; the Daihatsu's is conveniently located between the seats, where it won't provide an excuse for you to rub your girlfriend's leg.

The Daihatsu is considerably more comfortable than its opposition. Interior space is 8.5 percent greater: it seems more. Six-footers will find they have more room to stretch their legs in the little D. Because of its rather cramped cabin space, the Suzuki has a 50mm smaller diameter steering wheel, which magnifies steering effort. Although there isn't much difference, the Daihatsu's seats are marginally more restful than the Suzuki's — largely because of a large tubular brace which presses into one's spine with the seats pushed right back. We understand that this has been modified in more recent model LJ50s.

One further source of annoyance is the Suzuki door-frame design — each side-swipe bar is actually attached to the car (by a very suspect spring catch) instead of pivoting with the door! To get out without risking your future you must first lower one of the bars. Not only are they integral with

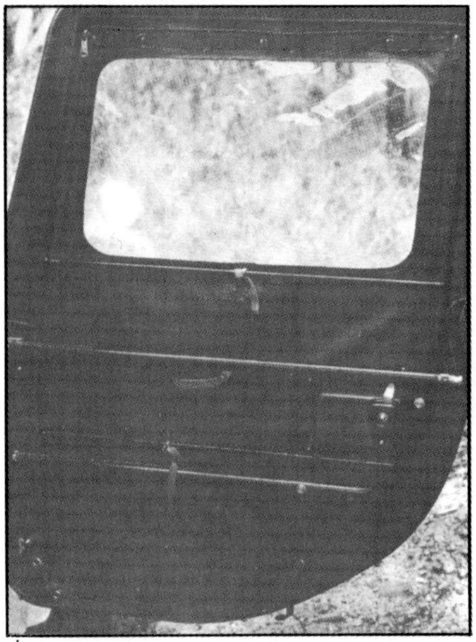

1. Daihatsu door-frame has two bars, zippered windows, whereas . . .

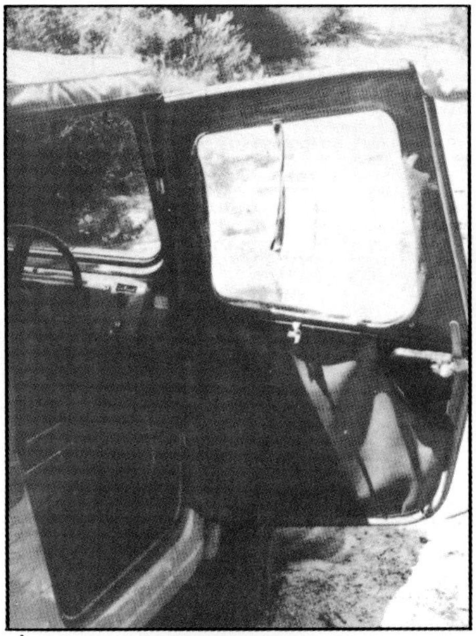

2. . . . . the Suzuki's is less structurally rigid, has unwieldy press-studs.

3. LJ50 exhaust extension still can't rid the cabin of that two-stroke smoke.

4. Large, oblong Suzuki mirror contrasts with round motorcycle Daihatsu mirror.

5. Those press-studs again! It's impossible to fasten the Suzuki's soft-top without clambering into the vehicle body.

6. Accessory Superwinch on Little D let us tackle obstacles we might have shied away from.

7. LJ50 cabin. Instruments are neatly arranged, gearshift stubby. Note lack of windscreen vent.

8. F10L boasts steering column lock, air vent. But gearshift is truck-like.

the doors in the Daihatsu, there is an extra pair of bars beneath them for added protection.

But perhaps the least pleasing aspect of the Suzuki is the way it induces claustrophobia with the soft-top *in situ*. Two oversights augment this sensation. Firstly, there is no windscreen vent to direct fresh air into the cabin (the Daihatsu has one in the centre of its cabin). Secondly, it's impossible to open the side windows from the inside. They're secured by press studs and the window rolls up. Daihatsu provides two zip fasteners with snap hooks at the top, so you can unfasten the window and tuck it into the door-frame while you're still on the move.

In heavy summer rain, with the demister going, the Suzuki becomes a real sweatbox, especially if you've neglected to switch off the hot water valve under the bonnet (the Daihatsu has a control in the cabin).

Removing the Suzuki's soft-top (including the doors) takes two people around 17 minutes, or five minutes longer than for the Daihatsu. Practice will reduce this time considerably. However, fastening the Suzuki's rear flap is so complex, it really has to be done from the cargo tray. Both tops rely extensively on tapes to lash the 'canvas' to its frame.

Daihatsu's snap hooks are once again easier-to-use than Suzuki's press studs and tapes. Moreover, the Daihatsu's top can be removed in sections, giving you a choice of top with no sides, sides with no top, no sides and top, or sides and top. With the Suzuki it's roll or nothing.

As a further hindrance to commuter pleasure the LJ50 suffers from an exhaust system which seemingly empties half its products into the vehicle interior. It's significant that we suffered the same problem in a hardtop LJ50V. Whilst never noxious enough to cause a blackout, it is unpleasant. The Daihatsu tailpipe does a much more accurate job of dispersing gases.

We can say that both soft-tops were amazingly waterproof. Some of the showers we drove through were little short of deluges, but the only moisture to enter either vehicle was a very slight trickle down the Suzuki's firewall — no more than you'd expect from a hardtop 4WD. Perhaps that jungle of tapes and tabs has its uses after all . . . .

Finally, we should mention that city security is bound to be a problem with both vehicles. The doors are not lockable, so there's not even the pretence of keeping light-fingered people out. The Daihatsu has steering column lock; the Suzuki locks on both the handbrake and the glovebox.

Out in the country you must resign yourself to an 80-100km/h cruising speed. The Suzuki has a definite edge here: it will climb most hills in fourth gear and will even broach the twilight zone of 110km/h! Absolute top speed for the Little D is about 102km/h, and you'll need to downshift for steep inclines. The low gearing and blunt profiles hinder speed bursts, although both vehicles returned creditable country fuel consumptions: 8.6 1 /100km from the Suzuki; 7.7 1 /100km from the Daihatsu.

Our test F10L was fitted with an optional push-button radio, which helped to while away the four-hour drive to Tea Gardens. An encounter with a low-slung eucalypt gave the D its first aerodynamically shaped accessory — a brushback aerial . . ..

Two speed windscreen wipers and an electric washer pump afford the D a visibility edge over the S, which has single-speed wipers and a hand-bulb washer.

Both vehicles offer acceptable range: look for around 400km from the Daihatsu (32 1 tank); 340km from the Sukuki (30 1

Above: the Daihatsu gave as much as any on the Big Hill, but failed at this point. You can't say our driver didn't try!

Below: fastening the Suzuki's soft-top . . . more of a hassle than need be on both vehicles.

tank). The Suzuki's CCI lubrication, which injects two-stroke oil directly to stress points, also uses around a litre a tankful. A 3.4 engine oil tank is located in the engine bay. It's hooked up to a red light on the dash which glows dully until the 0.4 litre mark is reached, when it burns more fiercely to alert the driver to the need for a top-up. You would imagine that this system would be foolproof, but a lot of Suzukis have seized because they have run out of oil . . . . .

With payloads of just 250kg each, even a lone passenger can affect the vehicles' hill-climbing and cruising ability. Our advice to owners is: trade-in your beer supplies on carrot juice!

Although it is possible to tow a small caravan or boat behind the cars, it's not recommended. Self-towing hooks are provided back and front on the Suzuki and at the rear on the Daihatsu, our test D was equipped with an electric Superwinch that we found was tough enough to shift a Landcruiser! It's possible to mount a very neat power take-off winch on the Daihatsu; there is also provision for this on the Suzuki.

In the rough

It was with great relief that we headed off the rutile road south of Seal Rocks onto the track that let to ten km of golden beach. The Suzuki had already shown up another side of its character: dirt road stability. Tauter suspension gives it a bumpier but safer ride than the Daihatsu, which pitches excessively at speed and demands massive driver concentration.

The track down through the sage-brush was rough and sandy and once again the Suzuki came up trumps. On off-camber sections the Daihatsu felt like it was going to tip over (thankfully, it never did) and this sensation was repeated on the 4WD-scarred sand.

Because of the narrow track of the vehicles compared to Rovers and Cruisers, it was impossible to follow in existing wheel ruts on the beach. To do so was to invite a spill, since one pair of wheels would catch in the rut, leaving the other pair scrabbling on the looser sand.

It wasn't long before we had progressively reduced tyre pressures to below 10psi. The Suzuki at last began to 'float' on the surface of the sand, and we found it quite possible to drive it in 4WD-H, or even 2WD-H at a pinch. This gave a top speed along the beach of around 70km/h. The Daihatsu, on the other hand, bit in and even in 4WD we found it impossible to use even third-high-except for short stretches at the water's edge. As an alternative, we tried third-low, which gave us a maximum speed of 45km/h and a most nerve-wracking ride.

When it came to climbing sandhills, the Suzuki was again way out in front, playing king of the castle to the D's dirty rascal. We must stress, though, that soft sand is the most of difficult of all terrain for a

1. LJ50 on our first major obstacle.

2. Soft-tops in situ: both 4WDs look trim, functional.

3. Daihatsu on our second major obstacle.

4. The only vehicle to conquer the first big dune: kitted Suzuki hard-top.

5. Daihatsu is slightly bigger than Suzuki, but nimble off-road.

6. Our third major obstacle: both vehicles crossed this!

4WD, and that on a more compacted surface (see pix) the Daihatsu gave as good as the Suzuki, was only marginally behind a kitted LJ50 van, and climbed much further than a widie-shod Cruiser. Fitting sand wheels and tyres would also minimise the difference between the two vehicles.

We figure the Daihatsu's inferiority in sand is a product of weight, and unsuitable gear ratio spacing. It's obvious that the much lighter Suzuki will 'float' more readily. In fact, the LJ50 is probably the best sandgoing 4WD in existence. But it would also help if the D's gear ratios were more evenly spaced, since third is just too far removed from second (see specifications). Presumably designer Sugitani had to use a tall third gear to compensate for lack of flexibility in top on the road.

Both vehicles utilise a single-lever transfer box, which offers 2WD-H, 4WD-H, N and 4WD-L. The Daihatsu's transfer case is attached directly to the rear of the main gearbox, whereas the Suzuki's is bolted to a more distant chassis cross-member.

We experienced no trouble with either transfer box, but did find that the Daihatsu's first gear synchro was not always smooth. On the other hand, the rather stiff action of the Suzuki's gearshift took some getting used to.

With the tops down and travelling in convoy, everything and everyone in the two vehicles was predictably covered in talc-like rutile dust, but it didn't matter somehow: we'd had a fantastic weekend and not even the long trip home could attenuate our memories of that virgin, unspoilt paradise.

Since we had not had the opportunity to compare the vehicles in other than sandy conditions, we were eager to pitch them against one of the **Overlander** test tracks near Sydney. But Fate had other ideas. It rained all that week, and when we finally drove into a northern bushland zone it was to find rivers instead of creeks, and cascades where there had been just trails.

Both 4WDs revelled in these conditions, but the Daihatsu had the edge. Such tiny engines have to be kept on the boil — wherever you are — but the bigger four-stroke was more responsive at low rpm and we found that usually we could use first and second H when the Suzuki was in 1, 2, and 3 L.

Some slippery sections that the Daihatsu would climb in one go took three attempts in the Suzuki — although we were always sure we would make it. Less rpm means more traction on slippery surfaces — it's as simple as that!

Moreover, that soft ride that we had found uncertain in the sand gave the Daihatsu the edge on comfort. Longer suspension travel also meant that we could get four wheels biting where three had to suffice in the Suzuki.

Additional braking force provided by the Daihatsu's four-stroke engine proved

Specification Overleaf
Text continued on page 42

Daihatsu F10L

Suzuki LJ50

Daihatsu F10L

Engine
Type: four-cylinder in-line ohv four-stroke, cast iron block with integral liners, alloy head. Forged con-rods with three-ring flat-top pistons. 15-55-55-15 degree valve timing. 93kg dry weight. PCV pollution control.
Bore x stroke: 68.0 x 66.0 mm
Displacement: 958cm^3
Carburettor: Aisan Kogyo Stromberg dual-throat, 24mm Venturi
Compression ratio: 9.0:1
Claimed max. power: 43.2kW (58 bhp) at 5500 rpm
Claimed max. torque: 78.7Nm (57.9 ft.lb.) at 4000 rpm
Bearings: copper-lead/ steel plain main and big end bearings. Press-fit gudgeon bushes.

Transmission
Internal gearbox ratios: 1st:3.707; 2nd: 2.167; 3rd: 1.413; 4th: 1.000; Rev: 4.093
High range: 1.307; low range: 2.361
Differential ratio: 5.571
Gearchange: all synchro four-speed floor-shift, single-lever transfer case.
Clutch: dry, 132cm^2 single-plate, diaphragm spring

Systems
Fuel: diaphragm type fuel pump through paper filter from 32 l steel tank
Lubrication: force-feed through trochoid pump and full-flow paper filter. Total capacity: 2.8 litres
Cooling: centrifugal water pump, radiator with cooling fan, 3.8 litres capacity
Ignition: 12V battery and coil, 1-3-4-2 firing order. Centrifugal and vacuum advance, NGK B6ES spark plugs
Air filtration: pleated chemical fibre element

Running gear
Wheels and tyres: 6.00 x 16 Bridgestone Ground Grip bar-treads on five-stud steel rims
Brakes: Front: d.l.s. drums, 254mm diameter; rear: s.l.s. drums, 254mm diameter. Parking brake: s.l.s. drum on rear drive shaft

Steering
Type: recirculating ball, 20.13 ratio
Turning circle: 5.1m (16.8ft.)
Turns lock to lock: 2.7

Suspension
Front: semi-elliptic leaf springs with double-acting tele shock absorbers
Rear: semi-elliptic leaf springs with double-acting tele shock absorbers

General
L x W x H: 3485 x 1460 x 1855 mm (137.2 x 57.5 x 73.0in)
Curb Mass: 995kg (2192 lb.)
Wheelbase: 2025mm (79.7in)
Ground clearance: 215mm (8.5in)
Track (F & R): 1200mm (47.2in)
Fuel consumption (open road): 7.7l/1100km (36.7 mpg)
Price*: $3988 excluding registration and TPI
Options fitted*: bull-bar, electric winch
Special equipment available*: free-wheeling hubs ($78); 18 litre fuel tank ($60); power take-off winch
Colours available: red, light green, olive green, white, off-white
Supplier: Daihatsu Distributors P/L, 286 Coward St., Mascot 2020
Manufacturer: Daihatsu Motor Co. Ltd., Osaka, Japan

Suzuki LJ50

Engine
Type: two-stroke piston-port triple, Advanced reed valve induction to prevent blowback. Cast-iron block with alloy head. Three-ring flat-top pistons. 66kg dry weight.
Bore x stroke: 61.0 x 61.5mm
Displacement: 539cm^3
Carburettor: 25mm venturi Solex single-throat
Compression ratio: 6.0:1
Claimed max. power: 24.6kW (33 bhp) at 5500 rpm
Claimed max. torque: 56.5 Nm (41.6 lb.ft.) at 3500 rpm
Bearings: four ball mains; needle roller big and small ends

Transmission
Internal gearbox ratios: 1st: 3.835; 2nd: 2.359; 3rd: 1.524; 4th: 1.000; Rev: 4.026
High range: 1.714; low range: 3.012
Differential ratio: 4.875
Gearchange: all synchro four-speed floor shift, single-lever transfer case
Clutch: dry, 134cm^2 single-plate, diaphragm spring

Systems
Fuel: diaphragm-type fuel pump from 30 litre steel fuel tank
Lubrication: CCI pressure-feed to stress areas from 3.4 litre two-stroke oil tank under bonnet. Plunger-type oil pump.
Cooling: centrifugal water pump, radiator with cooling fan, 4.1 litres total capacity
Ignition: 12V battery and coil, 1-3-2 firing order centrifugal advance, NGK B-7HS spark plugs
Air filtration: wet polyurethane element

Running gear
Wheels and tyres: 6.00 x 16 Bridgestone Ground Grip bar-treads on five-stud steel rims
Brakes: Front: d.l.s. drums, 210mm diameter; rear: s.l.s. drums, 210mm diameter.
Parking brake: s.l.s. drum on drive-shaft behind transfer case

Steering
Type: recirculating ball, 15.58 ratio
Turning circle: 4.6m (15.1 ft.)
Turns lock to lock: 3.3

Suspension
Front: semi-elliptic leaf springs with double-acting tele shock absorbers
Rear: semi-elliptic leaf springs with double-acting tele shock absorbers

General
L x W x H: 3180 x 1295 x 1710mm (125.2 x 51.0 x 67.3 in.)
Curb Mass: 700kg (1541lb.)
Wheelbase: 1930mm (76.0in.)
Ground clearance: 240mm (9.4in.)
Track (F & R): 1100mm (43.3 in.)
Fuel consumption (open road): 8.6l/100km (32.6 mpg)
Price*: $3350; van: $3595 (excluding registration and TPI)
Options fitted*: single roll-bar ($65)
Special equipment available*: power take-off $390 installed; PTO Warn winches $230-$291; roll-cage $200; tow-bar $20; tow-bar with bumper $98
Colours available: white, yellow, dark green
Supplier: Ateco Suzuki, 17 Sefton Rd., Thornleigh 2120
Manufacturer: Suzuki Motor Co., Ltd., Hamamatsu, Japan
*Prices quoted correct as of March, 1976

ABOVE: The interior remains the same as before with only a few minor changes in the area of instrumentation. There is also a new style of steering wheel. RIGHT: The special cloth trim is an Ateco Suzuki addition in Sydney. The seats have been improved slightly and offer slightly better support than those in earlier models.

SUZUKI'S 4 CYLINDER STROKE X FOUR

THE SUZUKI MOTOR COMPANY has opened a new era of automotive production for itself with the introduction of its first four-stroke motor.

The company has chosen to release the motor in the four-wheel-drive range where the diminutive Suzuki LJ50 - the two-stroke, three-cylinder model - has been taking a beating on the market place from the larger, bigger capacity, but still small, Daihatsu.

With a public release scheduled for October 26th, Suzuki has placed the new LJ80 on the recreational market just prior to one of the biggest selling periods of the year for this type of vehicle - the summer holiday period!

The most radical change in the new vehicle is, of course, the all new four-cylinder four-stroke engine. This is an extremely radical move for the Suzuki company which has , to our knowlege, never marketed a four-stroke engine. However, this does not mean that the engine is an experimental model. It has undergone several years of testing and development at Suzuki's giant research facility in Japan, before even the slightest suggestion was made that it even existed.

Suzuki has been customarily quiet about its existence until recently, denying on many occassions that the four-stroke had been developed. Stories were leaked that a bigger two-stroke was on the way, and it was a complete surprise to many that when the bigger engine finally appeared it was a four-stroke.

The apparent secrecy surrounding the development of the four-stroke was brought about by an obvious desire to keep the engine under wraps until the Suzuki engineers were totally satisfied that every possible problem had been sorted out. After all, the four-stroke engine - although only with a 797cc capacity - now makes Suzuki a competitor on the home market with all the other Japanese motor manufacturers in the domestic small car market. While the company's mini two strokes have always had a share of the mini-market in Japan, they've never really met with the same success as their competitors' mini-cars powered by the four-stroke engine. There's also Japan's tremendous smog problem to contend with - something not helped a lot by the relatively high pollutant exhaust from a two-stroke.

Outwardly, the LJ80 is distinguished from its smaller counterpart only by the flared rear guards, wider front guards and a high bonnet line with air-ducts across the nose.

The reason for the air ducts is obvious and when you stand the two vehicles side-by-side, the reason for the flares also becomes quite obvious.

The new model is 100mm (3.6in) wider in track all round. The LJ80 has a front track of 1190mm (46.5in) and a rear of 1200mm (47.4in) as opposed to the LJ 50's front track of only 1090mm (42.9 in.) and rear of 1100mm (43.3in.).

This increase in track has made the LJ 80 a more stable vehicle than the earlier model and has contributed to a much better steering feel.

In the short period during which I was able to drive the new model - both hard and soft-top - I found the greater

SPECIFICATIONS SUZUKI LJ80

MANUFACTURER: . . . . Suzuki Motor Co.,
MAKE/MODEL: . . . . LJ80 4 wheel drive
BODY TYPE: . . . . Soft-top (Hardtop)
SUPPLIED BY: . . . . Ateco Suzuki, Sefton Rd, Thornleigh.

ENGINE:
Cylinders. . . . . 4, in-line
Bore & Stroke: . . . . .62.0 mm (2.44 in) x 66.0 mm (2.59 in)
Capacity:. . . . . 797cc (48.6 CID)
Compression: 8.7:1
Aspiration:. . . .. .Single, downdraft Mikuni
Fuel pump: . . . . Mechanical
Valve gear:. .Single overhead cam
Maximum power: . . . . 41 bhp @ 5500 rpm
Maximum torque:. . . . . 59.8 Nm @ 3500 rpm

TRANSMISSION
Type/locations: . . . . 4-spd manual, high & low ratio, all-synchro
Driving wheels: . . . . .Two and four wheel drive
Clutch type: . . . . Single dry plate
Gear: 1st: 3.835
                                                            2nd: 2.395
                                                            3rd: 1.543
                                                            4th: 1.000
Final drive: 4.556
Transfer Case: .High range 1.563
                                                            Low range 2.571

SUSPENSION
Front suspension:. . . . . Leaf spring
Rear suspension: . . . . Leaf spring
Shock absorbers: . . . . .Double acting hydraulic
Wheels/Tyres: . . . . 6.00 x 16 - 4 PR

STEERING
Turning radius: . . . . 4.9 m (16.1 ft)
Steering gear box:. . . . . Ball nut

BRAKE SYSTEM:
Type:. . . . . .4-wheel, hydraulic
Wheel brake: Front: . . . . Two-leading
                  Rear: . . . . Leading and trailing
Parking brake:. . . . . Internal expanding on propeller shaft

CAPACITIES
Cooling solution: . . . . 3.8 lit
Fuel tank: . . . . 40 lit
Engine oil: . . . . 3.0 lit
Transmission oil: . . . . 1.0 lit
Differential gear box oil: . . . . 1.3 lit
Transfer gear box oil:. . . . . 0.9 lit

DIMENSIONS (HARDTOP IN BRACKETS)
Overall length:. . . . . 3170 mm/124.8 in (3170 mm/124.8 in)
Overall width:. . . . . .1395 mm/54.9 in (1395 mm/54.9 in)
Overall height:. . . . . .1845 mm/72.6 in (1685 mm/66.3 in)
Wheelbase:. . . . . .1930 mm/76.0 in (1930 mm/76.0 in)
Tread: Front: . . . .1190 mm/46.9 in (1200 mm/47.2 in)
                  Rear: . . . . .1200 mm/47.2 in (1200 mm/47.2 in)
Load deck size: Length:. . . . 930 mm/36.6 in (870 mm/34.3 in)
                  Width: . . . .1205 mm/47.4 in (1190 mm/46.9 in)
                  Height: . . . .1180 mm/46.5 in (1045 mm/41.1 in)
Ground Clearance: . . . . .240 mm/9.4 in (240 mm/9.4 in)

WEIGHT
Curb Weight: . . . . 705 kg/1554 lbs (750 kg/1653 lbs)
Weight Distribution:
                  Front: . . . . . . .410 kg/904 lbs (415 kg/915 lbs)
                  Rear: . . . . .295 kg/650 lbs (335 kg/738 lbs)
Gross vehicle weight:. . . . . . .1105 kg/2436 lbs (1100 kg/2425 lbs)
Seating Capacity:. . . . . .2 person
Maximum loading capacity:. . . . .250 kg/551 lbs (200 kg/441 lbs)

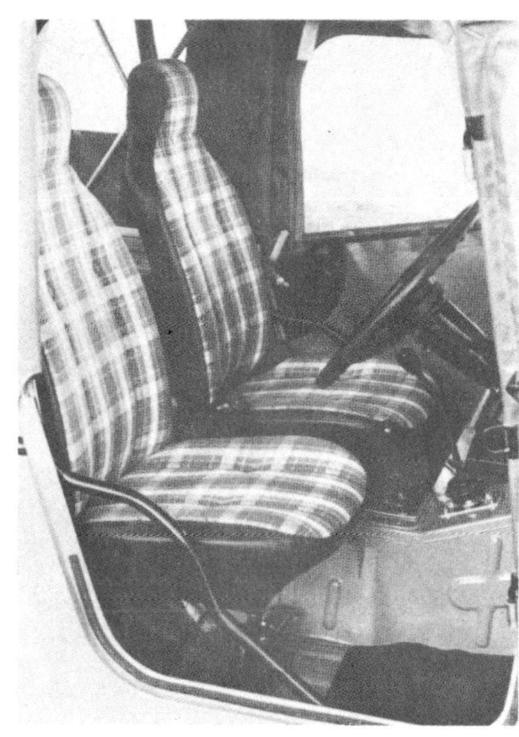

ABOVE & RIGHT: It's not until you look closely that you begin to pick the changes. Careful attention to detail will reveal that the front guards are much wider and the rear panels have been flared to cover the rear wheels. Otherwise, the dimensions are the same as for the two-stroke models.

track width had improved the handling and ride of the Suzuki immensely.It no longer had that "top heavy, wants to fall over" feeling when cornering and ride stability in rough going was much improved.

Powere from the little 800cc engine is quite remarkable.It puts out 41bhp @ 5500rpm, and allows much faster acceleration and easier cruising at highway speeds.But where it shows particular improvement over the two stroke is in its torque capability where it produces 59.8Nm @ 3500rpm (LJ 50 - 56.6Nm @ 3500rpm). While the actual figure shows little variation, the difference is in the work load on the engine.Where the two stroke will reach its peak and be straining in a load situation, then begin to die off - the four-stroke will continue to run without losing power almost to the point of stalling.

The single overhead camshaft engine is a lot quieter when running that the two-stroke and will no doubt overcome the problems of finding adequate supplies of two-stroke oil when in remote areas.

The marketers of the Suzuki in Australia feel the new model will put them back in the recreational and agricultural market place. Many people have been waiting a long time for the bigger engine to arrive, and with the new and somewhat unexpected development of the four stroke, the new model will doubtlessly win a spot in the hearts of the many Suzuki-freaks around the country who want that little extra get-up-and-go from their mini-4x4.

Unfortuanately the only thing we were not able to get before this issue went to press was the price of the new vehicle - Suzuki are keeping this totally secret until the day of release...not even wine, bribes and promises of lunch would prise it from their lips.

As far as the future of the LJ50 is concerned, it's planned to market the two vehicles side-by-side until current stocks run out.There is still a demand for the two-stroke, and if this demand continues it may be possible to continue to import and market the two-stroke for some time yet to come.

It will be interesting to watch the sales figures shape up in the next few months to come!

RIGHT: From the back the only noticeable changes are the flared guards. The wider stance of the vehicle doesn't show up unless the LJ80 is parked alongside an LJ50.

THE BETTER MOUSETRAP

Photography: Robbi Newman

It has happened at last! With little more than a whimper of publicity, Suzuki has entered the Clean Air Age with its new four-stroke 4WD, brand-new the LJ80V. And, whilst the transition from two-stroke triple to all-new four-stroke four is a major turnabout for any manufacturer, the new vehicle itself is surprisingly similar to the superseded model.

The move was obviously precipitated by the advent of the Daihatsu F20, released in Australia in June '77. According to the provisions of the NSW Clean Air Act, the two-stroke LJ50 was exempted from tough new exhaust emission levels until July, 1978. But months before the F20's release, Suzuki Japan would have known what was coming and may even have slotted a 1600 Corona motor into a Daihatsu F10 just to see how the new vehicle would perform. The news was all bad for Suzuki. Far from competing with the LJ50, the new F20 would walk all over it.

Suzuki knew that it was going to have to replace the LJ50 powerplant soon, anyway. What the F20 did was to accelerate the development phase. Daihatsu's incredible performance in the Australian market (Number Three in July, behind Toyota and Nissan) only hardened Suzuki's resolve. Production LJ80s began rolling out of the Hamamatsu factory in July. The only problem now was — when to release them?

Unfortunately for Suzuki and its agents, the Australian distributors were still holding large stocks of LJ50s, which since the introduction of the F20 had been predictably hard to move. Suzuki Japan would have liked to have announced the new model at the Sydney Motor Show in August. Ateco Suzuki (NSW) and MW Motors (Vic.) said No. We at **Overlander** were fortunate enough to obtain one of the handful of LJ80s in the country for testing in August, but the release date was pushed back to November. It was still a world first.

How much of a change is the new LJ80? Did hordes of 4WD devotees converge on the new model wherever we went, attracted like moths to a candle by the radically new body shape and throaty four-stroke exhaust note?

Not at all. In fact, we found we actually had to tell onlookers it was a new model — and open the bonnet to convince them. One group of four-wheel-drivers we passed on the long downhill run into Lithgow looked slightly askance at the unfamiliar sound of a Suzuki using its engine for braking, but otherwise the lack of interest was startling.

Let's hope the apathy is not reflected in sales figures.

Here are the changes made to convert the LJ50 to an LJ80. Many of these are based on recommendations from Australian Suzuki agents.

First, the engine transplant. The new design is a modern ohc 797cm^3 four. The crossflow head design and clean breathing means that it can meet exhaust emission requirements with only a minimum of anti-pollution equipment, so owners will not require university degrees to tune it. This is one benefit of starting from scratch with a completely new design. The pollution controls can be built into, rather than onto, the engine. It is certainly an advantage the LJ80 has over the F20, the engine of which is excessively complex, a typical example of conservative overkill. Holden has struck the same problem with its ageing six.

The Suzuki engine develops 30.6kW at 5500rpm and 59.8Nm of torque at 3500 rpm. Power is up 25 per cent on the LJ50's 24.6kW, but torque has increased only marginally (LJ50:56.5Nm at 3500rpm). Thus a 50 per cent capacity increase has resulted in only a 25 per cent power boost. This is not so unexpected. In the motorcycle world, it has long been acknowledged that more power per cubic centimetre can be obtained from a two-stroke than from a four-stroke. Suzuki has recently began the long process of converting its motorcycle range to four-stroke engines, and it has been an uphill struggle, fraught with double overhead cams and multiple carburettors. It could have gone the same route with the 4WD, but the complexity would scarcely have appealed to the farmers who are still the mainstay of the market. Rugged simplicity is the keynote of success in the 4WD market, not fancy valve gear and trick camming.

The engine has added another 20kg to

Opposite: we road tested LJ80V in Great Divide west of Lithgow. In this environment SWB vehicle was more than a match for its predecessor and for 'full-size' vehicles accompanying us.

SUZUKI
NSW
JHA·082 
Overlander
4WD
TEST

the kerb mass of the vehicle, less than expected (engine weight is 85kg). Body changes are minimal. Recognising the need for a wider track to cope with the higher cruising speeds expected of the new motor, Suzuki has widened the track front and rear by about 100mm (4in). To accommodate this, the front 'guards have been widened perceptibly and flares have been welded onto the rear wheel arches. There is also a tell-tale 'power bulge' in the bonnet that is sure to make the new bonnet a big-selling accessory item for LJ50 engine swaps.

These are the sole modifications to the body.

Below: Distributor runs off ohc, is right up under bonnet.
Centre: oiled foam air filter can be cleaned, re-used.
Bottom: new engine meets pollution standards without complex plumbing.

A minor suspension alteration has occurred. The rear shock absorbers, previously mounted inside the springs, have been shifted outboard. Some additional stiffening has been added to the chassis beneath the engine.

Inside the vehicle, improvements comprise: warning lights for the parking brake and brake wear; and a larger (and much more solid) rough-textured steering wheel.

As well, our test vehicle, an LJ80V, was equipped with Ateco Suzuki's "Off-Road Pack" — Stage Three bull-bar/sideguards, P/B radio, comfortable cloth-fronted seats and a not-very-attractive Go Faster stripe. We understand that the first shipment of LJ80's will only be offered with this pack, at an additional cost of $400 per unit. Standard vehicles will follow later.

The $64,000 question is: does all this add up to a better vehicle?

We would not be sticking our necks out if we were to state categorically that it does. The LJ80V is a much more pleasant round-town car than its predecessor, performs marginally better in most off-road situations, cruises at consistently higher speeds on the open road and returns more kilometres per litre. But it is not the fire-breathing cannonball Suzuki people originally led us to believe it would be. Despite the radically different motor, there is more similarity between this vehicle and the LJ50 than there is between the F20 and the F10 Daihatsus.

We had been promised that the 80 would 'see off' an F20 in straight-line acceleration. So we matched our 5000 km old Suzuki against a near-new, trade-plated Daihatsu, driven by a woman. Up to 30 km/h there was nothing in it, then the Daihatsu left the Suzuki gasping for breath. The F20 is a genuine 120 km/h vehicle; the LJ80 little faster than the

LJ50. At 105 km/h it runs out of puff. Admittedly, we ran the needle off the 110 km/h speedo of our test vehicle, but the gauge proved to be 10 per cent optimistic. Suzuki is to replace this speedo with a 130 km/h unit by November.

Both the diff ratio and the high range ratio have been altered in the new model. Overall reduction ratio in high top is 7.119, compare to 8.355 in the 50. Apparently the Japanese engineers were only convinced they should change to such tall gearing after a test session in Australia, during which they were forced to sit for eight hours straight behind the wheel.

What the gearing means is that the engine works much more easily on the open road. And noise level and fuel consumption are appreciably reduced. Moreover, the LJ80V is still much quicker off the mark than the LJ50V, a factor of considerable importance for weekday commuters and weekend overlanders.

From outside, the 797cm³ engine sounds like nothing so much as a Mini Minor, a vehicle which began its life as an 850. Since then there have been Mazda 800s, Fiat 850s, even an 800 sports car (by Honda). Thus, with kerb mass of only three-quarters of a tonne, the LJ80V *should be* nippy off the mark. An ability to keep up with or, as the occasion arises, to get ahead of the traffic is essential for relaxed commuting.

On the road

Out in the country, the 80 hums along at around 90 km/h, and is not badly affected by moderate hills, but steep climbs (like Kurrajong) will still send the driver scrabbling for second gear. The primary box in this vehicle is identical to that in the 50, and as such is imprecise, even spongy. Surprisingly, considering the taller gearing, speeds through the gears are no different from those of the 50: 60 km/h in second, 80 km/h in third. There is more get-up-and-go in top than previously, which is handy for overtaking, but this is still a drawn-out and protracted procedure.

One considerable improvement is in on-road handling. The effect of the wider track is immediately apparent, and over-steer has been reduced. It is difficult now to push the vehicle beyond its safe limit, although the tyres (Yokohama bar-treads on our test vehicle) are uncomfortable on moist surfaces.

The noise level in the cabin is lower than previously but an appreciable number of decibels still filters through the firewall. The amazing thing is that from inside the vehicle this noise sounds little different from the two-stroke: high-pitched and demonstrative.

Hand-in-glove with the improved fuel consumption (down 10 per cent, and no burnt two-stroke oil) goes a big-bore 40-

litre fuel tank, 10 litres up on the 50. This affords a cruising range of around 450km—at last adequate for outback use. When you consider that under the same conditions the F20 is returning perhaps 14.1l/100km, and has a range of only 280 km, the LJ80's 8.7l/100km (32.6 mpg) looks particularly attractive. No other current 4WD can come close to that fuel economy. It is a selling point Suzuki is bound to capitalise on. Ateco claims the vehicle will run on standard fuel, but with a compression ratio of 8.7:1 it appears to prefer super .

We would have liked to have seen Suzuki enlarge the luggage compartment along with the engine, but we guess this would have been prohibitively expensive. At 200 kg, the payload remains unaltered. Other changes that would have been beneficial include a hand throttle and a tripmeter. The only vehicle Suzuki could now claim to complete with is the F10 Daihatsu (still being sold in some country areas). In our opinion, the LJ80 is a vastly superior vehicle to the F10.

In the rough

Suzukis have always shone off-road and this new vehicle will only enhance the marque's reputation.

Improved low-down torque characteristics coupled with taller gearing have given the 80 a hill-climbing ability unknown to the 50. The 50 was geared too low in first, and too high in second for long, loose slopes. In the back-blocks of Sunny Corner, near Lithgow, we proved the 80's superiority convincingly in some of the most punishing terrain in NSW.

The track led up one of the steepest, roughest hills one could imagine, covered with rocks ranging from pebble to boulder-size. We tackled it in first low, with the tyres down to 70 kpa (10 psi). Unquestionably, this gear would have proven too low on the LJ50 for the job. But we were able to use half-throttle on the 80, with plenty of revs in reserve for tough sections. The 80 still bounced a lot (with only 750 kg to keep the wheels on the deck, that is inevitable), but confounding all the pundits it clawed its way to the top without stopping. A Toyota Land Cruiser which attempted the same climb afterwards banged and cracked its transfer case.

On the steep downhills the new vehicle evinced another of its features: the four-stroke exerts considerable braking force on the wheels. On all but the most vertical slopes we were able to coast down in first low, foot off the brake pedal. This was impossible with the 50. If engine braking is not of the calibre of a Nissan or Toyota, it is certainly dirt tracks ahead of the previous model.

However, here our test vehicle exhibited an exasperating vice. The transfer level jumped out of low range under engine braking. This may have been a fault of our test model; Ateco Suzuki claims it is a function of newness; we fear it may be a genetic one, undiscovered in the LJ50 because of the impossibility of using the two-stroke engine as a brake.

Water crossings are no more arduous than previously: the new Suzuki still has a nylon cooling fan, mounted close to the radiator (dangerous), but the distributor runs off the rear end of the camshaft, well up out of harm's way, and the foam air filter, which is a new elongated design, is located above the cutaway engine bay. A word of warning: Suzuki brakes (d.l.s./s.l.s. drums) do not like water.

In the sand the Suzuki feels little different from its predecessor; the four-ply Yokohama tyres are of similar tread pattern to the Bridgestone Ground Grips fitted to our previous test Suzuki LJ50V

Below: basic instrumentation is similar to LJ50s. Speedo dial will reach 130km/h on production models.
Bottom: suspension mod: rear shockers have been moved outboard of springs.

SPECIFICATIONS: Suzuki LJ80V *(LJ50V specs in italics)*

Engine

Type: four-cylinder ohc four-stroke, alloy cross-flow head
Bore x stroke: 62 x 66mm
Displacement: 797cm^3 *(539cm^3)*
Compression ratio: 8.7:1
Claimed max power: 30.6kW (41bhp) at 5500rpm *(24.6kW at 5500rpm)*
Claimed max torque: 59.8Nm (44.0 ft.lb.) at 3500rpm *(56.6Nm at 3500rpm)*

Transmission

Internal ratios: 1st: 3.835; 2nd: 2.359; 3rd: 1.543; 4th: 1.000; Rev: 4.026
High range: 1.563 *(1.714)*; low range: 3.012 *(3.012)*
Diff ratio: 4.556:1 *(4.875)*
Gear change: all-synchro four-speed floorshift; single lever transfer case
Clutch: dry 134cm^2 single-plate diaphragm spring

Systems

Fuel: diaphragm-type fuel pump feeding from 40-litre *(30-litre)* steel tank, Mikuni 32PHD carburettor
Lubrication: gear-driven oil pump, full-flow paper oil filter; 3.0l wet sump
Cooling: 3.8l radiator/water jacket; four-blade nylon fan
Air filtration: wet polyurethane element
Electrical: 12V/35AH battery, 35A alternator, 40/50W headlights

Running Gear

Wheels and tyres: 6.00 x 16 Yokohama four-plies on five-stud steel rims
Brakes: (front): dls drums; (rear): sls drums; (parking brake) mechanical drum on tailshaft

Steering

Type: recirculating ball, 15.58:1 ratio
Turning circle: 9.2m (30.0')
Turns lock to lock: 3.3

Suspension

Front: five leaf springs with double-acting tele shocks
Rear: five leaf springs with double-acting tele shocks

General

LxWxH: 3170 x 1395 x 1660mm (124.8 x 54.9 x 72.8 in) *(3170 x 1295 x 1695mm)*
Kerb mass: 750kg (1653 lb.) *(730kg)* Payload: 200kg (440 lb.)
Wheelbase: 1930mm (76.0 in.)
Ground clearance: 230mm (9.0 in.)
Track (F&R): 1190/1200mm (46.8/47.2 in.) *(1100/1100mm)*
Fuel consumption (range): 12.3l/100km*-8.7l/100km (23.0-32.6mpg)
Top speed: 105km/h *(100km/h)*
Base price: around $5400 with Off Road pack
Special equipment fitted: ORP/Stage Three bull-bar, P/B radio, cloth-front seats; dress stripes (cost: around $400)
Colours available: red, mustard, white, dark green.
Supplier: Ateco Suzuki, 17 Sefton Rd, Thornleigh, NSW 2120
*Includes 50 percent off-road use.

Left: always
attractive Suzuki
styling is enhanced
by bull-bar. We are
not so sure about
the stripes and
seats.
Opposite:
diminutive Suzuki
is dwarfed by new
Ford 4WD, our
other test vehicle
this issue.

(see **Overlander,** Vol. 2, No. 2): great in mud, hopeless in sand. Fortunately, the vehicle is still light enough to gain flotation even with the tyres at their normal pressure (115 kPa/17psi). Fitting sand tyres will confirm that the 80 is still the best over-sand 4WD available, and its dune-climbing ability has been enhanced by the new motor and gearing.

A fringe benefit of the new configuration is the additional stability conferred on the vehicle by the wider track. This will prove especially useful on the beach.

Conclusions

Unlike the new Daihatsu, the LJ80 is not radically altered from its immediate ancestor. But it is in many ways improved. All the old features that we liked about Suzukis: one-piece rear door, light steering, tight turning circle, tailshaft parking brake, etc. are still there, and there is no doubt that the new motor is better than the two-stroke both off- and on-road.

What is surprising is that Suzuki did not go to a 1000 or even a 1200 cm³ engine. For all its easy running, the new power-plant is still tiny. There would surely have been room for a larger motor without crowding the engine bay or making the vehicle unsafe on-road.

Our guess is that Suzuki no longer wished to compete head-on with Daihatsu. This new vehicle still has only half the engine displacement of its previous competitor, retails for $600 less (Daihatsu recently reported a $150 price increase), has a 50 per cent advantage in fuel consumption and—provided the engine is durable—should also cost less in maintenance bills.

The LJ80 is a more pleasant on-road vehicle than its predecessor, but it is still not a long-distance strider of note. For this reason, we feel that the benefits of the revamp are reflected more strongly off-road than on.■

Tiny table-top

Suzuki's latest — tiny, cute and extremely versatile!

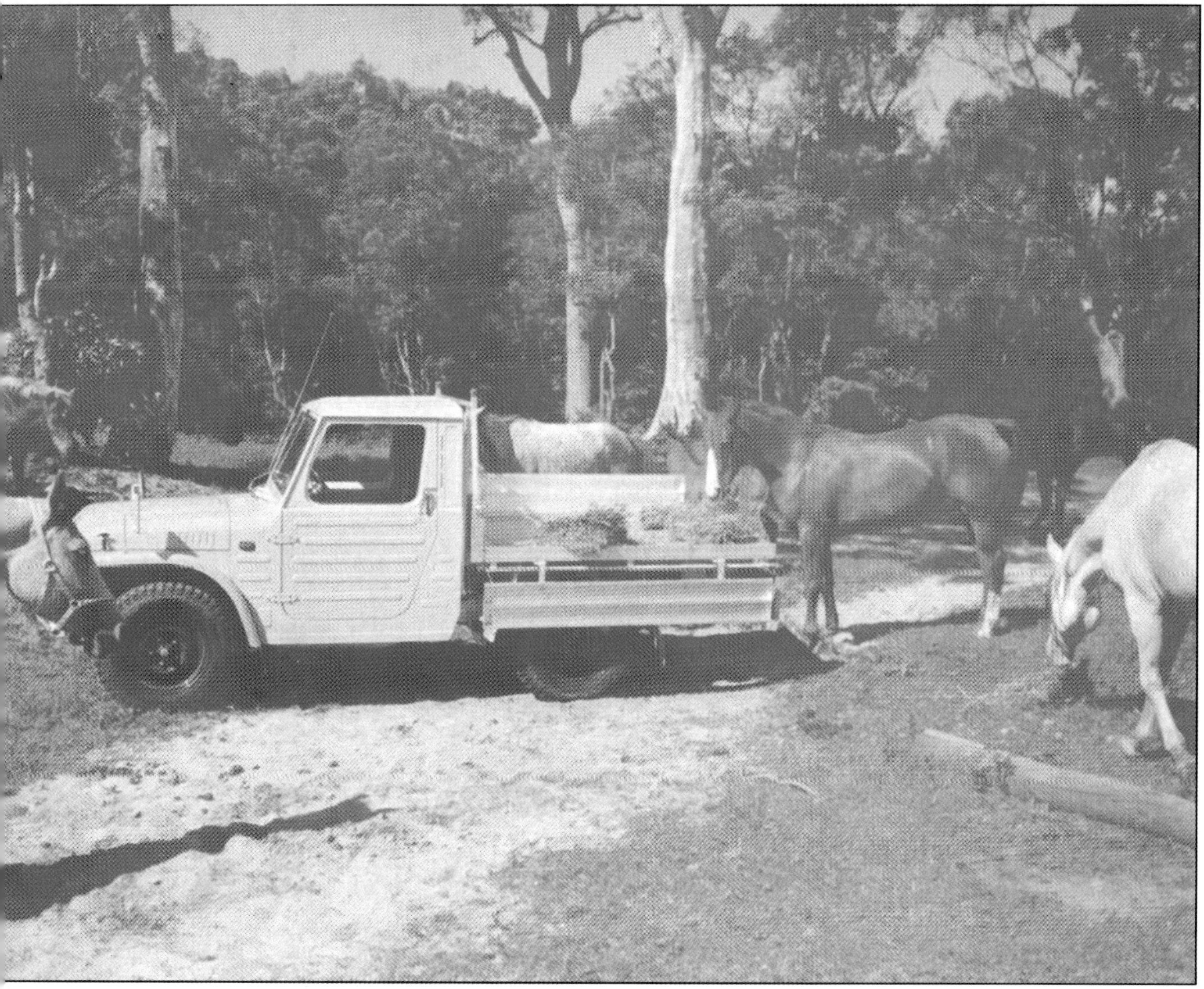

A "VARIATION on a popular theme", is probably the best way to describe Suzuki's latest variation on the LJ80 four wheel drive The newest innovation is a diminutive pick-up truck. A new cabin has been designed to allow for a cab/chassis application with a choice of steel or all-alloy tray available. With tray fitted, the little pick-up looks very much at home in an agricultural or goods carrying application.

In most states, the pick-up or LJ81 as it is designated, will have a 1.7 metre (5ft 6in) tray, but in NSW the tray length has been extended to 1.8 metres (6f5.).

Buyers in New South Wales have another added advantage. While the brochure describing the vehicle gives its carrying capacity as 250kg (550lb) at 41 degrees of slope, the NSW Motor Transport Department calculates its capacity at 440kg (968lb). This figure is arrived at by finding the difference in weight between the Aggregate Vehicle Weight plus 5 percent (1260kg) and the Tare Weight (i.e. unladen weight of 820kg). So, New South Wales buyers have in fact two slight advantages over their interstate compatriots.

Another important change to what remains as the standard model is the 270mm (10.6in) extension of the wheelbase. This allows, of course, for the

ABOVE: Interior layout is plain and simple and exactly the same as all other LJ80 models.
BELOW: The all-alloy tray is light and strong. The sides drop all round to allow easy access to the table-top.

try to be of usable length, but also contributes greatly to the ride capability of the vhicle.

It would be very interesting to see a long wheelbase hardtop!

The ride in the little pickup is excellent, most of the short wheelbase cho chop has been rectified by the extra length.

The additional wheelbase length also contributes to handling and reduces potential body roll dramatically. The cab/chassis or tray top unit is also fractionally (5mm) lower in overall height than the short wheelbase hardtop model.

Overall length is the only other dimension to change, and the LJ81 is a full 450mm (17in) longer than anything

SUZUKI LJ81

ENGINE

Type:	Four-stroke, water-cooled
Cylinders:	Four, in-line
Bore & STroke:	62.0 mm x 66.0 mm
Capacity:	797 cc
Carburation:	Single throat Mikuni 32 PHD
Compression Ratio:	8.7 to 1
Fuel Pump:	Mechanical, diaphragm type
Valve Gear:	Cogbelt driven SOHC
Maximum Power:	30.6 kW at 5,500
Maximum Torque:	59.8 Nm at 3,500

TRANSMISSION

Type:		Four speed, manual, floor change
Driving Wheels:		Rear or all
Clutch:		Single dry plate
Gearbox ratios:	1st:	3.835
	2nd:	2.359
	3rd:	1.543
	4th:	1.000
	Reverse:	4.026
Final Drive Ratio:		4.556
	Low Range:	2.571
	High Range:	1.563

SUSPENSION:

Front:	Live axle, semi-eliptic springs
Rear:	Live axle, semi-eliptic springs
Shock Absorbers:	Double acting telescopic

Wheels:	16 x 5.
Tyres:	600 x 16 x 4 pl

BRAKES

Type:	Dual circuit hydrauli
Front:	Drum (two leading shoe
Rear:	Drum (leading/trailing shoe
Parking Brake:	Mechanical on rear drum

STEERING

Type:	Recirculating ball and nu
Ratio:	15.6 to
Turning circle:	5.5 metre

DIMENSIONS AND WEIGHT

Wheelbase:	2200 mn
Front Track:	1190 mn
Rear Track:	1200 mn
Overall Length:	3620 mn
Overall Width:	1395 mr
Overall Height:	1680 mn
Ground Clearance:	240 mn
Kerb Weight:	.810 k

CAPACITIES AND EQUIPMENT

Fuel Tank:	40.0 litre
Cooling System:	3.8 litre
Engine Sump:	3.0 litre
Battery:	12 V 35 A
Alternator:	.35 A

else in the four wheel drive Suzuki range (in NSW the longer tray in fact extends overall length by 584mm or 23in).

The only other variation is pricing. These prices were correct in NSW as of February 13th, 1978 and are retail prices with no allowance for sales tax rebates. The basic cab/chassis was $5050; the pick-up with steel tray $5175, and the pick-up with all-alloy tray was $5450.

So there it is — the Suzuki LJ81 pick-up. It's an excellent compromise for those who want a small delivery vehicle and a weekend RV, and it's ideal for the man on the land as a back-up unit for those tasks which don't require the load carrying capabilities of the bigger four wheel drives.

Cross-country performance of the Suzuki is more impressive than when the vehicle is on the hard. It has generous suspension travel, very effective damping, and seems to have no difficulty in finding adquate grip on soft going

Suzuki LJ80V

A handy little pony for the farmer

WHEN YOU talk to a farmer about his transport requirements, it is appreciated that his needs are rather different from what might be imagined. Most of all, he just wants a mechanical horse: there isn't the supposed need to be lugging bales of hay and other produce about the farm — all that is done by the tractor. What the farmer needs is simply the personal transport that will be one hundred per cent reliable in all weathers — something that won't need a lot of attention, and won't get stuck just because it happens to be wet and muddy, or deep in snow.

In this light one can see the appeal of the Suzuki, fulfilling the role traditionally taken by the Land-Rover; it offers the same capability in the personal transport role, albeit without the load carrying capacity for which the bigger vehicle is justly famous.

Because of the maid-of-all-work functions to which a vehicle like the Land-Rover tends to be put, they have to be very strongly built and inevitably heavy. The Suzuki LJ80V, by making no attempt to fill the lorry side of the duties, and concentrating on personal transport only, is much lighter, and weighs just 16½ cwt. It can thus get away with an engine of only 797 c.c. capacity, bringing benefits all round — not only in fuel economy. At the same time, it has to be admitted that its abilities are strictly limited: it makes no claims to be a tractor as well.

Seen thus in perspective, it is still a vehicle of wide appeal. It has seats for two, can take two more occasionally at the back in modest discomfort that would be accepted for short trips, and it also has the capacity to take a reasonable load — up to the 400 lb limit.

Performance
At best off-road

We expected it to be rather a drag taking the Suzuki on the 100-mile trip to the MIRA proving grounds, but it proved less tedious than had been feared. Although the performance falls away abruptly once 50 mph has been reached, the Suzuki goes gallantly on to just over 60 mph and cruises at that speed without protest. Occasionally on a downgrade we saw the speedometer move up to just over 70 mph, but this was accompanied by a degree of thrash that discouraged one from going consistently on full throttle.

Much of the time the speedometer needle is seen at 65 mph, which seems the optimum cruising speed and is in fact a reasonable enough pace for such a vehicle, equivalent to true 60 mph. Where the shortage of power was noticed with greatest embarrassment was when a lorry was caught up on a motorway, running at a speed just below the Suzuki's natural pace. One would tend to wait until it was well clear behind, and then pull into the third lane to overtake, and all would go well until the vehicle was hit by the wind spill from the front of the overtaken lorry. It would then lose its momentum and the driver would find himself in the awkward position of being stuck in the passing lane, running alongside the other vehicle on full throttle, and unable to do anything about it as traffic began to build up behind. With a little forewarning, one learns to reserve the overtaking bid for downhill slopes.

In contrast, the performance in town traffic is decidedly lively. The clutch takes up smoothly and cleanly, taking the vehicle smartly off the mark, and the gear change is extremely quick with well-spaced ratios which make the best of the available power. Anyone who wanted to try could easily see off the Suzuki, but in general traffic running acceleration from rest to 30 mph in 6.8 sec is quite respectable. The gear change has a very narrow gate, so that the lever almost seems to go in a straight line from second to third. One has to avoid the temptation to change like this otherwise it goes inadvertently back into first; slight pressure to the right is advisable.

Synchromesh is good in most conditions, but can be beaten producing a crunch of gears if it is hurried too much, especially when changing down into second quickly. Strangely it was more effective into first gear, and on the one or two instances when first was found in mistake for third, the gear engaged without protest.

To the rear of the main gear lever is the subsidiary control for the transfer gearbox and four-wheel drive control. Normal position for this lever is forward but it is simply pulled back one notch to engage four-wheel drive. Only slight extra heaviness at the steering reminds the driver that he is still in four-wheel drive on the hard, but the lever can be knocked forward to disengage the front drive without any need to stop. The lever is moved to the left and then rearwards again to engage low ratio which is, of course, automatically in four-wheel drive. This drops the ratio in the transfer

---

Suzuki LJ80V
Lightweight 4 x 4 runabout for farm or estate, offering minimal but adequate carrying capacity for two and a modest amount of equipment or load. Superb little engine and gearbox, but rather atrocious ride especially when unladen. Not to be regarded as a substitute for a Land-Rover, but acceptable where a lighter and more economical vehicle is needed instead.

PRODUCED BY;
*Suzuki Motor Co Ltd,
Hamamatsu-Nishi,
PO Box 1,
432-91 Hamamatsu,
Japan.*
SOLD IN THE UK BY:
*Suzuki GB (Cars) Ltd,
87 Beddington Lane,
Croydon,
Surrey CRO 4TD.*

gearbox from the normal 1.56-to-1, down to 2.57, and maxima in the indirect gears at 7,000 rpm with low engaged are 15, 22 and 33 mph, instead of 22, 35 and 52 mph.

Familiarity with a number of cross-country vehicles leads one to expect that low range is hardly ever necessary, and can be kept in reserve for the occasional very steep climb, worse than 1-in-3. With the Suzuki, however, one has to allow for the small size of the engine rather more, and be more ready to change into low range for tackling thick mud or other tricky going — otherwise it can fail for sheer lack of power.

In low range with first gear

hard acceleration, but it is acceptable with the character of the vehicle.

Economy
Good for a 4 x 4

With its small overall dimensions and an efficient little engine of only 797 c.c., one tends to expect much better economy than is likely to be realised. It has to be appreciated that two driven axles and the associated transfer gearbox and duplicated running gear do consume a lot of fuel, while low gearing and a chunky box-like shape are also not the best for economy. But in relation to what is normally expected of a

with a fair amount of play in the system, but it did not prove any problem to keep the Suzuki in lane on a rather blustery day on the motorway. It scores in cross-country pounding, when there is scarcely any feed-back of wheel shocks through the steering. The turning circle is very stately at 33ft. 10in., but this does not make turning and manoeuvring as bad as may be feared thanks to the commanding visibility and the almost total lack of overhang at the rear. When reversing towards a parked car, it is a brave man who does not overestimate the rear length and allow about two feet more than necessary.

ever to be worked excessively hard. They cope extremely well indeed, and we were most surprised to find that 80lb pedal load achieved a 1.0g stop even when the track was swimming with water in heavy rain.

It was also commendable that even with its short wheelbase, the Suzuki pulled up all square without any trace of slewing in these conditions. Brake pedal effort brings good and steadily rising efficiency, in progression. The handbrake works on the transmission, just behind the transfer box. It makes a lot of noise and vibration if used as an emergency brake, but is capable of a very adequate 0.3g stop,

engaged, however, it has outstanding climbing ability, and it will plough through sticky mud so deep that the front differential is pushing a furrow through it. With this amount of reduction the Suzuki will not fail for lack of power — only lack of grip, or a sensibly prudent driver frightened by its climbing attitude, will halt it.

On the properly surfaced 1-in-3 test hill, the LJ80V had just enough power to move off in first gear high ratio, with judicious clutch slip. In low ratio, of course, a restart here was no problem at all.

Finished with the same sort of engineering neatness that characterises their motor cycles, the engine is beautifully made, and a mechanic's delight when it comes to maintenance work. The distributor is camshaft-driven and easily reached, and the camshaft itself is overhead, with belt drive. We were particularly impressed at how clean the under-bonnet compartment remained after a number of spectacular passes through a small brook during photography. Starting is very good and there is seldom need for a second try; a manual choke is fitted, which can soon be pushed in after a cold start, and gives good fast idle to prevent stalling.

This little engine is as free-revving as one would expect, but it does run through some vibration periods when revved hard. At low speeds it is extremely quiet, and the driver may even think it has stalled when he stops in traffic. There is a fair amount of roar in the upper speeds or in

four-wheel drive vehicle with big tyres and high ground clearance, the Suzuki is relatively good.

It did not go below 20 mpg while we had it — and if that does not sound much it must be appreciated that in cross-country work consumption tends to be assessed in terms of gallons per hour, with astonishingly few miles covered. Overall consumption for the full test, at 25.3 mpg, was therefore very reasonable.

Driven in spirited fashion but with not too much off-road work involved, the user can expect to clear 25 mpg, perhaps reaching 30 mpg for that unhurried trip to the market. Compression ratio is 8.7 to 1, but the engine runs happily on 2-star regular fuel without any snags of pinking or running-on. The filler has a lockable cap, and the tank holds 8.8 gal; the resulting range is only about 150 miles but is perhaps adequate for this kind of vehicle.

Road behaviour
Good for the liver

They say that too much opulence and comfort are bad for health — well, there's no problem of that with the Suzuki. The suspension uses tough leaf springs front and rear with live axles, and with the short wheelbase as well the ride is decidedly choppy. Even roads that one always presumed to be fairly well surfaced provoke a lot of lively reaction at the back end of the vehicle; but the ride softens noticeably when there is a full load on board.

Steering is by worm and nut,

On corners there is always the feeling that the vehicle wants to run wide, and the driver always seems to be tugging the front round. Above a certain degree of steering pull, however, there is a potentially hazardous swing to oversteer, which needs to be borne in mind in any attempt to hustle the vehicle along too hard. It would be all too easy for an inexperienced driver to overdo it and be caught out, resulting in a spin if the tail swing is not corrected in time.

Brakes
Very adequate

Although we could only reach 50 mph at the end of the quarter mile in standing start acceleration, it was felt that we should still run through our brake fade test procedure. A small increase in pedal load was noted, but the test is scarcely a severe one, nor is there sufficient power or high enough gearing for the brakes

while on the test hill it proves extremely effective. Its limitation is that with the vehicle pointing down the hill, there was not enough traction and the Suzuki slid steadily down dragging its locked wheels behind it. As there is no centre differential, it proved a complete answer to this to engage four-wheel drive, and the handbrake was then as effective as any we can ever recall testing.

Behind the wheel
Basic but adequate

We came to enjoy threading the Suzuki through traffic, since its narrow width of just under 4ft 7in, and the high seating position, mean that the driver misses no opportunities to go — motor cycle style — to the front of the queue, and he has no excuse for ever being caught out in the wrong lane. Well placed mirrors also help, and the all-round view is very good. In cross country

The "V" version of the LJ80 has this neat three-door steel body; there is also the canvas tilt model. Door windows wind down to open, and the rear side windows open outwards at the trailing edge

Impeccably finished for such a vehicle, the engine is delightfully neat and affords excellent accessibility

work the narrow width is again an advantage, allowing the Suzuki to pass down some overgrown tracks that would stop a wider vehicle.

A simple metal facia panel confronts the driver, with neat double instrument block seen through the top of the wheel, with speedometer on the left and fuel and temperature gauges in the matching dial on the right. The choke is positioned in the centre, and there is the unusual refinement of separate tell-tale lights for handbrake and for brake fluid level.

The steering wheel is neatly made with sturdy two-spoke construction, and the ''beep'' horn is sounded by the centre button. Lighting switch is on the right, with right-hand dip and flash lever beneath the wheel. The headlamps proved very adequate, with quite good dipped beam. There is an interior light over the driver's door, but no courtesy light switch.

The seats are unexpectedly comfortable, giving good lateral support and holding the occupants well in place when pounding rough terrain. The gear lever is well placed to be reached without stretching, and the transfer lever is equally accessible. A little plan on the centre tunnel explains its functions, in English.

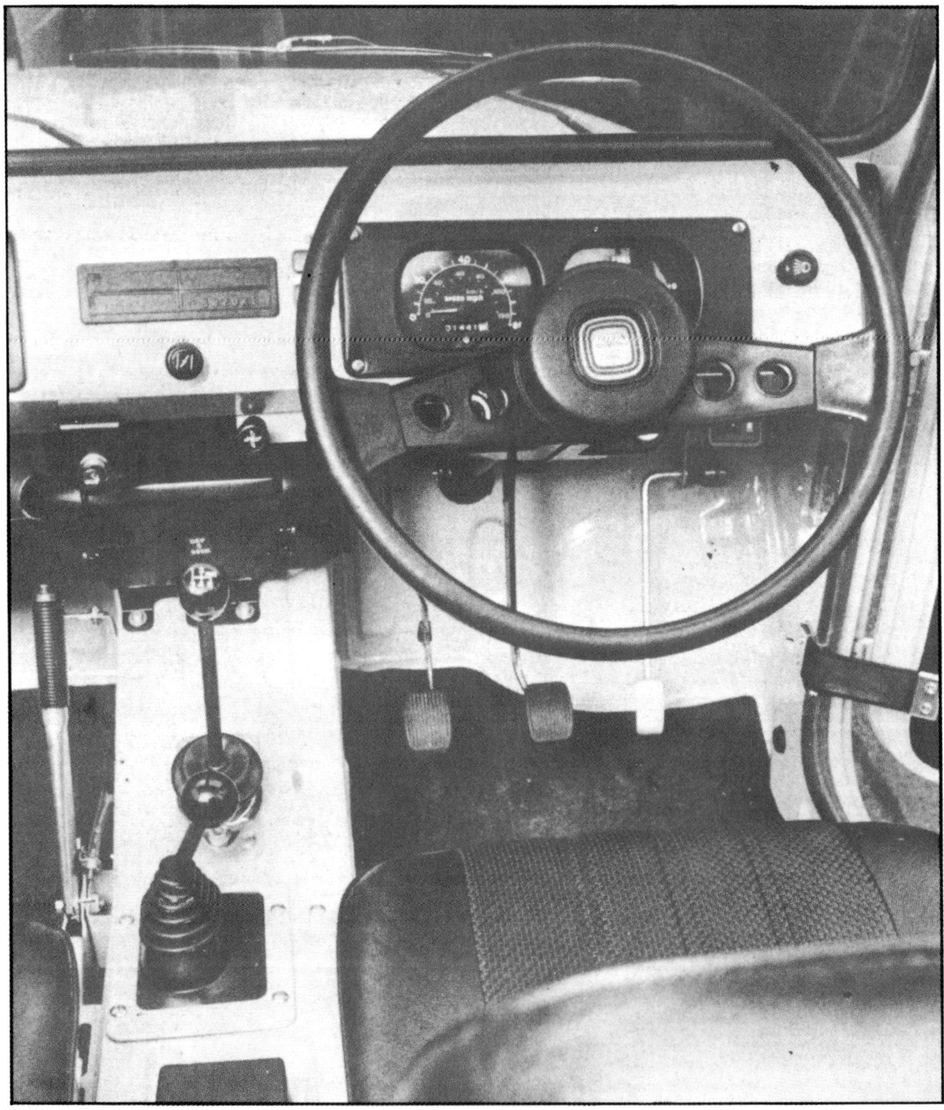

Living with the Suzuki LJ80V

Normally the bonnet is secured by two positive and easily released external rubber spring catches, and the bonnet has no stay: it is either held up with one hand during a quick dipstick check, or pushed gently back to lean against the windscreen. As already mentioned, accessibility is a delight, and will be appreciated by everyone who has to work on the engine. To secure the bonnet, there is a locking release pull inside the glove compartment, but this might be more effective still if the compartment were lockable, which it is not.

A useful toolkit including an admirable ring spanner for undoing the wheel nuts, lives in the facia locker. There is also a parcels shelf beneath.

A simple water valve heater is fitted. It has recirculatory or fresh air control, and a turn knob on the left side of the unit switches the water valve on or off — as usual, without any intermediate setting. The outlet flaps can also be closed if required, to send all the incoming air to the screen for demisting. In addition, there is quite an effective fresh air vent with control knob beneath the facia. The heater has a two-speed blower, quiet on the slower speed, but this does not boost the vent, which is by ram effect only. Rear side windows can be opened outwards at the trailing edge for extraction.

It seems a little crude to see the handbrake warning light switch revealed, with its feed wire enclosed in transparent plastic, but this is not out of keeping with the functional nature of the vehicle.

The spare wheel is mounted on the back door, where it is held by three wheel nuts. Many owners would probably want a more thief-proof mounting. Both front and rear doors are lockable from outside with the key, or by pressing down the lock button (side doors only) and closing with the outside handle pulled up.

Effective but simple windscreen wipers clear the screen adequately and work at two speeds, controlled by a simple rotary switch on the left of the steering column. It is pushed in to work the electric screen washers. Even on wet roads, the rear window did not become too dirty to see through.

Built very much for a purpose, the Suzuki LJ80V fulfils its utility function extremely well. It does not have the Land-Rover's appeal of an aluminium body, but in all other respects it serves very well as a scaled-down Land-Rover with the benefits of compactness and no doubt

Cross-country performance of the Suzuki is more impressive than when the vehicle is on the hard. It has generous suspension travel, very effective damping, and seems to have no difficulty in finding adequate grip on soft going

wer running costs. It has con-derable appeal for the farmer small-holder who wants inex-avagant go-anywhere trans-ort, or for the off-road leisure arket where running costs are ven more important.

he Suzuki ange

Two versions of the Suzuki ross-country vehicle are avail-ble: the LJ80V as tested, with eel estate body and opening il door, which attracts £244

worth of Special Car Tax; and the LJ80. The second version is a good deal cheaper (total £3,200), because it has remov-able canvas tilt body and so es-capes SCT. It has a sturdy roll-over hoop with rear support struts, and its windscreen can be folded down flat on to the bonnet in the fashion of the original Jeep. Quite different, but using the same splendid little engine, there are also the ST80 vans, with two wheel drive, mid-engine, and choice of three bodies.   □

HOW THE LJ 80 V PERFORMS

MAXIMUM SPEEDS

Gear	mph	kph	rpm
Top (mean)	68	109	5,800
(best)	69	111	5,870
3rd	52	84	7,000
2nd	35	56	7,000
1st	22	35	7,000
In low transfer:			
Top	49	79	7,000
3rd	33	53	7,000
2nd	22	35	7,000
1st	15	24	7,000

TEST CONDITIONS:
Wind: 5-10 mph
Temperature: 10 deg C (50 deg F)
Barometer: 29.7 in. Hg (1006 mbar)
Humidity: 98 per cent
Surface: wet asphalt and concrete
Test distance: 512 miles

Figures taken at 1,400 miles by our own staff at the Motor Industry Research Association proving ground at Nuneaton.

All Autocar test results are subject to world copyright and may not be reproduced in whole or part without the Editor's written permission

ACCELERATION

FROM REST

True mph	Time (sec)	Speedo mph
30	6.8	32
40	12.8	43
50	24.5	54
60	—	65

Standing ¼-mile: 24.6 sec, 50 mph
Standing km: 49.4 sec, 58 mph

IN EACH GEAR

mph	Top	3rd	2nd
10-30	17.0	9.3	9.1
20-40	25.4	9.8	10.6
30-50	27.0	18.7	

FUEL CONSUMPTION

25.3 (11.2 litres / 100km)

Autocar formula: Hard 22.8 mpg
Driving Average 27.8 mpg
and conditions Gentle 32.9 mpg

Official fuel consumption figures
(Not required for four-wheel drive vehicles)

OIL CONSUMPTION

(SAE 10W / 40) Negligible

WEIGHT

Kerb, 16.6 cwt / 1,860 lb / 842 kg
(Distribution F/R, 53.6/46.4)
Test, 20.0 cwt / 2,235 lb / 1,014 kg
Max. payload 440 lb / 200 kg

PRICES

Basic	£2,929.78	**Total on thd aroad**	**£3,762.00**
Special Car Tax	£244.14		
VAT	£476.09		
Total (in GB)	**£3,650.50**	**EXTRAS** (inc. VAT)	None listed
Seat Belts	Standard	**TOTAL AS TESTED**	
Licence	£50.00	**ON THE ROAD**	**£3,762.00**
Delivery charge (London)	£55.00		
Number plates	£7.00	Insurance	Group 3

SPECIFICATION

ENGINE

	Front, rear-wheel drive plus engage-able front-wheel drive; no centre diff
Head / block	Aluminium / cast iron
Cylinders	4
Main bearings	5
Cooling	Water
Fan	Fixed
Bore, mm (in.)	62 (2.44)
Stroke, mm (in.)	66 (2.60)
Capacity, cc (in³)	797 (48.63)
Valve gear	Ohc
Camshaft drive	Toothed belt
Compression ratio	8.7-to-1
Ignition	Contact breaker
Carburettor	Mikuni 32 PHD Single
Max power	40.5 bhp (SAE) at 5,500 rpm
Max torque	44.1 lb ft at 3,500 rpm

TRANSMISSION

Type	Manual four-speed all-synchromesh with transfer gearbox
Clutch	Diaphragm spring

Gear	Ratio	mph / 1000rpm	In low ratio:	
Top	1.0	11.52	1.64	6.9
3rd	1.54	7.5	2.54	4.5
2nd	2.36	4.9	3.88	2.9
1st	3.84	3.0	6.32	1.8

Final drive gear Hypoid
Ratio 4.55 (transfer gears: high, 7.12, low 11.72)

SUSPENSION

Front — location	Live axle
— springs	Semi-elliptic
— dampers	Telescopic
— anti-roll bar	No
Rear — location	Live axle
— springs	Semi-elliptic
— dampers	Telescopic
— anti-roll bar	No

STEERING

Type	Recirculating ball, with damper
Power assistance	No
Wheel diameter	15.8 in.
Turns lock to lock	2.9

BRAKES

Circuits	2, split front / rear
Front	8.26 in. dia drum
Rear	8.26 in. dia. drum
Servo	No
Handbrake	Centre lever, on transmission

WHEELS

Type	Pressed steel disc
Rim width	4.5 E
Tyres — make	Dunlop
— type	Roadtrak Major crossply tubed
— size	6.00-16 4-ply
— pressures	F: 17; R: 17 psi (normal driving)

EQUIPMENT

Battery	12V 35Ah
Alternator	35A
Headlamps	90/80 watt
Reversing lamp	Standard
Hazard warning	Standard
Electric fuses	6
Screen wipers	2-speed
Screen washer	Electric
Interior heater	Water valve
Air conditioning	Not available
Interior trim	PVC seats, PVC headlining
Floor covering	PVC mats
Jack	Scissors type
Jacking points	4, base of each leaf spring
Windscreen	Laminated
Underbody protection	Galvanised steel and vinyl sealant

Suzuki vs Daihatsu

Continued from page 23

useful in the slimy conditions and on pebbled down-grades. However, both vehicles had such efficient brakes (before the water crossings) that any advantage was minimal.

Two river crossings failed to make any impression on the vehicles apart from drowning the Daihatsu's brakes. But in deeper water it would be necessary to disconnect the nylon cooling fans to prevent them being pushed through the radiators. With the Daihatsu you can simply slip the fan-belt; on the Suzuki you must unbolt the fan. Radiator blinds would also help. Because of its slanted cylinder block, the Suzuki also has its distributor mounted right up on top of the engine and out of water's way; the Daihatsu's is more conventionally located alongside the vertical block.

It took all our skill to drive up the far bank of the second creek crossing. You had to make a sharp left-hand turn and position the front wheels on two rocks before making the run up the bank. The trouble was lining up the vehicles in the first place. The Suzuki's lesser turning circle helped, but its engine's lack of low-down grunt caused it to stall three times before it finally conquered the climb.

If the Daihatsu did not exactly sail through, it did make the traverse in only two attempts — and the engine never missed a beat!

We were concerned about the underneath of the vehicles, since there were many protruding rocks and logs in the creek-bed. Neither 4WD has a skid or splash plate but both have their engines fairly well tucked up out of harm's way. The Daihatsu has a thicker box section chassis which provides greater protection both from splashes and from hard objects. We were intrigued subsequently to find the Daihatsu's engine bay nearly clean, whereas the Suzuki's was liberally coated with mud.

The Daihatsu's differentials are also offset from centre, whilst the Suzuki's are located equidistantly from the wheels. Once again, they are more vulnerable to knocks. The two-stroke, however, has superior overall ground clearance.

Up front, the Daihatsu's radiator is recessed into the bodywork whereas the Suzuki's is squashed right into the snout of the vehicle, where it is susceptible to abuse even with a bull-bar fitted. The Daihatsu has a built-in roll-bar; the one illustrated on the Suzuki is an optional extra.

We have already mentioned the additional protection afforded by thehe Daihatsu's door-frame design. Both vehicles are fitted with lap-belts; we'd like to see a lap-sash arrangement integrated with their roll-bars.

A very solid through-bolt with 15cm Q.D. handle prevents the Daihatsu's spare wheel from taking its own outback excursion; Suzuki's less sturdy system should not fail but it is definitely harder to use. It is also possible to open one side of the Daihatsu's tailgate without disturbing the spare tyre; the LJ50 has a single gate.

However, two things not in the little D's favour are its fuel tank, which bulges below the centre floorpan (Suzuki's also bulges, but at the rear of the vehicle); and its car-type bonnet lock (the Suzuki has two side clamps which are much less likely to snap open in rough going). Also expect the LD's rear number-plate bracket to take a battering.

Access to the Suzuki's engine components is not up to the Daihatsu's standards, but by slanting the block the Hamamatsu engineers have cleverly gained maximum space from a small engine bay. There is room, in fact, in both vehicles to slot in a larger engine, and we think they would both benefit from such an upgrading.

Suzuki already has available to it a 750cm³ water-cooled two-stroke triple and the RE5 rotary; Daihatsu might be able to purchase a 1200 or 1400 four, perhaps even with an overhead cam.

This section of our test shattered no beliefs but added something to our understanding. To return to our original assessment of the two vehicles: the Suzuki is a better fun machine; the Daihatsu more suitable for the farm. If you want a city-based all-roads vehicle, you're probably better off with the hard-top Suzuki; Daihatsu is to release a similar version of the F10L later this year.

Now doesn't that all dovetail together beautifully? After all, Daihatsu is a workhorse-based company (trucks); Suzuki leisure-orientated (motorcycles) . . . . ■

SUZUKI LJ-80 SPECIFICATIONS

PRICES

Basic list	
Suzuki LJ-80	See text

GENERAL

Curb weight, lb (test model)	1740
Weight distribution, %, front/rear	55/45
Wheelbase, in.	76
Track, front/rear	46.9/47.2
Overall length	125.4
Overall height	65.7
Overall width	54.9
Ground clearances (test model):	
Front axle	7.7
Rear axle	7.7
Fuel tank capacity (U.S. gal.)	10.6

ACCOMMODATION

Standard seats	2 individual vinyl-covered front seats

INSTRUMENTATION

Instruments	speedometer, odometer, fuel, temperature
Warning lights	oil pressure, charge

ENGINES

Standard	48.6-cid OHC Four
Bore x stroke, in.	2.44 x 2.6
Compression ratio	8.7:1
Net horsepower @ rpm	41 @ 5500
Net torque @ rpm, lb-ft	44.1 @ 3500
Type fuel required	leaded or unleaded

DRIVETRAIN

Standard transmission	4-spd manual
Transmission ratios: 1st	3.83:1
2nd	2.35:1
3rd	1.54:1
4th	1.00:1
Synchromesh	all forward
Rear axle type	solid beam
Final drive ratios	4.56
Free-running front hubs	NA
Limited slip differential	NA
Transfer case	2-spd
Transfer case ratios	low—2.57:1 high—1.56:1

CHASSIS & BODY

Body/frame	welded steel body, ladder frame
Brakes (std)	front and rear drums, hydraulic
Steering type (std)	ball nut
Power steering	NA
Tire size (std)	165SR x 15

SUSPENSION

Front suspension	closed-knuckle beam axle, leaf springs, tube shocks
Rear suspension	beam axle, leaf springs, tube shocks

Which would you rather have:
Zero-60 in six seconds, or 30 mpg?

BY JON F. THOMPSON

Imagine a tough, versatile four-wheel-drive vehicle capable of traversing the most difficult terrain, a vehicle small enough to easily negotiate the narrowest trails, large enough to carry two adults and all their supplies, powerful enough to climb the steepest hills, and efficient enough to obtain fuel economy, in pavement running, as high as the low 30s.

Impossible, you say? Don't bet on that, and don't say ''impossible'' so loudly that the folks at Suzuki-Allarco, in Canada, can hear you. Suzuki-Alarco is enthusiastically importing the Suzuki LJ-80, pictured here on these pages, into Canada. The firm's enthusiasm is quite understandable, because the LJ-80 can do all those impossible-sounding things and indeed, can do them with a certain *élan*, a certain inde-

structible style, that makes the new LJ-80 driver suspect that he just may be rediscovering off-road driving. There are, of course, some important trade-offs. For instance, any 1700-pound vehicle that will obtain gas mileage of up to 35 mpg can be expected to be just a little, uh, anemic in terms of its highway performance. More about that later.

The Suzuki LJ-80 is essentially a second-generation Suzuki Brute. You may recall that during the very early '70s a few Suzuki Brutes—LJ-50s, in their proper designation—made it into the United States. Concentrated mostly on the West Coast, the Brute proved to be very small, quite sturdy, very economical, very slow, and because of its 300-cc two-cylinder, two-cycle engine, capable of producing some of the dirtiest exhaust emissions imaginable. With some reason then, the Brute's life-span here was very short.

So here we are nearly 10 years later. The folks at Suzuki, who 10 years ago

were renowned for their abilities with high-performance two-stroke motorcycle engines, have turned their not inconsiderable skill and expertise towards multi-cylinder four-cycle motorcycle engines. Suzuki's large motorcycles, the GL-750 and GL1000, 750 cc and 1000 cc machines respectively, are justly famous not only for their substantial power output, but for the integrity of their design and construction. So it seems that Suzuki's engineers have the mass-production, high-performance four cycle engine pretty well figured out. It stands to reason then that those engineers would turn their attention to the LJ-50. They did. They did not start from scratch. They did not need to, since the concept of the basic vehicle seemed sound enough. Mostly, they confined their activities to coming up with a suitable four-stroke powerplant. What resulted from those activities was a compact, jewel-like four-cylinder, overhead-cam engine using hemi-

SUZUKI

spherical combustion chambers and displacing 797 cubic centimeters, or 48.6 cubic inches. Obviously, any engine displacing just 48.6 cid can't make much power, at least not in stock trim; the LJ-80's engine doesn't: it makes 41 hp, at 5500 rpm and 44.1 lb-ft of torque at 3500 rpm.

Small though it may be, the little engine is a real marvel. A standard wet sump design, it features a crankshaft which runs in five main bearings. All the bearings, main and rod, are plane. The pistons work in bores of 2.44 inches, and have strokes of 2.6 inches. Compression ratio is 8.7:1, and fuel is fed to the combustion chambers by a single, tiny Mikuni-built Solex-type side-draft carburetor with a venturi bore of .945 inch. Fuel mixed by that midget carb is admitted into the combustion chambers by single valves situated in each pent-roof combustion chamber, and exhaust exits the combustion chamber by a single exhaust valve in each cylinder. Those valves are actuated by rocker arms which are driven by that single, center-mounted over-head camshaft. The cam is driven by a single, cog-toothed drive belt which runs off the front crankshaft pulley. All in all, this is a very contemporary arrangement. All that seems to be missing are the familiar (in this country) emissions control devices.

There are a few clever little touches, however, which keep this powerplant from being stone ordinary, touches which make very good sense indeed, given this engine's application. First of all, it is mounted very high in the LJ-80's chassis, so that there doesn't appear to be any way at all for even the most vicious rock to reach up and bite the oil pan, which is well protected by the front axle. Secondly, the engine's induction system is located well above the vehicle's front fender line. This means that to drown the engine out in a stream, a driver will have to get the LJ-80 into some seriously deep water.

Even if some driver does venture into deep water, he's going to have a very difficult time drowning out the ignition system, which is protected from moisture not only by all the usual methods— good distributor cap sealing, rubber boots everywhere—but by a clever arrangement which maintains a flow of warm, dry air through the distributor. This is supplied by a pair of plastic tubes which connect to the transmission gear case. Turbulence of the whirling transmission gears pumps that air through the distributor, helping it to remain moisture-free.

Sadly, none of this actually helps the engine make more power, and that is something that it could use. The folks at Suzuki-Allarco apparently agree, for they tell us that a kit aimed at doubling the little engine's output is in the works. That shouldn't be too difficult, since Suzuki's 850-cc motorcycle engine, though being similar to the LJ-80 engine only in size and in basic concept, makes an easy 70, maybe 75 horsepower with relatively mild camshafts.

The power made by the Suzuki's little engine gets to the ground via a straightforward little 4-speed transmission. The trans is a top-loader of sorts, but gear choice is not controlled by a shift lever

sticking directly down into the transmission case as per usual practice. Rather, gear choice is controlled by a remote lever mounted behind the transmission, and connected to it by a linkage system. This linkage system seems to work well enough, but also seems—well, flabby and imprecise, though we must admit, never in our brief though highly concentrated experience with the LJ-80 did we miss a shift because of it. The ratios, 3.8:1 for first gear, 2.35:1 for second, 1.54:1 for third and 1:1 for fourth, are cleverly matched to the engine's horsepower and torque, and displayed no large gaps in pulling power between gears.

The differentials reduce the final drive ratios by 4.55:1, but before that happens, all ratios are processed by the transfer case, which even in high range runs a gear reduction ratio of 1.56:1 and in low range a reduction of 2.57:1. What all this means is that even in high range, high gear and high engine rpm, you'll not obtain a great deal of top speed from an LJ-80.

That transfer case is mounted separately from the transmission, and is driven by its own short drive shaft, which has a universal joint on each end. It is controlled by a stubby little lever just between the Suzuki's front seats. The lever has a very light touch, and requires no effort at all for shifting, particularly when shifting between 2wd-high and 4wd-high. Suzuki recommends that while this shift can be made while the vehicle is underway, that the clutch be depressed and the steering wheels be pointed straight ahead. For the shifts into and out of low range, the Suzuki, like other 4x4 vehicles, must be at rest. Between the notches for 4wd-high and 4wd-low, Suzuki has provided a neutral PTO position.

Both the front and rear axles, with their standard, non-limited-slip, 4.55:1 gear sets, are of the solid beam type and both are suspended by semi-elliptical leaf springs, though the front leafs, like those on a Blazer, take a reverse bend. A light tube shock absorber helps control axle movement at each wheel. Locking front hubs are not available.

The Suzuki's brakes are, front and rear, rather tiny drum affairs which, while apparently up to some pretty hard use, are not able to cope with any amount of moisture. Thus, the first time you ford a stream in a Suzuki, or get stuck in mud of any depth, the brakes go away and stay away for a good while, even when the usual drying procedures are applied. More about this later. We'd be happy to see disc brakes applied to the Suzuki, at least up front, where most of the braking work is done.

Of additional interest is the fact that the Suzuki's emergency brake actuates a complete, double-shoe brake drum mounted on the final drive shaft just aft of the transfer case. Necessarily a bit higher in the Suzuki's chassis than the wheel brakes, it has a chance of remaining dry when the standard brakes get wet, and possessing ample power, it seems to be effective in emergency situations. A nice touch on the soft-topped version of the Suzuki, which of course cannot be locked up the way the steel-topped version can, is that a key-actuated lock is mounted on the emergency brake lever. Though a big enough guy with a big enough crow bar, or maybe a big enough hammer, could probably break the lock, the lock's sturdy construction seems to indicate that anybody trying to break it would have to expend considerable energy to do so.

Clothing all this mechanical paraphernalia is a welded steel body which in appearance is not unlike that of the Toyota Land Cruiser. This seems understandable; how many variations on this simple utility vehicle theme can there be, after all? Enough, apparently, so that the Suzuki at least maintains its own identity, when viewed from the front. Viewed from the side or the rear, though, it looks like a Jeep/Land Cruiser/Land Rover/whatever, but in 3/4 scale. There are several choices of form. The straight LJ-80 is pure vehicle, no doors, no top. The LJ-80-Q comes with steel doors and cloth top. The LJ-80-V comes with an integral, non-removable steel top, and the LJ-81 is a tiny, truncated pickup with a fold-down rear gate and bed sides that also fold down. We wouldn't expect the LJ-81 to be a rousing success in any Occidental country, for one sound reason: Its main feature is a disastrously low supply of interior room, a painfully short supply of leg room.

Not that the other models in the Suzuki lineup are all that roomy, but at least in them, the moderately-tall to tall driver is not forced by the LJ-81's rear

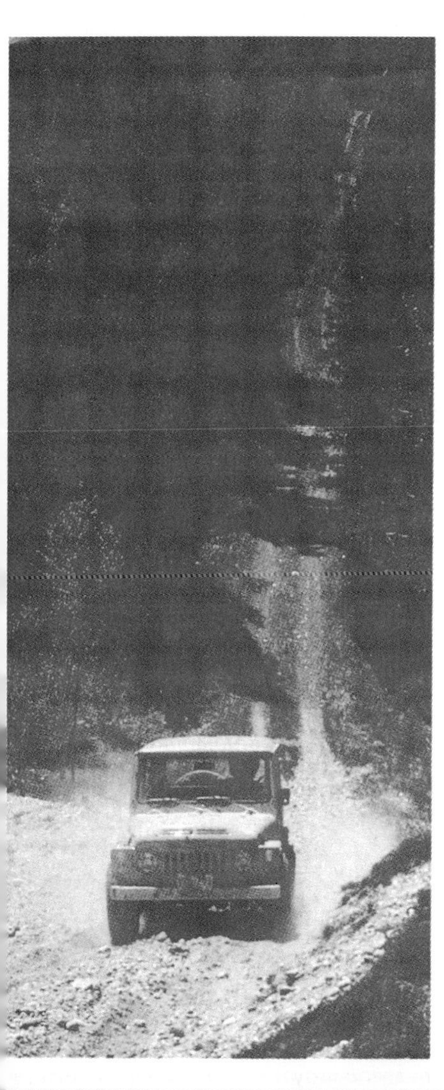

cab bulkhead to sit with his knees under his chin. Which is to say, unless you're quite short in stature, you're not going to fit into the LJ-81 at all.

Fitting into the other derivatives of the Suzuki, despite its relatively small size, is really not that much of a problem. While leg room is not found in copious quantities, it at least should be ample for most folks. Head room is more than sufficient and shoulder room also seems ample, being more-or-less on the order of the amounts found in VW Beetles: enough, but just enough.

As would be expected in a vehicle of this sort, the interior fitments are Spartan in nature and lacking in sophistication. The seats, for example, are tiny affairs which provide barely adequate comfort, particularly over relatively long hauls. The driver's seat is the only one which is adjustable fore and aft, though again, Suzuki-Allarco's representatives told us that a kit to fix that is in the works.

Once in the driver's seat and secured by the inertia reel-controlled seat belt-shoulder harness, the driver is confronted with a sporty little padded steering wheel which is connected to a ball-and-nut steering gearbox. The steering system delivers a turning radius of slightly more than 16 feet, even though the front axle uses closed-knuckle universal joints at the steering pivot points. Behind the steering wheel is a very plain dash featuring an absolute minimum of instruments: a speed-ometer/odometer on the left of the cluster, and on the right, a pod containing fuel and temperature gauges and oil pressure and generator warning lights, as well as high-beam and directional signal indicators. To the left of this cluster are the light switch and choke, to the right are the emergency brake and seat belt lights and the radio. So far, all straightforward.

Things get a bit more convoluted as we consider the heater controls. The fresh air/recirculated air, heater fan and defroster functions are controlled by three knobs below the center of the dash, but little of what you do with those knobs matters unless you've first turned on the flow of hot water to the heater by opening a valve on the left side of the heater box itself, mounted on top of the center transmission tunnel. Just aft of the heater controls is where the shift lever is found, and just aft of that lever is where the transfer case lever is found. The footwell provides ample room for the footwork required for correct operation of the clutch, brake and gas pedals, and even provides a little extra room for the feet—a bit of a surprise, given the overall size of the vehicle. The fact that all three pedals are very small undoubtedly helps.

Firing the LJ-80 up from stone cold requires little more than turning the steering column-mounted key and pulling out the dash-mounted manual choke. On the units PV4 was supplied

SUZUKI

The Suzuki's interior has all the basics, but not much more. Overall interior space is very limited but even though the seats are quite small comfort levels aren't as low as they might be.

with, two LJ-80-Vs and an LJ-80-Q, response was instantaneous, belying the fact that all vehicles were brand new, with less than 600 miles on them. One, in fact, had less than three miles on the clock when delivered into our hands, had received minimal dealer preparation, yet still started and ran like a charm. The engine starts with a throaty roar, and after reaching the operating temperature, ticks over at an even, smooth idle. Once out on the road, throttle response seems good, though with 41 horses pulling 1700 pounds plus passengers, how good can one expect the Suzuki's throttle response to be?

Around town and on paved highways is where the Suzuki's limitations are most felt. Though the driver's situation is overall a reasonably happy one, with modest comfort levels and good visibility, the Suzuki's vague little shifter, with its unclear detents and generally imprecise action, is a bit of a problem at first, and this is magnified by the fact that a driver must constantly use it to obtain even basically tolerable amounts of performance from that hard-working little engine. Eldon Edey, Dave Johnston and Vic Risling, Suzuki-Allarco's representatives on hand for our visit with the LJ-80, all verified that the vehicle doesn't really provide a fair reflection of its own performance potential until it has gone at least 1500 miles, and none of the vehicles PV4 sampled had. Still, all we can tell you is what we experienced, and that would be classified as generally poor highway performance, with top speeds in the 50–60 mph range and zero–60 times of—oh, say, an afternoon, unless you happened to be running downhill, in which case one reached 60 mph a bit sooner. Really, this is no freeway flyer, no commuter vehicle. The Suzuki is stable enough out on the highway, it's just bog slow, slow enough to hold up traffic in areas where passing is difficult, slow enough

so that a traveler had better plan for generous amounts of time travel. The one consolation is that with the Suzuki, he won't be spending too much time in gas stations, because with its 10.6-gallon fuel tank, the LJ-80 ought to be able to manage a highway cruise distance of at least 300 miles per tank. In all fairness, we should say that according to the men from Suzuki-Allarco, once it is broken in, the LJ-80 will cruise easily at 55–60 mph with a bit of throttle left over.

The vehicle's stiff little multi-leaf springs and its short 76-inch wheelbase also contrive to limit its highway comfort, providing a ride which borders on harsh. The short wheelbase exacerbates this condition by adding a certain amount of ride choppiness—short pitches fore and aft—to the vehicle's overall ride. The stiff springs and short wheelbase proved to be assets to the Suzuki off road, but on the highway, they serve to limit its overall comfort levels.

Obviously, highway cruising is not what this vehicle is for; it is for off roading, and to sample its potential, we flew to Calgary, Alberta, obtained a trio of Suzukis, and headed them west towards the Rocky Mountains, where we could play in the rough, remote foothills where off-road traffic is the exception rather than the rule. The area chosen consists of dense forests, criss-crossed by streams, rivers, and many, many

miles of what the Canadians call cut lines. We know them in the States as fire breaks, and no matter what you call them, their steep climbs and rough driving surfaces spiced with occasional meadows of swampy muskeg or acre-square areas of smooth, round rocks seemed an ideal situation for a vehicle like the Suzuki.

The most important discovery is that in spite of the LJ-80's marginal highway capabilities, we found very little in the way of rough country that would stop it. We got stuck once, in a large, flat meadow area under which was lurking

---

"With 41 horses pulling 1700 pounds, how good can you expect throttle response to be?"

---

muskeg—watery Canadian swamp land covered by grass. Our first attempt to cross this area resulted in an immediate stuck situation, and it was here that we discovered why we didn't like the oversized tires bulging muscularly out from under the Suzuki's minimal fenders. The exposed tire shoulders threw sticky, black mud in every direction— even into the Suzuki's interior, through the open windows—as we flailed around trying to extricate ourselves. With the help of a tow rope finally, we accomplished that task and skirted the mud to tackle some very steep hills. With one exception, the Suzukis climbed every hill they were pointed towards, though on a couple of occasions they ground to a halt halfway up the hill, progress impeded by the larger-than-stock tires and the poorer than normal gear ratio the large tires brought with them, and by the Suzuki's minimal low-speed power output. When halted this way, the standard procedure is to set the emergency brake, rev the engine, and once the revs were up, drop the clutch and peel out uphill. This sort of peel-out maneuver only serves to point out the vehicle's most glaring deficiency—its relative lack of low-end grunt. As mentioned earlier, the en-

The Suzuki's layout is unusual for several reasons: The engine sits up very high in the chassis, and the transfer case is separate from the transmission.

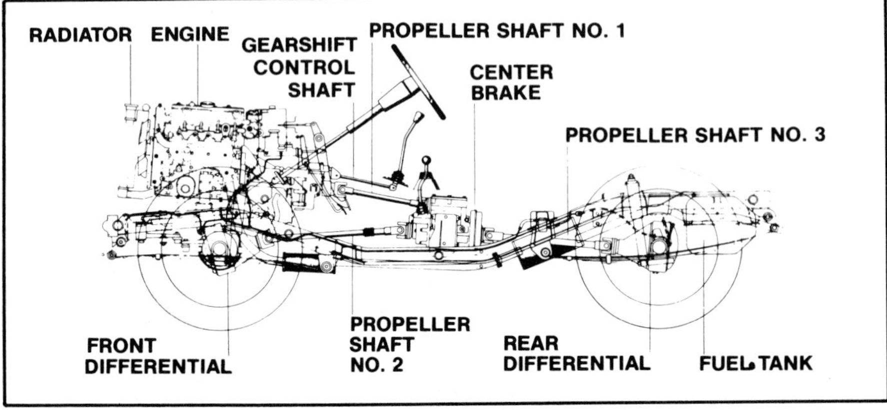

gine's torque output doesn't peak until revs reach a very high 3500 rpm, and this naturally translates to an unfortunate dearth of low-end pulling power, though in the LJ-80's favor, it must be said that because of the LJ-80's light weight and short gearing, it has enough chutzpah to make uphill peel outs necessary only on an infrequent basis. The one hill we were unable to climb was a special exception in that probably not many vehicles, no matter who built them, would have made it to the top. It was covered with slippery, loose, round rocks, and our vehicles were unable to find traction. This problem was solved by going around this area. Ordinarily we shrink from making new roads, but the Suzuki's light weight and general low

power levels mean that even if a driver tried to, he'd have a difficult time chewing up the terrain. When we did leave the road's surface, there were no tracks at all left behind, certainly no bad thing.

Through all of this the Suzuki seemed very well balanced and handled very easily. Steering effort seems just about right, though as might be expected from a system of this type, it didn't provide as much driver feedback as the best systems ought to. The vehicle's clutch action proved to be very light, and an overzealous foot on the clutch lever would bottom it hard on the Suzuki's floorboards. The vehicle's brake action also is very light and quite direct and linear in its response and all in all, the LJ-80's off-road handling is of a high order. It doesn't have enough power to get you into real trouble, and when trouble does begin approaching, the LJ-80 is nimble enough, and its

steering gear ratio fast enough, to help you avoid impending disaster. In fact, because of the LJ-80's generally good off-road handling, moments of near-disaster became quite easy to cope with.

During two days of very hard off-road driving, the only problem areas we encountered had to do with wet brakes and a bottoming front suspension. The wet brakes were obtained courtesy that first episode with the muskeg. From that time on, and despite a fresh adjustment, the vehicle involved had little brake pedal, and when the brakes were applied, it pulled strongly to the left.

As is the case with nearly every other factory-stock 4x4 unit we can think of, the front shock absorbers on the Suzuki proved not to be up to sustained hard use, allowing the front suspension to bottom quite hard on several occasions. Still, for this to occur the vehicle had to hit a pretty substantial bump, and do so at a not inconsequential rate of speed.

Really, we were quite pleasantly surprised by the Suzuki's off-road capabilities. Given that tiny engine, we expected its off-road performance to be disappointing at best, but this was just not what we found. Thanks to its very sturdy but still lightweight construction, that gutty little engine, and the ultra-low gearing of the transfer case, we soon learned that the LJ-80 is capable of going most places that full-sized 4x4s can go. In fact, because of its diminutive size—it is 55.7 inches wide and 125.8 inches long—is capable of sneaking between close-set trees and rocks, and of snaking down narrow trails that larger machines, even Jeeps and Land Cruisers, would never be able to handle. Considering the rate at which the

Suzuki sips gas, and considering the current state of fuel prices, the LJ-80 begins looking better and better to us. Like we said, it has some limitations, not the least of which involves its 400-pound carrying capacity. Still, 400 pounds of gear ought to do it for two people. Seating capacity for more than two is, at present, nonexistent, but like other trim and convenience items, the importers tell us that rear seats are in the works.

The folks at Suzuki-Allarco say they'll sell approximately 2000 LJ-80s and LJ-81s this year. The vehicle's base price is $6400 Canadian. The good news is that according to the importer, Suzuki's engineers are working on California emissions certification for the LJ-80 and once this happens, chances are very good that the unit will be sold in this country. This could happen, we were told, by 1980, maybe 1981. Hard to tell how much inflation we'll see by the time the Suzuki is introduced in the States, if indeed it ever is, and hard to tell how much money emissions engineering will add to the price. Still, if you want to daydream a little, look at it this way: The vehicle sells for $6400 in Canada, which has tighter tariff and tax laws than the U.S. As a result the importer says that if a comparable vehicle could be sold in the U.S. right now, it would probably go for from $4995 to $5495. In a day when 10-grand 4x4s and buck-a-gallon gas are common, we suspect that any LJ-80s that might become available in the U.S. would get sold immediately. And while the vehicle's highway performance levels might not satisfy everybody, we suspect that for hard-core off-road buffs, its off-road performance would more than tip the scales in favor of this little jewel.   ●

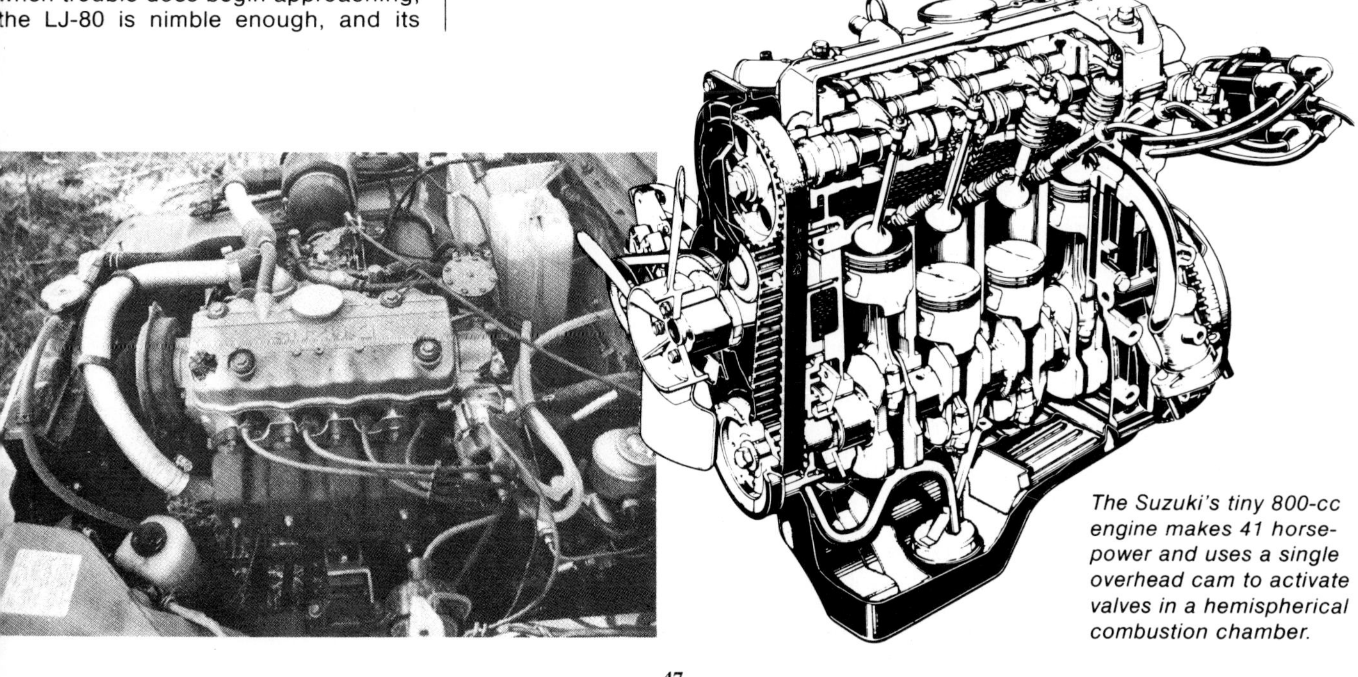

The Suzuki's tiny 800-cc engine makes 41 horsepower and uses a single overhead cam to activate valves in a hemispherical combustion chamber.

Suzuki's spring fever

Fighting for honours at the other end of the 4wd market is Suzuki's sub one-litre Sierra, with a $6350 price and off-road ability to match the big wagons on its side. But the suspension? It's a sneeze . . .

CONTRARY TO Suzuki's advertising jingle comfortable ride really isn't a feature of the new Sierra. And you wouldn't — or we wouldn't — buy it for the springs . . . One could buy a Sierra for its willing performance, its excellent handling, its thrifty fuel economy, its great off-roadability, and one could certainly be attracted by its undeniably good looks. But not its ride.

Everything is relative of course. The Sierra's ride may well be a marked improvement over its predecessor, the LJ80. Suzuki says so. It's several years since we've driven the LJ80 (tested WHEELS, June 1978). We criticised the ride then and time hasn't completely softened the memory. Anyway, the LJ80 connection is unimportant. What counts for the Sierra is how it rides relative to today's standards. And on that basis the Sierra's suspension scores only *Fair*. Regardless of what has been done, plenty of room remains for improvement.

The ride is very firm, strictly vintage in character, and becomes brutally harsh on sharp bumps, sending jarring shocks right through you. It doesn't have to be that way. With refinement it wouldn't be. It's not as though the Sierra is so small and light as to preclude supple suspension. Though still the baby of the 4wd field, the Sierra is bigger and heavier than not only the LJ80 but also some small sedans and ultra-light commercials, including the Suzuki Hatch, which ride better.

Aside from spoiling the ride through being too firm and poorly damped, the suspension allows the axles only very limited vertical travel, causing the Sierra to be unnecessarily susceptible to picking-up a wheel through sharp corners and over very high humps and hollows. When you get down to it, the suspension is the Sierra's least endearing feature among the few that strike negative notes.

The seats don't help. Only the driver's has fore-aft travel, but both have backrest adjustment. Trouble with the backrest is that when you push back into it for support the base of your spine contacts a hard bar. The cushion is too flat and thin for comfort. The only people who'll like them are the replacement seat specialists.

The Sierra needn't, and doesn't, comply with the whole Design Rules rigmarole. The wisdom behind the lack of steering lock and head restraints is debatable, and the use of ordinary fixed seat belts saves a little cost at the expense of convenience and perhaps safety. Inertia reel belts are easier and tidier.

Among the minor niggles is the absence of a warning light for the choke, the knob of which is hidden from sight, in usual Japanese fashion, behind a steering wheel spoke. Another minor demerit goes to the el cheapo plastic floor mats which don't fit well even when they stay in place, which is never for long. Suzuki must presuppose that serious Sierra drivers will throw the mats out while dress-up recreationers will replace them with carpet to enhance looks and help suppress noise.

Of rather more concern is the Sierra's habit of drawing exhaust fumes into the

PERFORMANCE

TEST CONDITIONS:

Weather	Cool, dry
Location	Castlereagh Drag Strip
Load	Two persons
Fuel	Super

SPEEDOMETER ERROR:

Indicated km/h	Actual km/h
50	49
70	67
90	87
100	96

FUEL CONSUMPTION ON TEST:

Check one	10.1 km/l(28.5 mpg) over 252 km
Check two	10.4 km/l(29.6 mpg) over 416 km

MAXIMUM SPEEDS IN GEAR:

First	41 km/h(7000 rpm)
Second	66 km/h(7000 rpm)
Third	89 km/h(6800 rpm)
Fourth	111 km/h(6000 rpm)

ACCELERATION:

Through the gears:

0-50 km/h	6.2 secs
0-60 km/h	8.4 secs
0-70 km/h	10.8 secs
0-80 km/h	14.7 secs
0-90 km/h	19.3 secs
0-100 km/h	26.1 secs
0-110 km/h	41.0 secs

In the gears:	Second	Third	Fourth
30-60 km/h	5.4	6.4	8.8
40-70 km/h		6.8	9.3
50-80 km/h		7.9	11.0
60-90 km/h		13.6	13.2
70-100 km/h			15.7
80-110 km/h			28.4

STANDING START (0-400 m)
22.3 secs

Sierra has size and weight advantages in sticky going; despite size engine is surprisingly flexible and responsive. Above: dash is simple but functional; poor seats but good room for two and luggage.

cockpit. The problem is at its worst with the soft-top's rear flap open. But we found it also occurs when the top is completely off and when it's fully on, especially when the door screens/windows are down. The gassing happens mostly during overrun but sometimes also when cruising. It needs attention. Changing the position of the exhaust outlet from the tail to the left side just behind the mudflap would be worth a try.

There's little else about the Sierra that needs changing. Apart from matters already mentioned it stands as a clear improvement over the LJ80 and a Good Thing in its own right. While it follows the basic mechanical design and arrangements proven over many years in Suzuki's 4wd series (which began in 1971 with 360 cm³ two cylinder two-stroke engine) the Sierra is virtually all-new.

The engine belongs to the same family as the 797 cm³ unit of the LJ80 and has opposingly inclined valves operated via rocker arms by a single overhead camshaft driven by a toothed belt. The large engine is identifiable by the ignition distributor facing the right instead of the left. Internally it has 65.5 mm bore and 72 mm stroke for 970 cm³ against the 800's 62 mm bore and 66 mm stroke.

The 970 doesn't hold much advantage in maximum power over the 800. The new version peaks with 33.5 kW at the same 5500 rpm at which the 800 gave 30.6 kW. But there's big difference in torque for where the 800 delivered 59.8 Nm at

3500 rpm, the Sierra boasts 73.5 Nm at 3000 rpm. That translates to much better performance, on and off the road, in spite of the new design being about 95 kg heavier and having taller gearing.

Few comparisons are needed to prove the Sierra's superiority. It takes 1.5 seconds less than the 800 for the 0-400 m run, takes 3.5 seconds less to reach 70 km/h from standstill and 7.3 seconds less to 90 km/h. The Sierra's advantage is clear for the In-gears times too. For instance it is 2.7 seconds quicker from 50 to 80 km/h in third gear, and in top gear takes five seconds less than the 800. In fact the Sierra is quicker from 30 km/h up to about 75 km/h than the Jeep Cherokee and Datsun Patrol in third and top gears, and also beats the Land Cruiser to that point in top gear.

Though the acceleration tapers off noticeably beyond about 80 km/h, the excellent flexibility and immediate response at low to middling speeds means that the Sierra's performance is seldom found wanting. On good roads it can be cruised quite easily, if noisily, at 90 to 100 km/h and will wind out to 111 km/h on the flat if you're determined.

The impressive performance hasn't been won to the detriment of fuel consumption. Given reasonably steady driving, we wouldn't be surprised if the Sierra was more economical than the LJ80. We didn't spare the Sierra during this test and it was hard driven much more often than not. In the circumstances, therefore, the Suzuki gave what we consider to be very good results. At 10.1 and 10.4 km/l for the respective stints, the Sierra gave almost exactly the same consumption as the LJ80 had given on its test. And on that basis we'd expect the Sierra to return around 12.4 km/l (35 mpg) as a rule.

The larger, gutsier engine has enabled the gear ratios to be revised, to good effect. The final drive ratio is increased to 4.111 (from 4.563) and the first three in the gearbox are considerably taller than before, meaning the gearing overall is higher than the LJ80's in spite of the transfer cogs being a little lower. And even with the wider but smaller optional FR78-15 tyres instead of the standard 6.00-16s, the Sierra comfortably pulls more km/h per 1000 rpm.

The fact that the Sierra can be wound to faster speeds in the gears is almost incidental to its cruising less busily and yet more responsively in fourth. But the faster you go the more you know it, of course, not least because of the growing audio accompaniment. By the time it reaches middling speeds the Sierra is quite vocal and thereafter becomes increasingly *Loud,* especially beyond about 80 km/h, from which point a grumbling resonance pervades the body. It's not intolerable but certainly is intrusive.

The soft-top may contribute something to the noise but one can't complain about the reasonable ease with which it is dismantled and erected, nor about the snugness with which it fits. The task is done fastest and easiest with two sets of hands yet isn't too slow and difficult for one person.

Although the $6350 soft-top half-door version has very good side curtains with zippered windows, buyers wanting the security and comfort convenience of proper doors with locks and wind-up windows will prefer the full-door soft-top for an extra $50. There's also an all-metal van version at $6550. Those three share the same wheelbase and other dimensions, whereas the table-top pick-up models and cab-chassis edition (from $6700 to $7100) have longer wheelbase and more length overall.

The variations share the same interior. It's amply roomy for two large people and has a plain yet not unattractive dash panel. The steering wheel is one of the few carry-overs from the previous model. Immediately ahead are two dials: speedometer with odometer and trip meter on the left, with water temperature and fuel gauges (plus sundry warning lights) on the right. At the middle of the panel are air outlets, heat/vent controls and the standard push-button AM radio. Ahead of the passenger's seat is a parcel tray and grab handle, with a glovebox which has a locking lid and more capacity than the 'boxes in most larger 4wds. The bonnet release is buried deep inside the glovebox. The bonnet, incidentally, is simply opened until it rests on the windscreen frame. There ought to be a security stay to prevent it blowing closed.

The Sierra has really good controls. The steering is light and reasonably direct, and its lack of vagueness is a welcome change among 4wd models in general. Indeed the Sierra handles conspicuously well, on the optional wheels and tyres anyway, and on smooth roads can be punted through corners and tight manoeuvres very enthusiastically without any suggestion of wanting to simply fall over, as earlier ones seemed wont to do. The brake pedal is a touch heavy perhaps, and not very progressive, but the brakes work well — in the dry at least. Deliberate applications are needed to restore braking efficiency after deep water crossings. The transmission type handbrake is very effective. The gearshift is light and precise, almost sporty to use, and the straight-line transfer shift is simplicity itself.

It all adds up to an obviously attractive small 4wd which — ride apart — has become a very reasonable vehicle and good fun for everyday on-road driving, even for moderately long stints behind the steering wheel.

And for rough road/off road 4-wheel driving the Sierra can be summed up in one word . . . brilliant. Suzuki's 4wd series has always acquitted itself well in trying conditions, and the Sierra is by far the best yet in that respect. It'll go virtually anywhere the big 4wds can. And, in tight terrain, some places they can't. So if you want the Sierra's imposing dual-purpose versatility, you'll take it for the drive, not for the ride. □

SPECIFICATIONS

MAKE	**SUZUKI**
MODEL	**SIERRA**
BODY TYPE	**Half-door soft top**
PRICE: Basic	**$6350**
As tested	**$6685**
OPTIONS FITTED	**Styled 15-inch wheels, FR78-15 tyres, wheelarch flares — $335 package**

ENGINE:

Cylinders	Four
Valves	SOHC
Carburettor	One sidedraught
Compression ratio	8.8 to 1
Bore × stroke	65.5 × 72 mm
Capacity	970 cm³
Max power	33.5 kW at 5500 rpm
Max torque	73.5 Nm at 3000 rpm

TRANSMISSION:

Type	Four-speed all-synchromesh, plus two-speed non-synchro transfer

Ratios:	Gearbox	Overall High (Low)	km/h-1000 rpm High (Low)
First	3.163:1	20.676 (35.316):1	5.9 (3.4)
Second	1.945:1	12.717 (21.725):1	9.6 (5.6)
Third	1.421:1	9.290 (15.870):1	13.1 (7.7)
Fourth	1.000:1	6.535 (11.164):1	18.7 (10.8)
High transfer	1.590:1		
Low transfer	2.716:1		
Final drive	4.111:1		

CHASSIS:

Constuction	Steel body, separate chassis

SUSPENSION:

Front	Live axle, semi-elliptic leaf springs
Rear	Live axle, semi-elliptic leaf springs
Dampers	Telescopic

STEERING:

Type	Recirculating ball
Turning circle	9.8 m
Turns lock to lock	3.75

BRAKES:

Type	Drums front and rear

DIMENSIONS:

Wheelbase	2030 mm
Track, front	1190 mm
Track, rear	1200 mm
Length	3410 mm
Width	1395 mm
Height	1690 mm
Kerb mass (weight)	800 kg
Ground clearance	240 mm

FUEL TANK: 40 litres

TYRES: FR78-15 Bridgestone RD702

Remember the Johnny Cash song, "One Piece At A Time," about how he built a car from spare parts. Well, it seems that Roger Downward of Reno, Nevada, took the lyrics as sage advice and did just that.

Roger's mix and match project began as a docile Suzuki LJ10 he bought to use as a utility vehicle to take along on vacation trips. However, after taking the truck on a trip to Utah, he discovered that the small 360cc engine did not have enough muscle for its intended purpose.

Instead of panicking, Roger initiated a rehabilitation plan designed to transform the truck into a peppy, practical off-road vehicle. First, he tried modifying the engine. When this didn't achieve the desired results, Roger decided that some kind of radical treatment was in order—an engine swap.

A trip to the local wrecking yard produced a Toyota 1200 engine with only 6000 miles on the clock. Requiring only minimal modifications, the engine fit easily into the stock engine compartment. After making a U-joint adapter with a Toyota spline on one end and a Suzuki spline on the other, the transmission bolted right onto the Suzuki's 2-speed transfer case. Knowing that an engine swap alone would not cure all of the truck's ills, Roger installed a radiator, electric fan

ONE FROM COLUMN "A"

A LITTLE BIT OF THIS AND A LITTLE BIT OF THAT— WHEN IT ALL CAME TOGETHER, A TOYUKI WAS BORN.

and a water pump from a Chrysler, a heater from a '72 Dodge Colt and rack and pinion steering from a '77 Fiat. In addition to this odd-ball collection, Roger added Toyota aftermarket headers to complete the underhood

puzzle.

To counter the added weight of the Toyota engine, Roger fabricated a Fiat/Suzuki leaf-spring suspension by removing two stock leaves from each side of the vehicle and replacing them with two leaves from a Fiat. The rest of the drivetrain, both axles and drum brakes are stock. The Toyuki rides on 5½-inch front and eight-spoke rear white steel Western wheels and H70-15 Remington Wide Brute mud and snow tires.

"The Suzuki is a fun vehicle for around town," Roger says. "It gets lots of looks from people who didn't think Jeeps came that small or with the steering wheel on the right side of the cab." And as for off-road use, its low center of gravity, light weight (about 1490 pounds) and small wheelbase (75 inches) make it a real performer.

The full-time four-wheel drive Suzuki does have one flaw that Roger is working on. Because the differentials put out a gear ratio of about 5.33:1, the engine is terribly overreved if driven over 40-45 mph. Around town roaming and off-road use is fine though, if kept below the 35-40 mph range. Roger hopes to remedy the problem by changing the front and rear differentials and axles over to Jeep ones, so that he can have locking front hubs.

A little more from column "J," please.

PHOTOGRAPHY: ALVIN TANABE

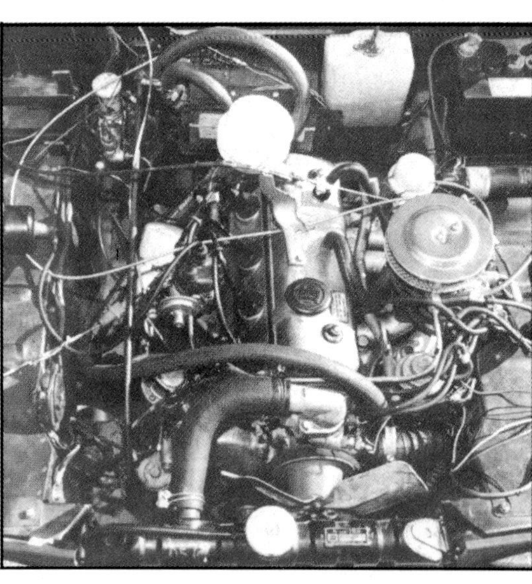

1. With its low center of gravity, light weight (1490 pounds) and small wheelbase (75 inches), the new Toyuki is a great off-road vehicle.

2. The Suzuki's 360cc engine proved too anemic, so Roger swapped it for a 1200cc Toyota engine and transmission.

3. The rack and pinion steering is from a '77 Fiat and is currently mounted on the front leaf springs. This setup transmits too many bumps to the driver, so Roger plans to remount it on the frame.

4. A new U-joint adapter fitted with a Toyota spline on one end and a Suzuki spline on the other end allows an easy match between the Toyota transmission and the Suzuki's 2-speed transfer case.

5. The cab remains stock. With the steering wheel on the right side, it gets its share of questioning stares.

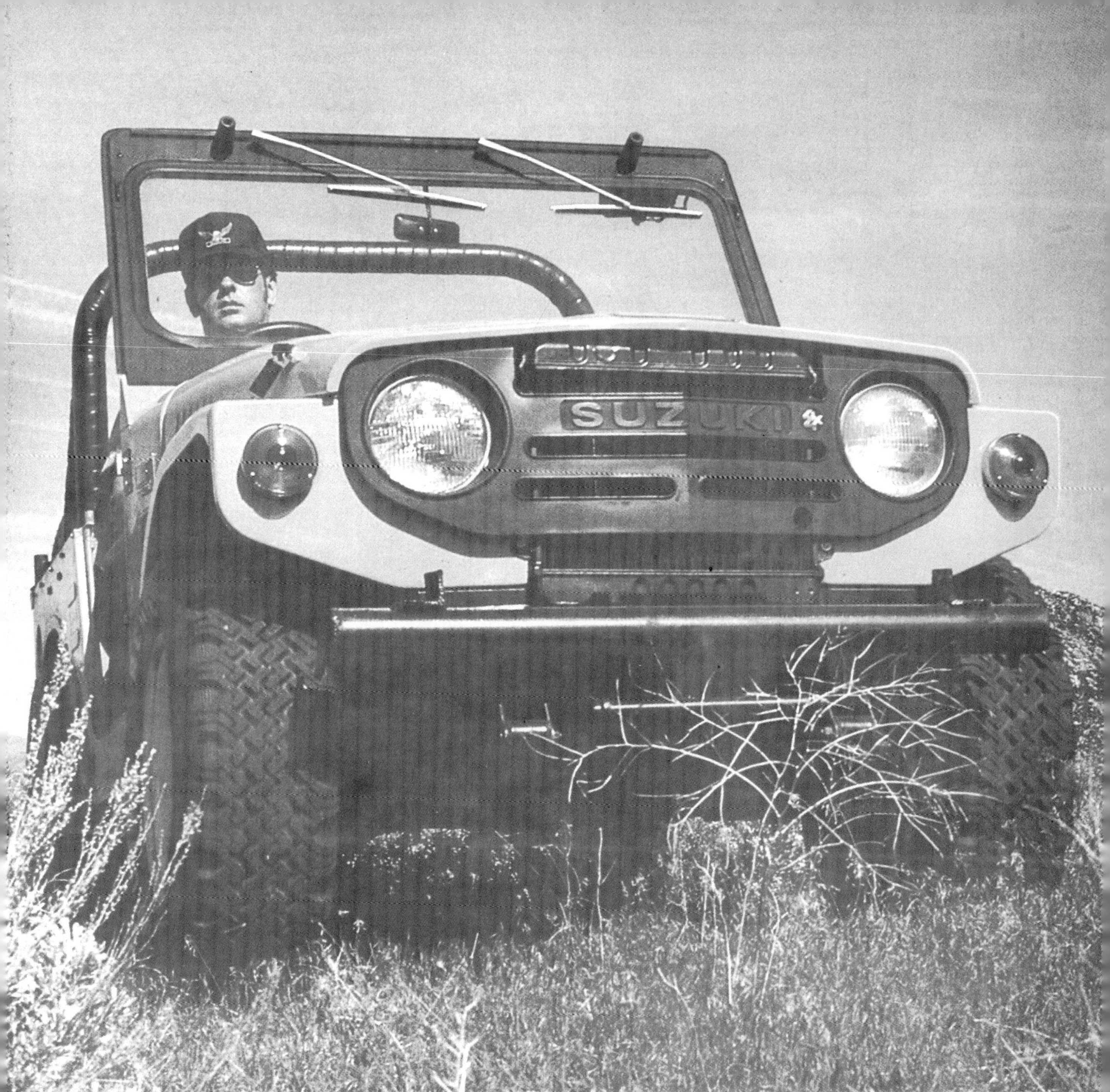
SUZUKI
REMINGTON
REMINGTON
WIDE BRUTE
SUZUKI
LTL SUZI

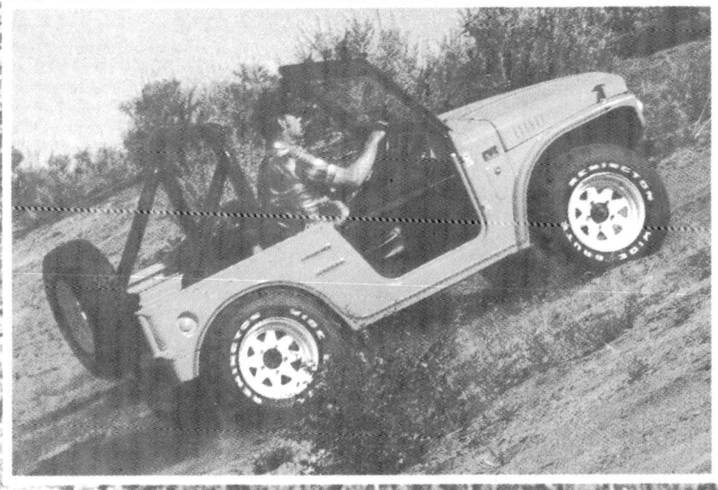

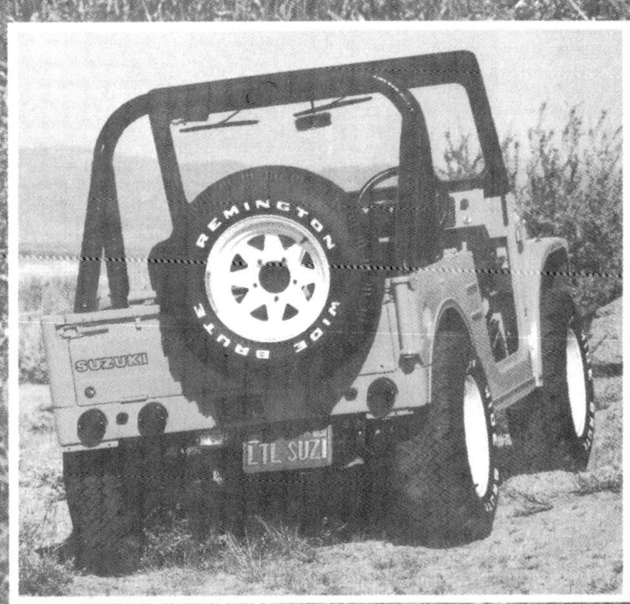

Smith'S

SIERRA

TEXT/PHOTOS: RAY BARKER

A shade more than ten grand will buy you a very stock standard Landcruiser SWB, MQ Patrol or dual-cab Hi-Lux. The same amount of money will also buy you a Suzuki Sierra decked out to turn more heads than a grand slam tennis match.

Such a Sierra belongs to Sydney radio executive Philip Smith. Philip needed a four wheel drive for weekend scuba diving and for getting around his parents' country property. The vehicle also had readily to accept the role of an economical town car during the week.

According to Philip, the Sierra well and truly exceeds his expectations, and he says that one of the most pleasant surprises of all is that he can legally park on city loading zones while he makes quick calls to see clients.

The bright yellow exterior of Smith's Suzuki is complemented with a chrome bull-bar, AVM front hubs, dark-tinted windows, chrome roof rack and a fine, colour-co-ordinated stripe. However, the most striking feature is the new Sunraysia modular wheels. These 15 x 6 wheels are the latest thing from Sunraysia and can be purchased in a variety of annodised centre finishes. Sierra buyers who order the "wide wheel model" need only buy the modular wheels, as the standard radials readily accept the one-inch-wider Sunraysias.

Interior comfort has been enhanced with the addition of front and rear carpet that is easily removed for cleaning, a fold-away, rear, bench seat, and Falcon "S-Pack" cloth trim over an extra layer of foam padding. The el-cheapo radio has been replaced by an AWA Clarion AM-FM radio cassette with speakers mounted in the side panels.

The fully integrated air conditioning keeps people in, and the Challenge burglar alarm keeps people out.

Only one thing annoys Philip, and that's the never ending number of people who come up to him with questions about the vehicle. Now he can tell them to buy BUSHDRIVER.

SUZUKI
LQG·058
NSW - THE PREMIER STATE
PETE GEOGHEGANS

SUZUKI SJ410P

With its outstanding cross-country capability, and reasonable road performance, Suzuki's new "total mobility" estate car brings 4wd into the supermini price bracket

"TOTAL MOBILITY" is a concept that you either love or hate, with no middle ground. Those whose idea of pleasurable motoring revolves around sports-style standards of performance and handling are improbable converts to the idea of a vehicle which will carry a driver and three passengers up steep, slippery rutted-chalk bostals; or plough happily through floodwater up to its high-set door sills. Conversely, those who either need or want to get along the beaten track (or off it!) may look equally askance at expensive cars that offer high standards of dynamic performance, but which will be stopped in their tracks simply by wet grass or a flooded road.

To some extent, it is an urban/rural divide. Any villager knows that there are times of the year when a conventional car offers no mobility at all: and if your home happens to be at the end of an unmade, hilly road, those occasions are more frequent than the average town-dweller ever suspects. In such situations you don't want refinement: you want wheels!

If you have a deep pocket, of course, there's no problem. You simply buy a Range Rover and get the best of all worlds. But not every countryman is rich enough to be able to join the Range Rover waiting list ... An altogether more utilitarian vehicle, which can be purchased for no greater outlay than that required for a fairly mundane saloon, is an acceptable answer, and it is primarily to that market that the Suzuki SJ410P is intended to appeal. This almost jeep-like, cobby four-seater estate, with its £4,599 price tag, combines an endearing go-any-where ability with reasonable passenger comfort. What's more, it undercuts any possible rivals by nearly £1,000.

In fact, the Suzuki could justly be claimed to be in a class of its own. Unlike its more expensive competitors, it is a genuinely *small* car, only 1.4 inches longer than a Metro (at 135.4in overall, including the externally-mounted spare wheel) and noticeably narrow at 57.5in width. It is, however, high-sided (66.5in high) and with the 9.1in ground clearance necessary for serious cross-country work it has a somewhat precarious appearance that is not wholly misleading.

The power unit is a new in-line "four", of 970cc, with belt-driven single overhead camshaft. Of cross-flow type, with hemispherical combustion chambers, this long-stroke (65.5mm bore × 72mm stroke) unit develops 45bhp DIN at 5,500rpm, and produces a maximum torque of 54.2lb ft DIN at 3,000rpm. Drive is through a single-plate clutch and a four speed and reverse gearbox, with synchromesh on all forward gears, and then by a short exposed prop shaft to a two-speed constant-mesh transfer gearbox. From this, exposed prop shafts take the drive to live axles at front and rear, the rear drive-shaft also carrying the drum-type transmission brake.

Internally, the SJ410P is neat and rather less utilitarian in layout than its slab-sided exterior might suggest. Perhaps it is stretching comparisons a little to describe it as "a miniature Range Rover", but the basic philosophy is similar even if the scale is markedly different. The driver and front passenger are reasonably well pro-vided for so far as creature comforts are concerned. The seats are comfortable, and give adequate support for average-sized adults.

One 6-feet-plus tester found the short backrest of the driver's seat extremely painful within five miles: by contrast, a 15-stone tester of medium height rated it as extremely comfortable over distances of more than 50 miles. The driver's seat is adjustable for position and backrest rake; the passenger seat, also has rake adjustment, but, no fore/aft movement, as it is mounted on a parallelogram linkage to make ingress to and exit from the bench-type rear passenger seat easier. This rear seat, though of fairly rudimentary proportions, in fact proves to be surprisingly comfortable, and rear legroom remarkably generous. It is marred, however, by lack of toe-room under the front seats.

In the front of the passenger compartment, the SJ410 appears to be as well trimmed and equipped as any "utility" rivals, such as the Fiat Panda, the smaller Citroëns, or the BL Mini. The facia is neatly padded and vinyl-covered; the small dashboard carries an easily-read speedometer, a fuel gauge and temperature gauge, and warning lights for oil pressure, alternator charge, turn signals, brake fluid level, parking brake, and main beam. A hazard warning mode, rear foglamp and cigarette lighter are all standard, as is a typically-complicated Japanese fresh air/recirculating heater and fan-boosted fresh air ventilation system, and a radio with push-button selection. The glove box is lockable, and the front windows are of wind-up type rather than the sliding panels one would expect on a utility car. The rear windows have over-centre catches on their trailing edges, and the side-hinged rear door has both external and internal lock handles. When the rear door is opened, it gives access to what must be the world's smallest boot — little more than a slot, in which a briefcase might just fit. The rear seatback, however, folds forward to increase luggage

capacity with only driver and passenger aboard, and for extra carrying space the entire rear seat can be hinged forward after removal of its two securing thumbscrews.

Controls are simple. The gearchange is operated by a long, tapered floor-mounted lever: the transfer box — which selects two-wheel drive; four-wheel drive, high ratios; or four-wheel drive, low ratios — by a stubby floor lever just forward of the centrally-set handbrake. The horn button is incorporated into the padded centre of the perforated two-spoke steering wheel, and wipers and lights are actuated by individual stalks set on opposite sides of the steering column.

The choke control is placed just to the left of the column, and it is there to be used. Full choke is essential on start-up, and since the choke is linked to the throttle mechanism it must then be set halfway to prevent over-revving. The engine on our test vehicle seemed to need several minutes to warm up before the choke could be pushed fully home without the risk of stalling.

The clutch action is light, and the gearbox delightfully quick and accurate. While changes between high-ratio and low-ratio four-wheel drive can be made only with the car at a standstill the transfer gearbox can be used to switch between two-wheel and four-wheel drive on the move.

The Suzuki powerplant is almost silent at tickover, and it proves to be as smooth — if not quiet — in operation throughout its considerable range Obviously, a vehicle of this type is no ball of fire, as a 0-60mph time of 29.9 sec confirms, but in town traffic the SJ410 proves to be adequately nippy while on the motorway it needs only a down-gradient of positively railway-engineering proportions to enable it to reach and then maintain a genuine 70mph. What is more impressive however, is the Suzuki's ability to drop down to 10mph in top gear and to pull away again briskly and without transmission snatch. Traffic driving is made even easier by the fact that it can trickle along in bottom gear, with the clutch fully home and the driver's foot hovering just above the accelerator. Put the transfer gearbox lever into "Low-4" position, and the same performance could be repeated uphill ...

While noise is no problem at restrained speeds and relatively low engine revs — save for a noticeable resonance around 25mph in third — it becomes more than just obtrusive at main-road speeds, while on the motorway the considerable drumming from the under-bonnet area makes the radio totally redundant.

The ride — as one would expect from a 79.9in wheelbase vehicle with live axles and stiff leaf springing front and rear — is very lively on all but the smoothest of surfaces, and a recirculating-ball steering mechanism, deliberately set up loose to lessen kick-back on cross-country going and controlled by a telescopic hydraulic damper on the drop arm, does not provide the ultimate in accuracy. In combination the stiffness of the suspension and the lack of feel in the steering make it essential to learn the car's handling characteristics before pressing it into corners. Once the trick of applying lock

Comfortable, but businesslike: the Suzuki's passenger compartment is well laid out for the car's dual role

Minimal luggage space inside the fully-opening rear door can be notably increased by folding the rear seat forward

The engine compartment remained reasonably clean after a cross-country expedition — including the muddy watersplash (top right)

little early and beginning to take it off again early is acquired the handling is satisfactory enough, though on wet or twisty roads it proved best to change into four-wheel drive. In that configuration, the car's dynamics improve notably, the steering becoming almost neutral.

However, road use is only one facet of "total mobility", and on cross-country going the little Suzuki really comes into its own. We tried it on greasy mud, slippery chalk, in water splashes with soft mud and ruts lurking below a foot or more of floodwater, on leaf-mould, and on the MIRA cross-country course. Nothing stopped it, and nothing even looked like stopping it. In "Low 4" it bounded up the rutted chalk of a South Downs track, leaping from hummock to hummock like a surefooted mountain goat. The suspension soaked up all the punishment that was thrown at it without crashing or bottoming, and the steering — perhaps a bit hit-and-miss on tarmac — became accurate, and easy for the driver to hold under constant hammering. In an off-road context, the ride, too, was remarkably comfortable. The front inertia-reel seat-belts locked the driver and front passenger into their seats, while a rear-seat passenger, unbelted, was able to steady himself sufficiently by grasping

the handgrip just above each rear window.

The only question mark was over the braking. Downhill, it is possible to get a 4wd vehicle "sledging", and applying the brakes exacerbates the problem. Suzuki frown upon the use of the transmission brake with the SJ410 on the move, but applying it did in fact allow well-controlled descents of steep, greasy slopes to be made without difficulty.

Both on the rough and on the road, the Suzuki's commanding driving position and good field of vision — apart from rather thick B-pillars, and the intrusion of the rear-mounted spare wheel in the rear window — make it easy to place the car accurately, and to enjoy the view over the hedges when cruising along the country lanes that are its natural habitat. But why no dipping mirror for night use?

One does not, of course, get anything for nothing, and as with all high-

built 4wd vehicles the poor aerodynamics bring with them a penalty in fuel consumption. An overall figure of little more than 25mpg could be bettered by many a 2-litre saloon, and this is an aspect that might be thought to put the SJ410 out of court. However, it needs to be viewed in the context of its rivals — the 21mpg overall of the Niva, for

example: or, on a more exalted plane, the Range Rover's inability to better 18mpg. More gentle use of the throttle would, of course, produce an improvement, but even at a steady 50mph we could record only 28.1mpg.

It is the one aspect of an otherwise individual and personable car that might call the concept into question.

Motor Road Test No 62/82 ● Suzuki SJ410P

PERFORMANCE

WEATHER CONDITIONS

Wind	0-8 mph
Temperature	36°F/2°C
Barometer	30.3 in Hg/1026 mbar
Surface	Damp tarmacadam

MAXIMUM SPEEDS

	mph	kph
Banked circuit	65.9	106.0
Best $\frac{1}{4}$ mile	66.7	107.3
Terminal Speeds:		
at $\frac{1}{4}$ mile	56	90
at kilometre	64	103
at mile	66	106
Speeds in gears (at 6,500 rpm):		
1st	25	40
2nd	40	64
3rd	55	88

ACCELERATION FROM REST

mph	sec	kph	sec
0-30	6.0	0-40	4.4
0-40	10.0	0-60	8.6
0-50	16.5	0-80	16.0
0-60	29.5	0-100	35.8
Stand'g $\frac{1}{4}$	23.1	Stand'g km	45.5

ACCELERATION IN TOP

mph	sec	kph	sec
20-40	12.0	40-60	7.3
30-50	14.0	60-80	9.3
40-60	21.5		

FUEL CONSUMPTION

Touring*	27.6 mpg
	10.2 litres/100 km
Overall	25.3 mpg
	11.2 litres/100 km
Govt tests	27.0 mpg (urban)
	31.1 mpg (56 mph)
Fuel grade	85 octane minimum
	2 star rating
Tank capacity	8.8 galls
	40 litres
Max range	243 miles
	391 km
Test distance	1,290 miles
	1,945 km

*An estimated fuel consumption computed from the theoretical consumption at a steady speed midway between 30 mph and the car's maximum, less a 5 per cent allowance for acceleration.

NOISE

	dBA	Motor rating*
30 mph	72	18
50 mph	79	30
70 mph	—	—
Maximum†	84	41

*A rating where 1=30 dBA, and 100=96 dBA, and where double the number means double the loudness
†Peak noise level under full-throttle acceleration in 2nd.

SPEEDOMETER (mph)

Speedo	30	40	50	60	70
True mph	27	36	46	55	65

Distance recorder: 2.2 per cent fast

WEIGHT

	cwt	kg
Unladen weight*	16.7	848
Weight as tested	20.4	1,036

*with fuel for approx 50 miles

Performance tests carried out by Motor's staff at the Motor Industry Research Association proving ground, Lindley.

Test Data: World Copyright reserved. No reproduction in whole or part without written permission.

GENERAL SPECIFICATION

ENGINE

Cylinders	4 in line
Capacity	970cc (59.2 cu in)
Bore/stroke	65.5/72.0 mm (2.58/2.83 in)
Cooling	Water
Block	Cast iron
Head	Light alloy
Valves	Sohc
Cam drive	Belt
Compression	8.8:1
Carburetter	Aisan 80000
Bearings	5
Max power	45 bhp (DIN) at 5,500 rpm
Max torque	54.2 lb ft (DIN) at 3,000 rpm

TRANSMISSION

Type	4-speed manual plus 2-speed transfer box; 2 or 4 wheel drive
Clutch dia	7.1in
Actuation	Cable
Internal ratios and mph/1,000 rpm	
Top	1.000:1/11.9
3rd	1.421:1/8.4
2nd	1.945:1/6.1
1st	3.163:1/3.8
Rev	3.321:1
Transfer	
High	1.590:1
Low	2.716:1
Final drive	4.111:1
	(6.534 effective overall)

BODY CHASSIS

Construction	All-steel
Protection	Tuff Kote Dinol under-body protection (6 year warranty)

SUSPENSION

Front	Live axle carried on longitudinal leaf springs, with telescopic dampers
Rear	Live axle carried on longitudinal leaf springs, with telescopic dampers

STEERING

Type	Worm and ball, with hydraulic damper
Assistance	None

BRAKES

Front	Drums, 8.7 in dia
Rear	Drums, 8.7 in dia
Park	Drum, on transmission
Servo	None
Circuit	Split front/rear
Rear valve	Yes
Adjustment	Manual

WHEELS/TYRES

Type	Steel, $5\frac{1}{2}$ x 15 in
Tyres	195 SR15
Pressures	20/20 psi F/R (normal)
	20/26 psi F/R (full load)

ELECTRICAL

Battery	12V, 30Ah
Earth	Negative
Generator	Alternator, 35 Amp
Fuses	4, plus fusible link
Headlights	
type	Tungsten
dip	80W total
main	90W total

Make: Suzuki   **Model:** SJ410P
Maker: Suzuki Motor Company Limited, Hamamatsu-Nishi, PO Box 1, 432-91 Hamamatsu, Japan
Concessionaire: Heron Suzuki (GB) Ltd, 46-62 Gatwick Road, Crawley, West Sussex RH10 2XF
Price: £3,692.00 plus £307.00 Car Tax plus £600 VAT equals £4,599.00

SIERRA SOPHISTICATION

Suzuki has released a luxury pack that points to a new era in the 4WD market place. TONY LOVE reports.
Photography: GEOFF BROWN.

WHEN the Suzuki Sierra pulled up alongside its co-contenders in Overlander's 1981 Four Wheel Drive of the Year, the judges had been wholeheartedly surprised by its performance during long stretches of outback touring. It had also excelled off the road.

One judge remarked ... "If I were travelling constantly over rough territory, then the Sierra would be my first choice ... it's the perfect vehicle for the farmer, in the traytop configuration, and there's a certain trendiness, too, in owning a Suzuki. It is both for the man on the land and for city mannequins".

Others concurred: "It was fun to drive,

which includes the bounces and the dust ... I can see farm and recreational users plumping for it every time ..."; and "The Suzuki Sierra does the job it is aimed at very well ... it's still king of the tiny tots of 4WD."

At that stage the Sierra had only been on Australian roads for a few months, but now, with more than a year's driving, the king of the tiny tots has undergone several changes to accommodate the public's criticisms.

The foremost of those were the seats ... considered dangerous and especially so for weightier drivers. This problem, also noted by Overlander's

judges — a bar that dug into the lower back — has now been rectified and the seats made more comfortable with extra foam padding.

In the softtop version problems were also found with exhaust fumes entering the rear of the vehicle. To combat this, the exhaust pipe has now been lengthened.

The year has also highlighted unexpected market trends for the vehicle's N.S.W. and A.C.T. distributors, Ateco Suzuki.

Most people involved with 4WD marketing had assumed the RV boom finished in the late seventies, since then sales having been dominated by farmers and miners, as well as the family buyer.

The Sierra, with its streamlined appearance, was an obvious attempt to clean up in the RV section of the market ... especially the hardtop, which boasted the best look of all the models.

Top left: The 970 cc engine remains the same.
Left: No enhancements to the dash, but Scheel rally seats and SAAS padded steering wheel boost comfort levels.
Above: Free-wheeling hubs give greater versatility.

Ateco Suzuki itself decided to market towards the city buyer, with any sales in the country regions thought of as a bonus. The radio slogan "Four Wheel Jive" was definitely a young person's pitch, and the public responded with sales of the softtop exploding. It was seen as much more of a fun machine than the hardtop, and distributors have been unable to keep up supply.

As a result they have found themselves with an excess of hardtops, and to get those moving a limited edition of 50 luxury packs has been designed.

For a recommended retail price of $7820, the car now boasts most importantly, Scheel rally seats, a sporty SAAS padded steering wheel, twin, long-range Bosch driving lights, quartz halogen headlights and guards, free wheeling hubs, wide wheels shod with Bridgestone steel radials, a spare wheel cover, rust prevention treatment, and resistant carpet and special coloured striping.

The new model comes in white, yellow, blue and silver.

Ateco claims this special equipment is worth around $2000 but have only added $700 to the standard price.

Not bad value and additions that make the Sierra a grander tourer to boot. The Scheels are a boon on longer trips, providing stability to the driver who ordinarily would be bounced around a fair deal . . . the Suzuki is that sort of vehicle! The radials and padded steering wheel give a better feel for the road . . . both in and around town, and on longer hauls. In the mud, however, watch it!

The FWHs provide flexibility and eventually will add to the Sierra's already excellent fuel economy. Although our test vehicle was still in its first 1000 kays, it recorded an average of 9.2L/100km, including some off-road work with the hubs locked in.

Despite the Sierra's proven off-road

ability, this luxury package is obviously directed at the 'city mannequin' set . . . not quite the aggressive marketing many passenger car manufacturers have undertaken, but one still aimed at combating falling sales figures.

Between July, 1981 and June, 1982, when Ateco Suzuki had budgeted to sell 1700 Sierras, it was able to sell 2,056. However, between July and October last year these figures dropped to only 418.

Where it had budgeted to sell 40 steel and aluminium tray Sierras in October last year it managed only 10. Earlier in the year figures were passing 30 to 40 a month in the rural areas, but with the drought progressively worsening, the farming sector has all but dried up.

This problem is affecting all distributors of 4WDs and Suzuki's approach could well be followed by other manufacturers. If you're in the market for a new off-roader this could be the best time to buy.

SUZUKI SJ 410 Q 4x4

Even with 100 per cent duty, the price of this tough mini 4x4 is attractive. But while it's impressive off-road, it's not really a dual-purpose vehicle...

IT says a great deal about the cost of Japanese vehicle manufacture, and the vagaries of international exchange rates, that a tough, attractive lightweight 4x4 like Suzuki's SJ 410 Q — the subject of this test report — can be retailed (as a Special Import) for as low as R8 890. Even after being brought in fully assembled — incurring shipping costs and 100 per cent import duty — it can still be sold at a price low enough to catch the youth/fishing/surfing market, at which its designers aimed it, offering

KEY FIGURES

Maximum speed	112 km/h
1 km sprint	43 seconds
Terminal speed	107,5 km/h
Fuel tank capacity	40 litres
Litres/100 km at 80	7,65
Optimum fuel range at 80	526 km
*Fuel Index	9,9
Engine revs per km	3 123
National list price	R8 890
(*Consumption at 80, plus 30%)	

an attractive alternative to the larger, heavier and more expensive 4x4s that don't look nearly so much fun.

NO TOY, EITHER

True, it's not a real workhorse: it's only 3 430 mm long and 1 460 mm wide with a wheelbase of 2 030 mm and a mass of 840 kg. But it's no toy either. Its combination of low mass, narrow track and large wheels on long travel suspension, powered by a lively 970 cm^3 s-o-h-c "four" driving two or four wheels through a transfer box, enables it to pick its way over really rough terrain, or churn through soft deep sand that would cause some 4x4s to struggle, if not to stop.

It will zip through gaps that would halt full size vehicles in their tracks and with its front hubs locked and "low range" engaged, it will conquer very steep gradients indeed with no signs of undue stress.

Thus priced and sized, this Suzuki can be fairly claimed by GMSA (who import and distribute it) to "bridge the gap between the scrambler motor cycle and the conventional 4x4", for its overall running costs should be modest, compared to those of most comparable vehicles.

However, anyone considering a purchase should bear in mind the fact that this ingenious lightweight is *primarily* contrived for off-road use — where it acquits itself impressively — and in our view it is not an acceptable "second car", despite its low fuel consumption, in two-wheel-drive form on tarmac.

Unless, that is, you are willing to accept the snags of high noise levels, limited cornering stability, sluggish acceleration and a bouncy ride of the type that would induce car sickness in anyone prone to this problem.

The high ground clearance, short wheelbase, narrow track and soft suspension — the factors that work so well in the rough — limit the vehicle's safe cornering speeds when it's driven 2WD on tar — a point that has to be borne constantly in mind, when you first drive it.

"AVOID SHARP TURNS"

In fact, Suzuki advise, in their driver's handbook, that you should "avoid sharp turns on the road" (when the short wheelbase will cause the rear end to hop) and "if at all possible, approach corners cautiously — more slowly than a conventional road car"...

The vehicle's high c of g and narrow track also call for caution when negotiating *across* a steep slope — something off-roaders tend to avoid as much as possible. As a matter of interest, Suzuki claim a maximum "lateral tilt" angle of 45° for the SJ 410 Q, and this specification is impressive.

On good tar, the ride is smooth but noisy, for even with high range/high ratio engaged, the overall gearing is low (19,21 km/h per 1 000 revs) and the engine is always "busy". Just over 5 200 r/min is required, for example, to cruise at 100 km/h — which is just 12 km/h below its true maximum. Moreover, on undulating tar or a concrete road, the Suzuki pitches and bounces rhythmically as its long travel suspension struggles to control the relatively large wheels, which involve an unfavourable ratio of unsprung-to-sprung mass, and for many buyers these drawbacks would preclude its

The little Suzuki has strong, modern and compact styling and its large wheels help off-road traction. The spare wheel (inset) is mounted on the side-hinged rear door.

SUZUKI
CAR TEST
SUZUKI
SUZUKI
CAR
TEST

Interior treatment (above) is simple but practical with clear, logical layout. The short lever engages high/low ratios and 2/4WD with a smooth action. The little 970 cm³ "four" (below) is a willing performer and provides surprising off-road punch.

ratio, 2WD) to H4 (high ratio, 4WD) with a short throw, or from H4 to N (neutral) then on to L4 (low ratio) — a shift that requires the Suzuki to be stationary with the front wheels pointing straight ahead. To engage 4WD, the front hubs must then be locked but, of course, there is the option of using the low ratio with 2WD, if this is not done.

POWERFUL HEATER

There is a powerful heater that we found difficult to adjust for gentle warmth — even a few mm on the control lever produced a blast of heat — and a three-speed fan powers an effective distribution system, with a split level facility and good demisting capabilities. There is a locking cubby and a useful parcel shelf beneath the fascia.

Two exterior mirrors are provided, in addition to the normal interior mirror, and both side windows wind up, though the left hand door has no key lock: the only access, when the vehicle is locked, is through the driver's door.

A massive integral roll-over bar loops across in line with the front seat backrests and a short cloth trimmed folding seat, suitable for occasional use, is mounted between the rear wheel arches with its backrest (when erected) close to the vehicle's full width back door. This is side-hinged for easy access and carries a spare wheel vertically, clamped to its outside surface, so that half of it projects above the bodywork when the hood is off.

350 KG LOAD CAPACITY

Once they are in, the rear passengers have plenty of leg room where the floor drops behind the front seats and with the rear seat folded flat, there is 1,1 m² of load area. The vehicle has a quoted load capacity (including occupants) of 350 kg.

The front windscreen folds flat, if required, after releasing clips on either side of the dashboard and unscrewing two corner stays. The hood, which has large rectangular rear screen and side windows, is secured, when erected, by a wrap-round, press-stick system and tightly braced by tubular stays at the rear.

Projecting forwards from the top of the windscreen are two rubber "buffers" which serve two functions: they provide a safe rest for the screen when folded flat and they also support the rear-hinged bonnet, when this is folded up for access to the engine compartment. However, as no stay is provided, you need to park facing into a prevailing wind, if it's a strong one, or the bonnet could easily be blown closed. . .

Front and rear driving lights are given heavy tubular protection from off-road damage but the overall effect is neat, with heavy bumpers integrating mildly recessed light clusters. Both reverse lights and rear mudflaps are fitted.

The little alloy-head cammy motor

use as a dual purpose vehicle or second car.

TWO MODELS AVAILABLE

Two models are being imported by GMSA — the open (vinyl hooded) version as tested and the SJ 410 V, which is mechanically similar but has an all-metal two-door body. Both versions use white off-road wheels shod with steelbelt radials.

The test car was finished in bright red, with gold side flashes which set off its modern, chunky styling very effectively. Access to the front passenger compartment is gained via two steel hinged doors, much like a normal bakkie, and the two cloth upholstered bucket seats — the driver's adjustable for rake —

are fitted with "basic" seat belts which are not inertia reel. The floor is sensibly covered with rubber.

Set behind a largish, vinyl trimmed steering wheel is a simple plastic trimmed fascia incorporating a binnacle with two round apertures — one housing a 120 km/h speedometer with trip and the other, fuel and water temperature gauges and warning lights for high beam, charge and oil pressure.

There are two stalk controls — one for wipe/wash and the other for lights and indicators — and the three pendant pedals are well spread and light to operate.

A longish gear lever controls a conventional four-speed gearbox and a stubby lever controls the centrally mounted transfer box, shifting from H2 (high

Practical materials — vinyl, rubber (on the floor) and moulded plastic — are used in the interior, while conventional seat belts are provided in front (left). Access to the rear seat is limited (right), but once there, occupants have ample room. The little 4x4 is likely to spend much of the time "topless" anyway, and hop-in access over the side is easy enough.

spins to life eagerly and the Suzuki moves off happily in second (high range), its gearshift light in action and the clutch a little sudden, but strong and "clean". The manual choke can be pushed most of the way in almost immediately, unless the weather is really cold, and the recommended speed ranges in high range are from 0-30 km/h, from 5-50, from 10-70 and from 30 to the 112 km/h maximum. With L4 engaged, the maxima fall to 15, 30, 40 and 60 km/h.

QUICK STEERING

The recirculating ball steering is reasonably precise and nice and quick, off-road, with 3,5 turns from lock to lock in a 10,4-metre turning circle.

Noise levels, as our tables show, were high and road performance, in H2, proved to be sluggish. The Suzuki takes a shade under 33 seconds to reach 100 km/h from rest, for example, and 43 seconds for the standing kilometre. . .

Fuel consumption off-road would obviously vary greatly with the conditions. On tar, in H2, we recorded good figures for a vehicle of this type, ranging from only 6,4 litres/100 km at a steady 60 km/h to 10,8 at 100.

The unboosted brakes required only moderate pedal pressure and provided good feel. The vehicle remained directionally stable while producing figures ranging from 4,3 seconds to 5, in our ten-stop programme.

TEST SUMMARY

The Sukuzi SJ 410 Q emerged from our rigorous test session as an impressively efficient mini off-roader which is bound to prove extremely popular with such recreational users as fishermen, surfers and hunters as well as with people like surveyors and rangers whose work takes them into the bundu. Its off-road capabilities are limited by its small size and the range provided by its 40-litre fuel tank, but not by much else and it appears to have the simple, robust construction required for reliable operation in severe conditions.

Its striking good looks, gay finish and modest price (for a 4x4) give it special appeal in the youth market, but those specialised design features that make it so efficient off-road also limit its value in a dual-purpose role.

So small a vehicle just couldn't do both jobs and do them well — the compromise would have weakened its performance — and its designers have wisely concentrated on one. **(Graphs overleaf)** ●

SPECIFICATIONS

ENGINE:
Cylinders . . . . four in line
Fuel supply . . . . Aisan single choke downdraught
Bore/stroke . . . . 65,5/72 mm
Cubic capacity . . . . 970 cm^3
Compression ratio . . . . . . 8,8 to 1
Valve gear . . . . .s-o-h-c
Ignition . . . . . coil and distributor
Main bearings . . . . five
Fuel requirement . . 93-octane Coast, 87-octane Reef
Cooling . . . . water

ENGINE OUTPUT:
Max. power I.S.O. (kW) 33,5
Power peak (r/min) 5 500
Max. usable r/min 5 500
Max. torque (N.m) 73,5
Torque peak (r/min) 3 000

TRANSMISSION:
Forward speeds . . . . . .eight (two reduction gears)
Gearshift . . . . .floor
Low gear . . . . 3,16 to 1
2nd gear . . . . 1,94 to 1
3rd gear . . . . 1,42 to 1
Top gear . . . . 1,00 to 1
High reduction 1,59
Low reduction 2,557
Reverse gear . . . . 3,32 to 1
Final drive . . . . 4,111 to 1
Drive wheels . . . . .four-wheel-drive, free wheel front hubs

WHEELS AND TYRES:
Road wheels . . . . . . pressed steel
Rim width 5,5J
Tyres FR7815

Tyre pressures (front) . . . .140 kPa
Tyre pressures (rear) . . . . .140 kPa

BRAKES:
Front . . . . .discs
Rear . . . . .drums
Hydraulics . . . . .dual circuit, pressure limiting valve at rear
Handbrake position . . .between seats

STEERING:
Type . . . . .recirculating bal!
Lock to lock . . . . 3,5 turns
Turning circle . . . . . .10,4 metres

MEASUREMENTS:
Length overall . . . . .3 430 mm
Width overall . . . . .1 460 mm
Height overall . . . . . . .1 690 mm
Wheelbase . . . . .2 030 mm
Front track . . . . .1 220 mm
Rear track . . . . .1 220 mm
Ground clearance . . . . . .230 mm
Licensing mass . . . . .840 kg

SUSPENSION:
Front . . . . .live axle
Type . . . . .leaf springs
Rear . . . . .live axle
Type . . . . .leaf springs

CAPACITIES:
Seating . . . . four
Fuel tank . . . . .40 litres
Load area . . . . 1,1 m^2
Load rating . . . . .350 kg

WARRANTY:
12 months or unlimited km.

TEST CAR FROM:
GM South African.

ACCELERATION

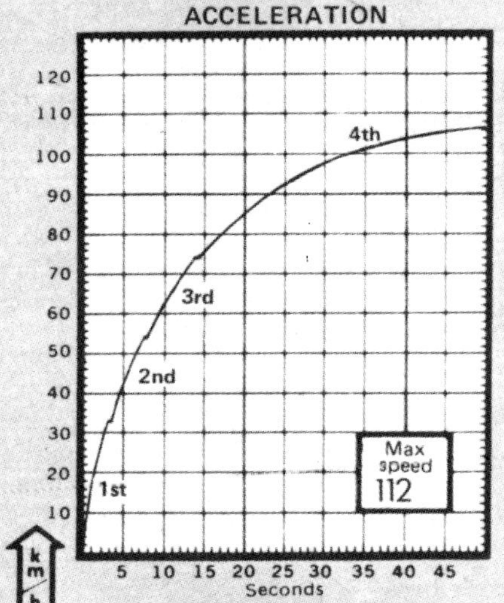

BRAKING DISTANCES

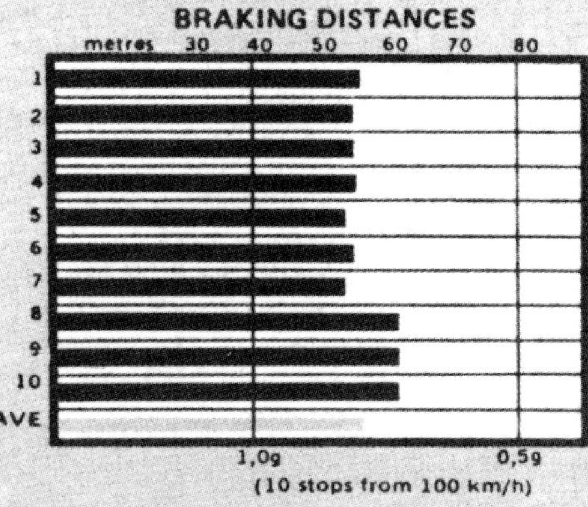

NOISE VALUES

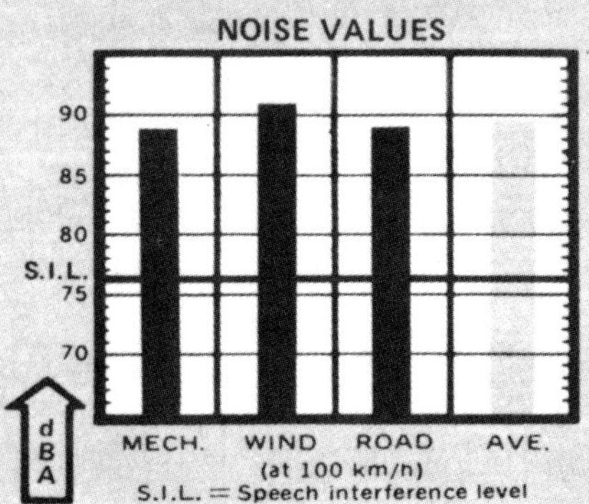

test Suzuki SJ 410 Q

PERFORMANCE

MAKE AND MODEL:
Make . . . . .Suzuki
Model. . . . . SJ 410 Q

PERFORMANCE FACTORS:
Power/mass (W/kg) net. 41,35
Frontal area (m^2) 2,47
km/h per 1 000 r/min (top) . . 19,21

INTERIOR NOISE LEVELS:

	Mech.	Wind	Road
Idling	.59	—	—
60.	.78	—	—
80.	.84	86	86
100	.89	91	89
Average dBA at 100			

ACCELERATION (seconds):

0-60. 8,9
0-80. 16,3
0-100. 32,9
1 km sprint 43,0
Terminal speed 107

OVERTAKING ACCELERATION:

	3rd	Top
40-60	.4,3	6,4
60-80	.6,1	7,4
80-100	.N/A	16,5

MAXIMUM SPEED (km/h):
True speed 112
Speedometer reading . past maximum
indication

Calibration:

Indicated:	60	70	80	90	100
True speed:	54	64	74	83	92

FUEL CONSUMPTION (litres/100 km):
60. 6,4
70. 6,9
80. 7,65
90. 8,75
100 10,8

BRAKING TEST:
From 100 km/h
Best stop 4,3
Worst stop 5,0
Average. 4,5

GRADIENTS IN GEARS:
Low gear . . . . 1 in 4,0
2nd gear . . . . 1 in 6,2
3rd gear . . . . 1 in 9,0
Top gear . . . . 1 in 14,3

GEARED SPEEDS (km/h):

	High	Low reduction
Low gear	.33 .	. . . 21
2nd gear	.54 .	. . . 34
3rd gear	.74 .	. . . 46
Top gear	106 .	. . . 66

TEST CONDITIONS:
Altitude . . . . at sea level
Weather . . . . overcast, windless
Fuel used 93
Test car's odometer 6 108

ENGINE SPEED

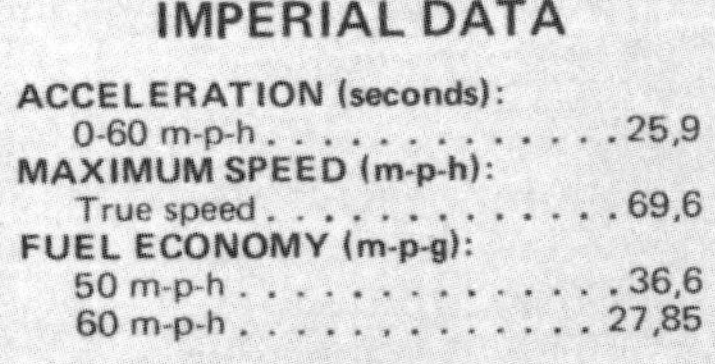

IMPERIAL DATA

ACCELERATION (seconds):
0-60 m-p-h 25,9
MAXIMUM SPEED (m-p-h):
True speed 69,6
FUEL ECONOMY (m-p-g):
50 m-p-h 36,6
60 m-p-h 27,85

GRADIENT ABILITY

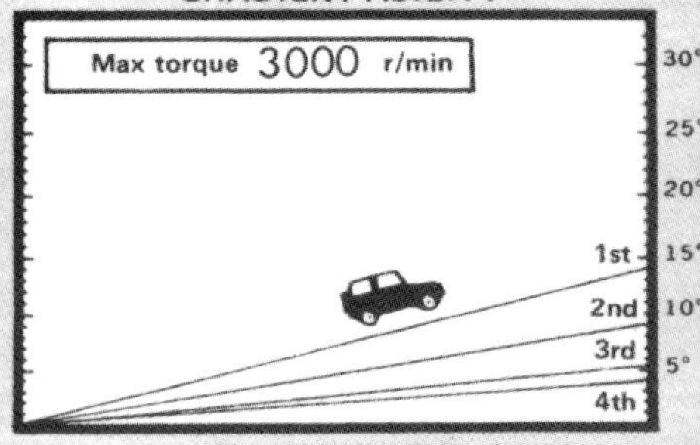

CRUISING AT 100

Mech. noise level . . . . 89 dBA
0-100 through gears. . . . 32,9 seconds
Litres/100 km at 100 10,8
Optimum fuel range at 100 . . . 370 km
Braking from 100 . . . . . . 4,5 seconds
Speedometer error . . . .8 per cent over
Speedo at true 100 108
Odometer error . . . . . 1 per cent under
Engine r/min at 100 . . . . 5 205

"Dear Sir..."
Guess what! Our family has acquired a little Suzuki 4WD as a second car

The author at the wheel of the Suzuki

HONESTLY, I was petrified! Fancy being handed a brand-new SJ410QX — that's the rag-top version of the little Suzuki "jeep" — and being *told* to hop in and drive it home. Husbands!

Mind you, it really looked the part. Black, with a white hood, and red trimmings. Really butch, in its way, but that first drive was an eye-opener. I learned more about me than about the car . . .

For a start, I've only been used to conventional runabouts. Minis, and things, where you sit almost brushing the road. I just wasn't prepared for climbing up into a vehicle, and having this commanding driving position, where you can look over the other gals in their — well, Minis and things — and over the hedges as well. The things you could see!

Mind you, that was the least of my worries! I was too busy trying to learn how to *steer* the device. I know that there's a world of difference between driving on main roads and on the farm tracks which are the Suzuki's stock in trade, but I simply wasn't prepared for the difference in handling between our new 4WD and the cars I'd driven previously. At first, I felt that I'd never make it go where I wanted. You see, on the rough-stuff there's always a lot of kickback as the wheels drop into pot-holes or lift over hummocks, and if the steering was *too* direct you'd be into the ditch in no time. So, it has to have a fair amount of play, and on the Suzuki they've even added a hydraulic damper to take some of the shocks out of it. Fine. But on the road that means that you have to twiddle the wheel a quarter of a turn before it has any apparent effect at all, and until you're used to it you just sit there wondering if it's really connected to the wheels. Leastways, I did.

It doesn't take long to pick up the trick, of course. You have to telegraph your punches: start turning into a bend just a little earlier than you would normally do with a conventional car, and start straightening up earlier too. That way, it goes round nicely enough. If you don't, then you sit there sawing away at the wheel and wondering if you're going to end up in the oncoming traffic stream, with everybody shaking their fists and screaming rude words about women drivers. You know the score!

The odd thing is that, get it on the sort of going that any farmer's wife is used to — and you know what our farm tracks in Sussex are like, even if they're a doddle compared to yours — and it completely alters its character. You can place it to an inch, even when you're bouncing your way up a bostal in which the ruts in the chalk are eighteen inches or more deep.

I've found the same thing with the suspension. Remember the old cart springs — well, leaf springs is the real name for them, I'm told, though I've always used the other term. Now, the Suzuki is quite unsophisticated down below. Cart springs — all right, hubby dear, *leaf* springs, if you insist! — at both ends, with good old-fashioned live axles, just like I used to have on my '36 Morris Eight only double, and better controlled. So, of course, when one wheel goes up the other has to come down. Fact of life, isn't it. And that means that every time you hit a bump the axle tilts and tries to steer the car the other way. You soon get used to it, and on the rough stuff that springing is *fab*. You can go bucketing over surfaces that remind me of Grannie's washboard and, though you'll get bounced around a bit if you don't keep the speed down, you don't really *feel* anything. Snag is, on the far gentler

Ready to go . . . high driving position gives the driver an excellent view.

humps and bumps that you get on our country lanes — and the County Council don't seem to have spent a penny on maintenance for years! — the little car just seems to go berserk. "Himself" keeps murmuring darkly about changing over to Koni dampers, or taking a leaf out of the springs: but personally I hope he doesn't play around with it. It's stiff, Goodness knows, and can be quite uncomfortable after 40 miles or so if the surfaces are none too good, but I'm not at all sure I'd like to take the risk of spoiling the overall balance of the car, which is good. Mind you, I'll probably develop the biceps of an all-in wrestler keeping it on line, but I'd be very loth to risk that wonderful off-road performance

Driver's eye view of the Suzuki. Controls are well laid out.

when all you have to do is knock five mph or so off your usual cruising speed to get a quite acceptable ride.

Not that Himself has got the message, yet. When he takes the wheel, and pushes me into the passenger seat, I know I'm going to endure the old rally-star act. I don't get scared — well, I do, but I try not to show it — while he's trying to zoom the Suzuki round the corners. Snag is, it's not really built for the great he-man act — it's a bit tall and narrow — so Nev and I get bounced around like peas in a none-too-secure pod. It's not easy for passengers, riding in a zippy but hard-sprung car with a short wheelbase, if the driver reckons he's all set to take on Walter Röhrl and his Quattro. Again, it only needs a few mph off the speed, and the 410 rides well enough and, frankly, on our sort of trips — ten, perhaps fifteen, miles at a stretch — you don't really save any time by blasting round the bends. Oh, the car will do it all right: it's very stable. But everybody is so much more comfortable if the driver's taking it that

little bit easier. I'll readily agree that the Suzuki's like a mettlesome horse: you've got to dominate it, and show it who's the boss. But then, I have to do the same with Himself . . .!

I've only tried it on a motorway once, and I was unlucky enough to hit on a day when there was a gale-force headwind. Well, you've only got to look at the Suzuki to see that it starts off with a fair old built-in headwind itself, so I wasn't really surprised that it took me all my time to crawl past lorries. When I hit the bow-wave, it was just as if somebody had suddenly applied the brakes. Just my luck, because Himself has whipped it up and down the M23 four or five times since, and has come in all smug and self-satisfied to report that it has cruised all the way at 70mph without a murmur. Men!

After all, what do they know about real utility driving? Do they do the shopping? Do they Hell! If they did, they'd know that there are aspects of a second family car which need a bit more consideration. Like, for instance, getting that load of shopping into the back. Much though I love our Suzuki — and I know that I'm going to sit down and bawl my eyes out like a kid when I have to part with it — this version isn't the world's best shopping car. If Himself had listened to me, we'd have had the hard-top version — it only costs a hundred quid or so more — in which you only have to swing open the back door and pop the carriers straight into the boot. Oh no, *he* had to choose the rag-top. True enough, it looks macho (whatever that may mean!) but I haven't found it to be really practical. Before you can open the rear door you have to unzip the hood and then free a line of pop-studs. And when you've done that, you have to fasten them all again.

True enough, the summer we've had there have been advantages. I've been driving around with just the rear of the hood rolled up, and the windows open, and its been cool, really cool . . . But with the hood down it was a real disappointment: too much back-draught, which sent my flowing locks flowing right into my eyes. And too much buffeting from the slipstream too. Mind you, it takes all the ingenuity and determination of a 14-year-old son to get the hood folded in the first place, since it has to be bodily removed. It's held in place by a combination of slots into which the hood slides, and Velcro strips which secure it to the window frames and the roll-over bar. I've met nothing like it since the one and only time Himself talked me into crewing his bilious little boat, and I had to wrestle with the sails. Come to think of it, even when it's up the hood cracks and rustles just like those boat sails did. No, it's the hard-top for me, every time.

Don't get me wrong, though. I *love* this little car, and I'm finding 4WD tremendous fun. I like the feeling that I'm never going to get bogged down, even if I venture into the slimiest corner of the 40 Acre Field. I like the feeling that I'm never going to be without wheels, even if we get another snowfall like — well, I'm not going to give my age away by saying when! I know that Nev complains (but not too bitterly) that he has to sit sideways in the rear seat to get sufficient toe-room — not so much leg-room: there's enough of that, but the space under the front seats is limited — and I know that the family dogs, who usually love cars, have to be cossetted because of the bumpy ride. And I know that you have to put your brain into gear, and not just the car, to get the best out of it.

But, there's so *much* to get out of it. The engine is a gem: a smooth little unit, of under 1,000cc, that will pull from less than 10mph in top gear right up to 70 or so without demur. A slick four-speed gearbox to match — though I wish it was a five-speeder, because at any speed in top it does feel terribly undergeared. A sturdiness of construction which makes me feel that it is safe and that it'll last forever. And the sheer fun of its "go anywher, go anytime" concept. I simply know that if I start a journey — any journey, over any sort of going, in any weather — then the Suzuki is going to get me through. I'd miss it terribly if we had to change to a conventional car.

And it's been doing a steady 28mpg overall on two-star petrol in everyday running; and will happily tow a one-ton load; and has had people stopping to knock at the door and ask for details about "that interesting car of yours". Can you wonder that I've come to love it? Happy days!

SHUNA HUNT

Left: Rear seat is spartan and when in use (left, below) load space is limited but when the seat is folded forward (below) quite large objects can be carried. Bottom pic shows the engine layout.

Right: A sunny day in Sussex — the Suzuki in its element down on the farm.

SUZUKI SJ410Q AT A GLANCE

ENGINE ●●●●●

970cc sohc "4" in line; alloy head, cast iron block; single carburettor; conventional ignition; 5 main bearings; 45bhp at 5,500 rpm, 54.2 lb ft torque at 3,000 rpm; 11.9mph/ 1,000 rpm.

TRANSMISSION ●●●●

4-speed + rev; transfer box with high/low ratios; no centre differential; live axles front and rear. Ratios (high) 1, 20.67 2, 12.71 3, 9.28 4, 6.53 rev, 21.7 (low) 1, 35.01 2, 21.73 3, 15.87 4, 11.17 rev, 37.10; locking freewheels optional.

SUSPENSION ●●●

Live axles on leaf springs, with telescopic dampers, front and rear; 195 SR15 tyres, 5½ x 15 in steel wheels.

BRAKES ●●●●

Front, 8.7in drums; rear, 8.7in drums; transmission brake, 7in drum; no servo assistance.

STEERING ●●●

Manual worm and ball, with hydraulic damper; 3.5 turns lock to lock; turning circle, 32.2 ft.

BODY ●●●

Steel 3-door, 4-seater; steel box-section chassis; hinged-back seats for driver and passenger; folding rear bench seat.

DIMENSIONS ●●●●

Length, 135in; width, 57.5in; height, 66.5in; wheelbase, 79.9in; angle of approach, 48 deg; angle of departure, 39 deg; ground clearance, 9.1in; loading sill height, 25in; max all-up weight, 2,756 lb; max towing weight, 2,205 lb; fuel tank capacity, 8.8 gal.

SERVICE ●●●

Every 6,000 miles. Times: 6,000 miles, 2 hr; 12,000 miles, 4 hr; 24,000 miles, 5.5 hr.

PRICE ●●●●●

£4,499 inc Car Tax and VAT.

IMPORTERS 47 dealers

Suzuki GB (Cars) Ltd, 46-62 Gatwick Road, Crawley, West Sussex RH10 2XF.

4Wheel Drive Star Scale
●●●●●=excellent ●●●●=good
●●●=average ●●=below average ●=poor

SUPER ZOOKIE

IF YOU'RE doing 85mph in top gear with the engine revving on the red-line and hills don't make any difference to your top speed, then you couldn't possibly be driving one of Suzuki's attractive little SJ410 off-roaders. Those little machines, though good fun off-road and quite sprightly enough for tootling around town, lose a lot of their charm when asked to make a motorway journey of any length. It's hard work trying to maintain the legal limit — 70mph comes up occasionally when the road is straight and windless but any sign of a hill and the needle drops back to 65 . . .60 . . .55 . . .

One way out of the problem is to wait for a National bus to come roaring by in the fast lane. If you're quick enough, you can tuck in close behind and get an 80mph tow for as long as it takes the bus driver to shake you off. Fortunately, there is another way. Allard Turbochargers, of Ross-on-Wye,

Herefordshire, can give the little Suzuki enough of a power boost to manage without the bus.

For a start acceleration becomes almost sporting — 12.3 seconds 0-60mph compared with the standard car's 22.3, and better than the Range Rover's 14.3. Flexibility is improved, too, cutting down the amount of gearchanging. At anything over 30mph it is quite feasible to leave the SJ410 in top gear, as it will accelerate strongly right up to 80mph or more. And it will stay at that speed quite happily regardless of motorway inclines — in fact so willingly does the turbocharged engine rev up that it has to be rev-limited to prevent extended red-line running in top.

There is little turbo lag, so that acceleration is smooth throughout the rev range. This is because the relatively low compression ratio of 8.8-to-1 does not have to be adjusted to handle the

turbo boost — the only requirement that the turbo car has to be run on premium rather than regular petrol and because the Japanese IHI reacts very quickly to changes in exhaust gas flow.

It is ideally suited to the small capacity of the engine — only 970cc in that it is one of the smallest production turbochargers in the world weighing less than 6lb complete with wastegate system. A backward curve blade design helps to give the unit an efficiency of over 72 per cent. Since turbine and wheel assembly are light and have low inertia, the turbo can respond quickly to the exhaust flow. Also because of the small capacity of the engine, the boost pressure can be kept low. The Allard conversion is set to blow to a quite moderate 6psi.

The standard carburettor is retained but with modified jetting. The carburettor is pressurised, which in

Left: There is plenty of room in the Suzuki's engine bay for the exhaust-driven turbocharger and its plumbing. Right: On the road the Allard turbocharger boosted top speed over the 80mph mark. The intercooler can be seen through the radiator intake grill.

Bob Cooke tries a Suzuki fitted with an Allard turbocharger

...n requires a high-pressure fuel pump ...nsure adequate supply plus a ...ulator valve to prevent oversupply. ...he basic conversion is available as a ...for just over £600; Allard or an ...ard-approved dealer will fit the kit ...an extra £115.

...here is, however, a second-stage, ...her performance kit which adds an ...-to-air intercooler and a larger bore ...e-flow exhaust pushing the basic ...ce up to just over £800. In this ...version the air-to-air intercooler is ...unted in front of the standard water ...iator and is linked to the turbo ...npressor discharge and carburettor ...intake by flexible, reinforced silicon ...se and aluminium manifolding.

...he turbocharger is mounted on a ...cially cast iron exhaust manifold ...h a large bore turbine exhaust ...charge pipe running back through ...replacement free-flow exhaust. Oil ...d for the turbo bearings is taken from the oil warning light switch tapping in the engine block, and a drain takes the oil back into the forward end of the sump.

Allard say the conversion can be fitted in around 10 hours, and requires little additional servicing apart from ensuring regular oil changes and air filter checks.

The version we tried had the "stage two" conversion and impressed us with its smooth, quiet delivery of power, excellent flexibility and top speed performance. The short wheelbase and off-road suspension makes the car a little jittery at speed along windy country lanes, but the brakes proved well up to the task of slowing the car for corners, and there was seldom any need to change down to get adequate acceleration to build up speed for the next straight section.

Engine noise is quite high when buzzing along at 70 or 80mph since it is revving away at nearly 6,000rpm. The engine could use a fifth gear or overdrive, but unfortunately Allard know of no suitable replacement systems. Raising the gearing by using bigger wheels is not a satisfactory solution since handling becomes tricky.

Allard claim that the performance boost does not cost a lot in fuel consumption terms. Consumption might be expected to drop from around 32mpg for the standard car to 27mpg for the turbo version, simply because the car is able to maintain high cruising speeds, thereby increasing the percentage of relatively thirsty driving. At lower speeds the increased efficiency of the turbocharger should result in better fuel consumption.

Allard Turbochargers are based at Unit 3, Alton Road Industrial Estate, Ross-on-Wye, Herefordshire HR9 5NB (telephone 0989 63963).

From left to right:
JX models feature two-tone trim panels.
An armrest would be welcome.
Front buckets fully recline and, with
headrests removed, would make an
emergency bed.
Sedate-looking grille hides the fact that
engine power is up 40%.
5-speed LWB can be distinguished by step
in roofline behind B pillar.
With roof fully removed, rear support
remains in place — handy for boards,
canoes, etc.
Rear window can be rolled up, but there is
no provision for rolling up the sides.

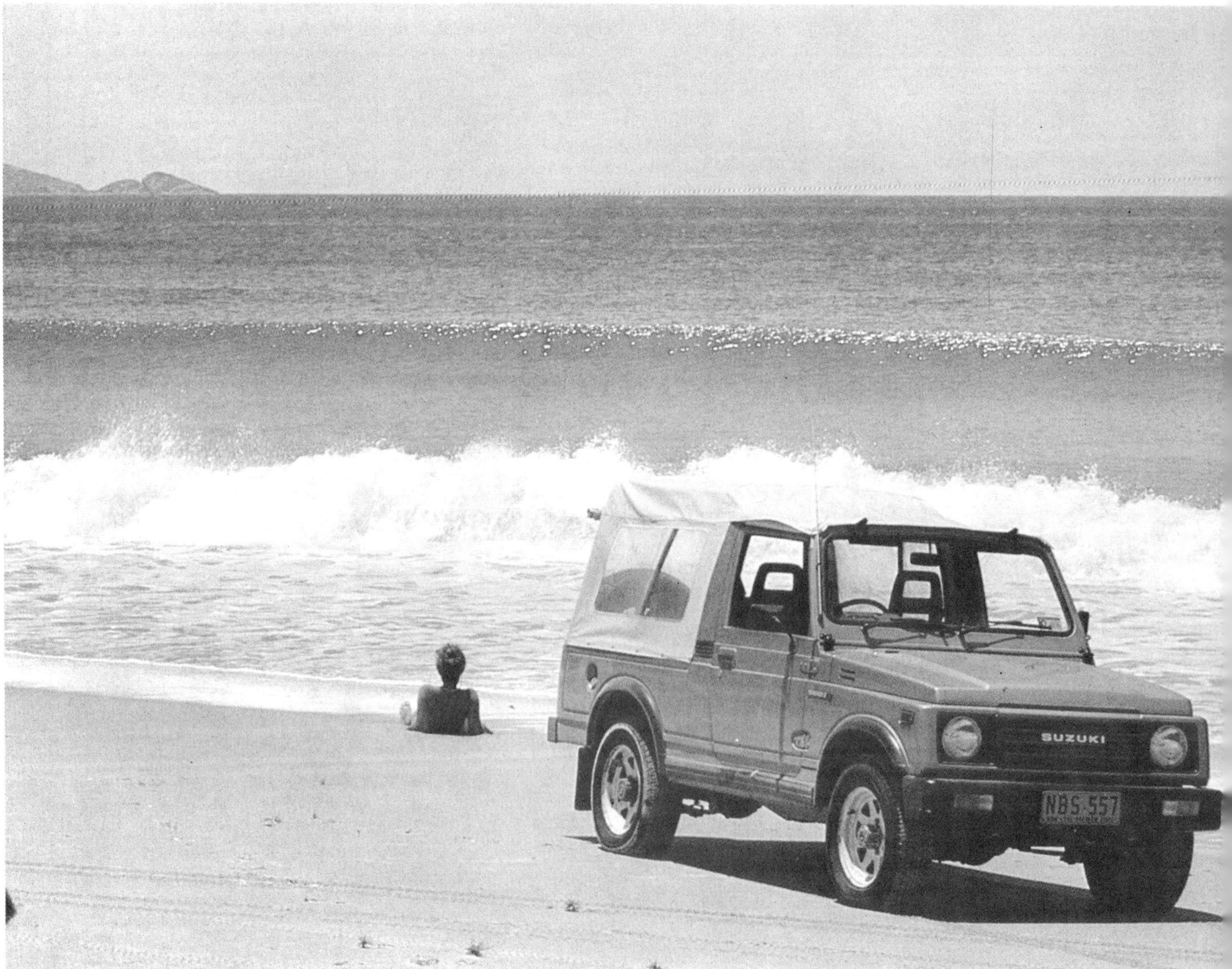

Since their release in 1981, the compact 4WD Suzuki Sierra models have been extremely popular vehicles. They have found homes with a very wide cross-section of buyers — from budget-minded students seeking the lowest-priced, most-economical-to-run 4WD, to highly-paid executives looking for something which might put a little bit of fun back into their weekends.

The Suzuki Sierra, especially in soft-top form, is to the eighties what the T Series MGs were to the early fifties — yet, even though the Sierra has been a real success story, many potential owners would have been put off by the Sierra's lack of comfort features, very mild performance from the one-litre engine, and the vehicle's inability to cruise the freeways at high speed.

Times have changed!

Like all of Japan's automobile manufacturers, the Suzuki Motor Co. Ltd doesn't waste time sitting on its laurels. No matter how successful a model may be, they know that today's market is highly critical, acutely aware of new trends and will not put brand loyalty in the way when it comes to deciding which vehicle best suits its needs.

Suzuki's commitment to continual improvement of the product has produced what must be one of the most competitive 4WDs in years, and certainly one of the leaders in terms of value for money.

The new 5-speed, 1.3-litre Sierras are available in similar configurations to what was offered in the 1.0-litre models. However, there are a few model changes.

At the top of the list, with a price only a few hundred dollars

Suzuki Sierra
1·3 litre JX

BY RAY & HELEN BARKER

short of ten grand, is a new, high-roof hardtop which is, at the time of writing, available only in JX trim. The soft-top JA or JX with half doors and clip-on side curtains will not be imported, as sales have revealed that the majority of soft-top buyers prefer wind-up windows. Interestingly, we hear that GM-H will offer this model in their Holden-badged Sierra, due for release in the first half of 1985 and rumoured to be called the Drover. If that is true, then GM-H have obviously not done their homework too well, and we predict that the half-door version of the Drover (drover's dog?) will be quietly discontinued.

As a "price leader", the very basic 1.0-litre, 4-speed, half-door soft-top will continue to be imported — in NSW at least. This model, which retails for $6,990 including sales tax, is by far the lowest-priced 4WD on the market (excluding Daihatsu's tiny HiJet things) and is ideal for farming, paper deliveries and as patrol vehicles etc.

The BUSHDRIVER test vehicle was the long wheelbase soft-top with JX trim. The long wheelbase is available ex-factory only in soft-top form, although several Australian companies make canopies to suit.

Continued on next page

When we picked up the JX, we had a close look at all of the new models. For our money, we could not see any reason for not buying the JX in preference to the JA. The $500 to $600 difference in price entitles the JX buyer to a well-designed factory rear seat, much more supportive and high-backed front buckets, padded instrument panel, comprehensive instrumentation including a tachometer, intermittent wipers, fancy door panels and seat inserts (vinyl in soft-tops and cloth in hardtops), full-length floor covering (vinyl in soft-tops, carpet in hardtops), sporty white spoked wheels, thick side bump strips and different badges — a lot of value for very few extra dollars.

Our test vehicle was finished in an attractive blue metallic ($60 extra) with a white roof and grey and orange interior trim. Black tops are available if you prefer that colour to white, but there is no option on the interior colour scheme. No matter what the exterior colour, all JX soft-tops have grey and orange trim. It sounds worse than it really is. We inspected all of the colours available, and only in the red vehicles did the interior trim appear to clash.

The easiest way to pick an LWB 1.3-litre from a 1.0-litre is to look at the roof. The 1.3's soft-top is noticeably stepped up just behind the front seat area, whereas the superseded LWB had a fairly even roofline.

Externally, the only changes are to the grille and bonnet. The old shark-toothed "real 4WD" grille has been replaced by a close-meshed, plastic affair which is more carlike than you would expect to see on a 4WD. We prefer the earlier grille — if only for its more macho appearance.

The 1.3's bonnet is noticeably higher to accommodate the new engine and to provide a "power bulge" effect.

Other standard equipment around the vehicle includes halogen headlights, manual free-wheeling front hubs, FR78-15 radials on sports wheels, front and rear towing eyes, the snugly-fitting soft-top and rubber bumpers above the windscreen which support the windscreen when lowered to the bonnet, or support the bonnet when raised to the screen.

It is the interior that has received the most noticeable changes. Gone is the black, flat, sheet-metal fascia panel and basic instrument panel. In its place is one of the simplest, yet smartest, fascias in any off-roader.

The steering wheel is now three-spoked and thick-rimmed. The gauges are big, easy to read and have orange lettering on a grey background. There are big, multi-adjustable air vents plus side vents for demisting the door windows. A centrally-mounted digital clock sits high in the padded dash.

A lockable glovebox of reasonable size is directly below the horizontal panic bar in front of the passenger's bucket seat.

Column-mounted stalks control the wiper/washers, the lights and the high/low beam operation.

As with previous models, there is an AM/FM push-button radio with one speaker in the front passenger's footwell. There is provision for a second speaker in the right-hand footwell, although the radio is not a stereo type and an extra speaker would only increase the noise level.

The main gear lever, transfer case lever and handbrake lever are all mounted on the transmission tunnel and, as with all of the Sierra's controls, are very easy to reach and operate.

However, of all the new interior appointments, it was the seats that impressed me the most. One week prior to the test, I pulled a muscle in the lower part of my back, and spent two days on the bed, unable to walk or move about. Then, when Ric Williams rang and said in his usual easy-going, unhurried manner, "You have to do this story. We are past the deadline already!" I knew that any protest was useless. I also thought that I might be starting the test in a Suzuki and finishing the test in an ambulance.

Nevertheless, although still in plenty of pain when we set off for five days of zooking, my back actually improved, and, by the time we returned home, I

Engine bay is superbly laid out. Note air intake running behind battery.

was brand new — something I least expected, and something which says a lot for the well-contoured and obviously quite comfortable front buckets in the JX model Sierras.

The only criticism I have of the front seats is that the left-hand one is not adjustable fore and aft. This means that, while the driver can slide the right-hand seat far enough back to please a six-and-a half footer, the passenger must be content with a lot less legroom. On this test I would have preferred to have been the passenger and let Helen drive, but my long legs demand that they be given plenty of stretching space.

Two people who did have stacks of legroom were. the kids in the back.

Suzuki mount the rear seat well back — a position that robs a lot of space from the cargo area, but one which ensures that even adults will be able to ride in the rear without too much discomfort. After having been back-seat drivers in all manner of vehicles over the years, our kids have become fairly experienced passengers. They are quick to comment on anything that they don't like. Surprisingly, they made no negative comments about the Sierra's seats at all — which, to me, must mean that the seating accommodation overall is pretty good for a 4WD and excellent for a 4WD with such compact dimensions.

On the trip, we were impressed by the forward vision over the stubby bonnet, but annoyed by the very big blind spot just behind the left-hand door. If you approach an intersection where the angle between the road you are travelling on and the road on the left is less than ninety degrees, you can be in real bother. The wide roll-bar and the vinyl material between the roll-bar and the forward edge of the rear side window effectively block out all vision to the left . . . dangerous if you haven't a front passenger to give you a report. Suzuki should either make the side window longer or move the forward edge right up to the roll-bar.

Other minor annoyances inside include the right-hand window winder which dug into my right knee and left a big, red mark (my fault for having long legs), the ventilation/heater fan which is excessively noisy, the absence of (a) a dimming control for the brightly-lit instruments, (b) a day/night mirror, (c) a cigarette lighter (to operate the tyre pump) and (d) armrests on the doors.

Oh, OK . . . you want to know how the machine goes.

Here we go . . .

On the test we carried two adults, two kids and enough baggage to support five nights of motelling. That means that, in the Sierra's luggage area, we had one very large suitcase, one normal-sized suitcase, a photo-equipment case, a vanity case, an electric iron (gotta keep up appearances, you know), a comprehensive first-aid kit, a snatch-um-strap, a Coleman type pump case and some other junk the kids decided to bring. We could have carried more had we kept the rear curtain down and loaded it in the vertical space.

For a Suzuki, that is a reasonable load, yet, by the way the 1.3-litre, four-cylinder engine handled it, I reckon we could have added fifty per cent more before it would have begun to struggle.

The 1.3 has forty per cent more poke than the 1.0 — and it shows! Second gear starts were the norm. Sitting on the

*argo area is limited but can accommodate
iree large cases.*

peed limit, whether it was 80, 100 or
10 km/h, was child's play. Steep hills
viped off speed quickly, but not any
nore so than you would expect in any
mall sedan of equivalent engine size.

The 1.3 engine is very similar to that
ised in the Suzuki Swift, a vehicle that,
lespite its super-economy claim to
ame, can outrun a Mini Cooper S from
ero to 100 km/h.

When Suzuki first introduced a four-
ylinder, four-stroke engine in the LJ80,
t was at that time (1977) one of
he cleanest-burning and most efficient
ngines in production. Their new,
igh-tech 1.3 is another giant step.
Developing 47 kW (13.5 kW more than
he 1.0-litre), the new design with its
ll-alloy cylinder block weighs in at
ust 78 kilograms. That's 172 pounds in
he old language — or just over 12 stone
n mum's bathroom scales.

The five-speed gearbox is a dream.
f it had any idiosyncracies (in my
ondition) I would have been well
ware of them in the first two days.
Third gear seemed to "come out" of
he slot at the slightest touch, but that
ould, more than anything else, have
een the way I was driving.

The long wheelbase offers a good
ide — much better than you would ex-
ect from a fairly light, leaf-sprung 4WD
ehicle. We doubt that anyone would
omplain of the ride and comfort in this
articular model. Naturally, the shorter
wheelbase Sierras would be choppier
n uneven surfaces.

Sierra's front disc/rear drum brakes
re now power assisted and well up to
he task of pulling the vehicle up in a
uss-free manner. The radial tyres also
ontribute to the excellent ride, hand-
ing and braking.

On the first leg of the trip, which
omprised about 100 km of suburban
raffic and 300 km of open highway,
he Sierra consumed 35 litres of petrol.

This converts to 8.8 L/100 km or 32
mpg — a good figure considering we
were pushing for maximum performance all of the time. The 40-litre fuel
tank should therefore provide a range of
approximately 450 km.

An annoyance at speed is the soft-
top. The air rushing past caused the top
to vibrate, which in turn urges the rear
zippers to undo. This, in turn, eventually leads to excessive flapping of the top
at the rear corners, and the unfastening
of the clips . . . complicated, but that's
what happens.

Actually, the soft-top on the LWB
is the one thing that spoils an otherwise
excellent vehicle. Suzuki retain the soft-
top by extensive use of Velcro self-
adhesive tabs — tabs that, after only
3,000 km, were looking worse for wear
and which I doubt would last out the
warranty period — especially if you take
the top off frequently.

The soft-top's side windows are non-
opening, and there is no provision for
rolling up the sides. This means that the
only way you can let the rear passengers
have some fresh air is by rolling up the
rear window and letting the air blast in
on the back of their heads . . . acceptable on a very hot day — and on a sealed
road. If you travel any distance along a
gravel road on a hot day, there are two
alternatives: leave the back down
and swelter, or roll the back up and get
the interior (everything and everyone
in it) coated in a film of dust.

With the top right off, everything
is apples — provided you can find somewhere to put the top and the three hood
bows — one small one from above the
front seats and two large bows from the
rear. The most-rearward roof support
actually doubles as a secondary roll-
bar and therefore remains fixed in
place.

In the rough stuff, the Suzuki performed as we expected it would. The
LWB is not as agile as its SWB counterpart, but nevertheless it is still a trim
package in the bush. The fifth gear
overdrive enables you to stay in low
range longer than would be pleasant in
the four-speeder. This means that low
range can be used for everything from
dead slow slogging to reasonable speeds
on trails.

We were quite alarmed at the way
the transfer case lever would vibrate in
certain conditions. It really gets the
rattles and shakes. We were also concerned for the fuel tank which has no
protection whatsoever, and for the rear
number plate bracket which scrapes
when you traverse any decent mound or
rock.

Our test included about one hundred
kilometres of beach driving — conditions in which all Suzuki 4WDs excel,
even when using 600 x 16 lug-type
crossplies.

We ran the tyres at normal pressures
for much of the time on the beach, and
had no hassles . . . not until we happened to be passing a lone couple sunbaking
in their birthday suits. Lo and behold,
just as we passed them to tackle an exit
track, the Suzuki buried down — a case
for all out, lower the pressures and have
a faster run at the section. I'm sure the
couple thought I bogged the Sierra on
purpose. I know from the look they had
on their faces that they did!

For rough-terrain work, the things
that impress about the Sierra include
the extremely well laid out engine bay
where a lot of thought has gone into
proper location for the air cleaner
inlet and the electrics, the removable
floor coverings which make cleaning out
the debris easier, drain holes in the floor
which allow you to hose the vehicle
out if necessary, plus a general no-
nonsense look and feel about the entire
vehicle which is reinforced by the first-
class quality of manufacture that is
typical of Japanese 4WDs.

In a variety of conditions which included town running, bush roads, bush
tracks and beach, the Sierra returned
8.5 L/100 km which is almost identical
to that achieved on the highway — proving that the Sierra is equally at home
pottering around or out for a jog.

Overall, the new, long-wheelbase,
1.3-litre 5-speed is so impressive that it
needs to be compared with vehicles
further up the scale . . . vehicles such as
the Daihatsu Rocky, Mitsubishi Pajero
SWB and the Jeep Renegade. Of course,
in many respects, those vehicles are
superior and could obviously tackle
heavier tasks, but when you look at the
price difference, the new Sierra shapes
up well . . . very well, indeed.

What a pity is has such a lousy
soft-top!

The Female View

*Size-wise, the Sierra was great for a
short time away for a family — provided you don't have to carry all the camping gear. A couple would find it ideal,
and if they really had to sleep in it, the
front seat (with the head restraints
removed) could be laid down flush with
the rear seat cushion.*

*I was disappointed with the steering.
It wasn't heavy or light or normal —
just vague. There didn't seem to be any
direct connection between the steering
wheel and the wheels. Somewhere along
the line it all goes wrong, and the faster
you go, the worse the steering gets.*

*Nonetheless, we are seriously think-
ing of buying one as a back-up vehicle.
It will have to be the long wheelbase
model, but it definitely will have to
have a hardtop fitted to it — right from
the first day we get it.*

The Suzuki has a lot to answer for. This magazine, for example.

Until its birth, off-roading by means of four wheels had largely been the territory of the green-wellie brigade, admission being by ticket only. With tickets taking the form of a variety of Rovers, the price was far from right.

The Suzuki changed all that.

But like any new messiah, it was a while before it was even taken seriously. Cast out for a year or two into the proverbial wilderness, the Suzi had time to gather its thoughts, study the antics of its British hosts, and mature from the ungainly LJ80 into the now-successful SJ410.

The copybook transformation from ugly duckling to all-singing, dancing, great white swan. Who's laughing now? Certainly not the British car industry. Suzuki's only trouble is they can't ship enough of the little things in to keep the buying public satisfied.

Hordes of grinning Orientals

Why did we ever mock it in the first place? Well, as I mentioned in last month's issue, it didn't quite fit in – sure, back in 1980 or whenever it first arrived, we could all have pictured hordes of five-foot tall grinning Orientals careering around their homeland in this

SWEET LITTLE SUZI

Suzuki's SJ410 certainly goes against almost everything said and done by UK manufacturers on the subject of off-road vehicles, but does it work? Russell Fisher explores the question.

shrunken imitation of a Jeep, but us big, macho Brits? Noooo....what we wanted was Power, and note the capital 'P'. Rugged, brute power.

At that time the name Suzuki was still associated almost solely with motorbikes, outboard motors, generators and the like – small, two-stroke and cheap. Fundamentally Japanese.

It's therefore really no surprise that the LJ80 was looked upon as being perhaps a little effeminate. More of us are laughing at the Sinclair C5 now than ever did at the Suzuki LJ80, but Sinclair's no fool, and neither were Suzuki.

Almost unforgivably twee

They knew that 4x4 had the potential to appeal to a wider audience, but that to succeed their vehicle had to be aimed at the bottom end of the market. Hence it's small, with a pint-sized engine, but who can match the price? Only Fiat have managed to do so with their Panda 4x4, and that's not in the same class. As I said, Suzuki are no fools...

So, what is it about the SJ410 that makes it so wonderfully popular? If, at least for the meantime, we forget the performance, handling and associated guff – after all, the vast majority of the motoring public rarely pay much attention to such detailed info – I think you'll find its success has a lot to do

with its appearance. In a way it's like the Mini or Citroen 2CV – almost unforgivably twee. Take it along to the nearest hotspot for womanizing, impress a likely candidate all night long with drinks and witty repartee, broach the subject of 4x4s just before taking her out to the carpark for the long run home, and she's still more likely to giggle and want to hug it at first sight than stand back in awe. Like I said – twee. *Teddybear* twee.

Given time we'll no doubt see Suzis adorned with a variety of disgusting Snoopy, Mickey Mouse, Nuke The Whale and Save The Bomb decals, driven by lightweight health food, nuts-and-pulse freaks in pink stripey dungarees and wire-rimmed spectacles. Pass the sick bag, Alice...

Yes, the SJ410 is indeed a functional, fairly attractive design, but the thought that it may well be appreciated and remembered for reasons of aesthetics rather than its remarkable capabilities makes me cringe. What a waste.

Well-aimed flak

It is an extremely capable little vehicle which, somewhat inevitably, comes equipped with most of the usual 4x4 bugbears – namely iffy handling and disgusting ride. Show me a 4x4 that doesn't have at least one of those and I'll send a full-size coconut, postage and packing paid.

Having been at the receiving end of a lot of well-aimed flak as a result of my 'first impressions' piece, I'll still stick to most everything I said in that short piece – it's too excitable for my long-term liking.

The problem is, if it's a problem at all, that I'm one of those poor, poverty-striken souls who has to live with their 4x4 on a day-to-day basis. Not for me the luxury of parking-up the everyday mode of transport in its cozy little garage and leaping into the stand-by 4x4 for a weekend of mud-plugging. No, my requirements dictate an all-rounder, and I'm not convinced that the Suzi cuts it as one of those – for better or worse, the SJ410 has been designed, I'm sure, primarily as a second car. Let's accept it as such and get on with it...

Boasting all of 970 cubic centimetres of swept capacity, the SJ410 is no

workhorse. On the other hand, it isn't a sluggard. The little engine may not be particularly familiar to us all, but, on paper at least, it appears quite straightforward. Four cylinders in line are pumped up and down courtesy of a five-main crank and fed with fuel and spark respectively by a plain and simple single carb and mechanical ignition system. In other words, there ain't much to go wrong, chaps.

Having said that, we only had the Suzi for three weeks or so – that may not sound particularly long, but Press road tests in the case of 4x4s are pretty, 'er, thorough shall we say, and if it stays in one piece through that, you can reckon on it holding together for a while longer.

Quick, snappy response

Performance from the Suzuki engine is quoted as being 45bhp at 5,500rpm and 54lb/ft of torque at 3,000rpm, and to be honest, we've no inclination to question those figures. What they both represent is a pleasing, buzzy response to throttle demand – no hesitation of any kind, just a snappy, quick effort from what is obviously a good little unit. It's the torque which took us completely by surprise – 54lb/ft is far from an earth-shattering torque figure (even the average Subaru boasts a cool 90), and it's highly unlikely that you'll ever be able to yank oak stumps out by the roots, but the point is that it never, ever felt like a mere 54. At 3,000rpm the 970cc lump is nothing short of just tootling along, but at those revs it will pull the hardware it's bolted to almost anywhere.

If ever you get the chance to have a bash with one of these toys, keep that magic 3,000rpm figure firmly in mind – stick religiously to it and you'll go far. The further, the better, etc, etc, etc...

If figures are to be trusted (when you work on the budget we do, they have to be...), from standstill to 60mph takes the Suzi almost 30 seconds – it felt quicker. Whether or not our's was a good 'un is difficult to tell, but my wristwatch-cum-teasmade/calculator clocked it at roughly 26, still far from maximum 'g' level, but respectable nonetheless.

Free of graunch, grind and groan

Top whack is reckoned to be 70mph or so, but again, the

SWEET LITTLE SUZI

drivers of the artics we terrorized on the nearby M1 would have something derogatory to say about that. The speedo clocked at least 83 on the flat, and it's also worthwhile to point out that progress at that rate of knots was generally without drama. Unlike our own beloved Niva (not that bloody thing again, we hear you cry...), cruising in the Suzi was a surprisingly comfortable affair free of almost any nasty mechanical graunch, grind or drone.

Granted, the aforementioned artics did tend to wreak vengeance by whistling past up the hills (things which prove a little too much for it to cope with at those speeds), leaving the SJ410 careering around in what felt like a cyclone of, if you'll excuse the expression, broken wind. Being high and a little lacking in the wheelbase department meant that even the slightest of sidewinds played havoc with straight-line progress, and we doubt that there's anything that can be done to solve the problem. You could slow down...

Fuel consumption, or rather the lack of it, is bloody wonderful. 30mpg and around 24 when thrashed. What else could you call it? Bloody wonderful.

Handling. Ah, yes...handling – an interesting point. I think the word which best describes it in this case is 'uncomfortable'. Sorry about that, folks, but the purpose of these tests is supposedly to tell the truth, and, as I failed in my last attempt to join the upper ranks of the Civil Service, that's exactly what I'll do.

Better dampers required?

Many of you may remember what the combination of multi-leaf springs and steeply-inclined dampers did to the rear of the old-style

970cc of brute force – without the ignorance!

Ford Escort – the combination gave rise to an extremely nervous, twitchy ride, and therefore some pretty undesirable leaps and bounds when the going got bumpy. Ford made a half-hearted attempt to solve the problem by mounting the dampers vertically and taming the harshness of the cart springs by using a version with only one leaf, but the Zebedee effect never really went away.

Unfortunately these nasty side-effects of such a mode of suspension are magnified by the featherweight nature of the Suzuki – there's very little weight available to tame the bouncy-bouncy tendencies of the springs, and the badly-mounted dampers can do virtually nothing to help.

A good set of up-and-downers from Mr Bilstein or

Mr Koni would be an advantage, but be very careful not to fit anything that's too stiff.

Roadholding is something completely different – *fantastic*. In reality I think a lot of this can be credited to the rubberware, 195x15 Dunlop SP44s, tyres so beloved of the rallying fraternity ten years or so ago. They are a close-blocked M&S tyre and use a relatively soft compound, both advantageous facts when there's a lot of roadwork involved, especially in the wet. Whether or not the soft nature of the rubber used means that you'll be contributing to safety in your area by coating the local highways in a thin layer of sticky black stuff remains to be seen, but we saw no significant loss of tread during our spell together, just

Interior of the current SJ410

the scrubbing-off of the square edges thanks to an overdose of enthusiastic cornering techniques.

It's a wind-up

These words of wisdom concerning handling and roadholding are, by the way, levelled at the Suzi SJ410 in two-wheel drive, the recommended mode of drive for road use. In case you didn't know, as a part-time 4x4 it would not be awfully clever to partake in the delights of the open road with the little Oriental bolide in four-drive. The lack of a central differential would lead to transmission wind-up and the eventual demise of some of the major drive line components. As it happens, the addition of pulling power from the front wheels does little to help handling but improves roadholding even more, but you still shouldn't do it. Got that?

I'm told that pulling one of these little machines up to a standstill before the arrival of the front disc brakes was an entertaining affair involving much adrenalin, foul language and searching for escape routes, but I'm happy to say that the aforementioned items now do a wonderful job. The only fault exhibited under heavy braking was a twitchiness in attitude, but that can be put down to the handling maladies covered somewhere above. Pedal effort required is minimal thanks to the servo.

I mentioned my dislike for the steering when I spoke of the SJ410 in the first issue, and, even after a further two weeks with the car, the remarks stand. I'd better be fair about it, however – there is absolutely nothing wrong with the steering in any way, in fact its nature is most likely ideal for the car, being extremely light. My own preference is for a heavier action which feeds more of a message about the terrain through to the driver's hands, but if you're unused to such muscle-building tillers the Suzuki steering gear should be just the thing for you – it certainly makes off-road driving a leisurely affair.

Four in comfort

The interior is fairly well-appointed, my only grumble being that the seat backs are a little on the short side. The SJ410 City and County is a four-seater – there is little

SWEET LITTLE SUZI

point in attempting to squeeze one more bod in the back, unless it's a child, as the two unfortunates on the outside of the rear seat will have to cope with perching on the unpadded wheel arches.

The rear seat folds away quite neatly.to provide a decent load area in the back, but in the upright position there is room to jam little more than a slim attache case down behind. The base of the seat is held to the floor by means of a couple of little wing-bolts – undoing these is simple enough, but be prepared for a frustrating job attempting to screw them back in. I eventually gave up and left the job to Suzuki themselves.

Off-road the Suzi really does come into its element – I can honestly say I've never driven anything that's felt quite so nimble, agile and therefore competent. My only complaint would be, again, the ride – forgiving it is not, and sutained periods off-road necessitated the unclipping of the inertia-reel seat belts if you wished to leave your kidneys intact.

I believe that a 1300cc version is due to arrive very soon, which should deal with any moans about a lack of go, and if the camera doesn't lie, foreign types have recently welcomed a long-wheelbase estate version. This latter variation on the SJ410 theme may provide the answer to my prayers, as an increase in length will not only mean my old English sheepdog will fit behind the rear seats, but also handling, ride and general stability may improve.

Would I buy one? Well, if I was in the fortunate position of being able to afford two cars, yes, I most certainly would. When the longer version arrives I may even be tempted to put the trusty Niva out to grass... **4x4**

Load space is limited, but there's no problem with legroom. Pics by courtesy of Colin Appleyard Cars of Huddersfield

SUZUKI LJ80

Secondhand

The first Suzi off-roader to arrive in the UK is now becoming prolific on the secondhand market. Just ask Ian Booth

Budget off-roading often starts with one of these capable 4x4 vehicles and consequently they're rarely advertised for long in local rags.

Introduced in 1979 the L580 was popular straight away as a leisure vehicle and for use as a second car for country dwellers, being especially popular with women as the steering is so light. The 76-inch wheelbase also makes it very easy to park and nip around in traffic.

A wheelbase that size coupled with leaf springing all round is the ideal recipe for a choppy ride. Although it certainly does deliver a rough ride, most owners are prepared to put up with it, as the little car has such outstanding off-road capabilities. Being so light and small, it can traverse bogs where Land Rovers and the like sink up to their door sills.

It has a similar 4x4 layout as a Landy with two-wheel drive for the road and 4x4 high and low range for off. The only real drawback is the engine size – a mere 797cc, but consequently very economical. It'll return at least 30mpg if you're canny, but would really only tow a light trailer – the sort of thing you might cart your camping gear around in. The other gripe for some folks might be the small rear area which was fitted with seats facing each other in some models, these being only really suitable for children.

Basically they're pretty much like small Daihatsus and all these complaints have been rectified on the newer SJ410 models which we will look at in the future. The standard front seats are plastic and seem to wear very well, indeed out of seven examples I looked at, only one had split seats in the front.

The dashboard and instrumentation are functional with speedo, and fuel gauge etc. There is a glove box and a radio is fitted to some models. The transmission tunnel separates the passenger from the driver, and it's surprising that really large frames can fit in comfortably – don't forget the Japs are traditionally small people! The soft top version comes complete with a roll bar and the windscreen folds flat for those rare summer days. The earlier models had a rather silly plastic door with a safety bar to stop you falling out, but these were draughty and flapped around and were soon dispensed with on the UK market in favour of the metal and glass door.

The actual soft tops are fairly well made and seem to last the test of time

Left: LJ80 soft-top. Spartan to say the least. Above: the Daktari paint job was never optional. Right: standard tyres were a bit naff in the wet

Above: Ron Hotson and open-top LJ80 during recent Hippenscombe night trial

and you either have a choice of a full hard top with rear door or one with side windows. Beware when looking at the latter, as this model was used by quite a few construction companies when building motorways, etc. Such a small vehicle could be well knackered by such use and you would need to look at the suspension very carefully.

Apart from a bit of plastic around the front lights the body is all metal and therefore prone to rust if abused. When I looked at older vehicles they really weren't too bad for rust but some had gone fairly badly along the seams and door bottoms.

The small four cylinder ohc engine is very capable and can stand a bit of revving, being very nippy when wound up, in fact it's a bit like driving a large Mini. Check for oil leaks, as gaskets appeared to be leaking on a few of the older models I looked at. Owners I spoke to were happy with overall engine performance and reported no major problems as long as regular servicing was carried out.

Have a good poke around on the chassis, especially at the rear around the lights, as this is the area which receives the clout when being abused off-road. The exhaust is mounted nice and high so really you only need to check it out on the blowing front.

Inside you should check the rear load are for any large dents in the floor to indicate whether any large loads had been carried, although the springs underneath should tell you this! One of the main rust areas on the LJ80 range is under the front mats. All the cars I saw had had a problem there at some time, although it can be rectified if sorted early enough. It's caused by the fact that people climb in with muddy boots and the water from them can't escape as there's no low sill as on the Landy. A couple of drain plugs and some sort of anti-rust treatment seems to do the job.

The tyres these cars were fitted with aren't a lot of bottle in the wet, so there's a strong possibility that older models will have different boots fitted. One chappy I saw had Range-Rover 205/16 tyres on and another had large American eight spoke wheels and equally large tyres fitted – check these out as some of them catch the body work when on full lock.

As said, most of these LJ80s are to be found in use as second cars, so you may be lucky and find one with a sensible mileage. Suzuki haven't flooded the UK with their wares due to import

SUZUKI

Above: you'll be lucky to find an LJ80 this tidy under the bonnet. Below: even the French still race 'em. This was taken on the Cimes

restrictions so you may need to look long and hard to find a nice one to suit your needs and pocket. The *Exchange and Mart* is quite a good place to start, as at least it gives you a price guide. Popular now with the Sloane Ranger set, prices have been pushed up a bit, especially as many have been graced with roll bars, etc.

As usual there is no real price guide, but earlier vehicles in running order should fetch around £1,000 to £1,500. I saw a W-reg 1981 full hard top vehicle in a garage recently and they were asking £3,000 for it and got it. Parts are fairly easy to come by through the ample dealer network and are fairly well priced.

So anyone looking for a small 4x4 vehicle with good economy need look no further than the little Suzi. If you don't believe how good they are, why not go along to an AWDC trial and see for yourself! It won't be an easy task finding yourself a secondhand Suzuki, as once someone's got one they grow attached to it. What better recommendation?
Ian Booth

`4x4`

81

UZUKI SJ410Q

Popular in town certainly, how does the little Suzuki cope when the going gets rougher? Push the latest 'Fully Accessorised' SJ410Q hard and you quickly find out.

It's when you come down with a crashing thump that bounces your feet off the pedals that you realise just how well the Suzuki SJ410 works as an off-roader. A crash-landing that should have been spine-jarring is reasonably soaked up by the simple, old-fashioned but compliantly effective suspension – with some help, of course, from the padded seats to this soft-top version, the SJ410Q. The Suzuki may be small, but it has the strength to match its good-looking, chunky styling ruggedly accentuated by the bull bar and in our test car's case the enormous steel cage that serves as a roof rack.

The little Suzuki goes well, too, considering the small size of the engine which is the same 970cc four cylinder producing 45bhp at a buzzy 5500rpm. That's enough to pull it up to around 70mph on the highway – 80mph if you can tuck into the fast lane quick enough to catch a tow behind a National bus – but something closer to 60mph is a little more prudent because the car feels very wandery and wobbly at that sort of speed.

People who buy an SJ 410 to do

SUZUKI SJ410Q

nothing more than look chic and tootle around town may critcise the imprecise handling at speed, but they should remember that the car is a real and remarkably competent cross-country vehicle, and the suspension and steering have been set up to cope with the knocks of rough and tumble driving — not high street posing. Hence the Suzuki has heavy-duty springing with relatively long vertical wheel movement, designed to allow the car to clamber over boulders and tree-stumps, but which unfortunately also means pronounced body roll when attempting to corner at speed on the road. The steering, too, is bushed and damped to preserve the driver's wrists from kick-back shocks as the car runs over sharp ruts and humps. Neither of these features is particularly good for high-speed highway stability or accuracy of line when careering along winding country roads.

The extras on the 'fully accessorised' model we drove included a sports-style, smaller-diameter steering wheel. Off-roaders usually get big-diameter, spindly steering wheels for two reasons — firstly because many basic all-terrain vehicles lack power steering and you need the leverage to get those heavy wheels into line, and also to reduce the effect of the kick-back that still gets through. In the Suzuki's case the switch to the smaller wheel did not present a problem in either case. The car seemed light enough to control during most manoeuvres and even the tough off-road thrashing we gave it failed to jerk the wheel from our grasp. Parking called for some strong-arm work, but not so much as to detract from the sportier look of the passenger compartment.

The Q is a two-seater soft top version of the SJ410, offered with a 'blind' tilt

The smart exterior appearance of the little Suzuki is not a disguise. Off-road ability is reasonable considering the vehicles specification, and price. Cross-country limitations only become noticeable on sharp decents with the Suzuki's lack of low down engine torque — understandable given the engine size.

traversed, it's the ability of an engine to punch out big, easy torque at low-down crankshaft speed that really matters.

The diminutive Suzuki unit manages 54lb/ft, but over a rather narrow band and peaking quite high up the rev range at 3000rpm. The result is that the SJ 410 tends to get beaten quite easily in mud if, for instance, it is expected to pull away up an incline, or to haul a heavy trailer from standstill, since getting enough oomph out of the engine to get the car going has it revving so fast that it becomes impossible to avoid wheelspin.

There is, of course, a way of overcoming both of these shortcomings — momentum. In other words, don't back off before going into that muddy patch, keep your foot down and let brute force take over where traction may fail.

The SJ410 might be a little too easy to get stuck in the mud, but in the dry it is a great fun off-roader. The transfer gearbox reduces the ratios of the four-speed transmission by 1.75 times giving the Suzuki the crawling power to scrabble up and down ridiculously steep slopes with ease. Four speeds in the main transmission is enough, both for on-road and off-road purposes. The car's highway top speed coincides pretty well with the engine's peak power speed of 5500rpm in fourth, and there's not really enough there to pull a usefully long overdrive gear; in the rough the peakiness of the engine means you'll be using the lower ratios to carry out most manoeuvres anyway.

The Suzuki is not meant to challenge the Land Rover as a tough all-terrain workhorse — it has neither the power nor the payload, nor for that matter, much space behind the seats to carry more than a few bags of potatoes or a couple of unhappy sheep. But it has good ground clearance, on knobbly tyres it will tackle

od at a very reasonable £4899 basic ice. The standard equipment list looks etty good too, with inertia reel front ats belts, two-speed plus intermittent indscreen wipers and lockable glove ox. It doesn't get a radio which is a pity; ough you'd never be able to listen to it hile chasing down the highway — ere's far too much engine and road ise, not to mention the deafening pping of the canvas tilt.

The most obvious extra on our test car as that roof rack. It seemed like a lot of pework just for somewhere to hang a uple of surfboards, but then how else ould you attach a roof rack to an open-pped car? It proved to be a pleasing and eful extra.

Most important, however, the roof rack es not interfere with the removal or placement of the tilt. That's an easy ough process, though it's not one of ose half-minute folding jobs. Studs ave to be released all the way round, lcro tabs released inside where the cloth tied to the roll-over hoop and stays and en the whole panel can be slid off, lded up and stowed away. We preferred iving the car in its open form, which is st as well because the tilt seems a little the flimsy side and we don't think it ould last for more than one busy ason.

One thing those town-only users ouldn't complain about is the quality of de in the sense that the suspension, though consisting of primitive leaf-rings all round, allied with the big-ameter wheels, will iron out most in the ay of a pothole or irregularity (or even e occasional kerb) with ease. The only oblem is likely to be the vehicle's ndency to pitch when running over a umpy surface because of its short heelbase. Again, though, this is a oblem which increases in severity with eed and requires little more than cking off the throttle to cure.

In off-road terms this translates into an ility to tackle tortuously rough and ugh going with surprising ease. Your assenger — the Q is marketed as a two-ater but a dinky little bench rear seat is ailable at £150.00 — now has a elcome grab-handle built into the car-yle dashboard, which is just as well cause the Suzuki pitches and bounces e a bucking bronco if it's given its head the rough. There's nothing too harsh or

crashy about its behaviour. though, because the suspension is designed to cope — and it does its job well.

There are limitations in the car's cross-country capability, however, one of these being that in spite of the evident compliance of the suspension there is still not enough overall axle twist. The other important limitation is the lack of low-down engine torque, an understandable shortcoming in such a small-capacity unit. Certainly, the Suzuki is small and light and has quite enough power to make it move as fast as any average owner would expect it to, but power often is not the most important factor in good off-roading. When the going gets slippery, such as when a particularly muddy patch or a stretch of wet grass has to be

Only 970cc, the diminutive engine manages 45bhp at a buzzy 5500rpm.

SUZUKI SJ410Q

your coarsely muddy farm field with adequate competence and it has the usual axle-deep wading ability in standard form. Understandably it sells well in those areas where the ability to move a few people about is more important than ultimate payload or a power takeoff facility; companies involved in forestry or mineral exploration find the car gives a useful blend of practicality and economy. In basic form, it also has a strong incentive in low price. Add all the extras that we had on our test vehicle, and the price certainly rises, but it still appeals.

Most private buyers have far less strenuous duties in mind, probably seeing the little off-roader as a characteristic alternative to a roadster-type sports car. It looks good in its mini-macho way, the roof rack will take any surfboard or windsurfer you'd care to throw at it and the four-wheel drive system is quite good enough to cope when actually taken to where it belongs — off-road.

Optional Extras

"Fully Accessorised" is something of a tongue-twister, but Suzuki GB (Cars) has made a great commercial success from offering a wide range of extras to allow owners to personalise their little Suzukis. Here we include a short list of some of the items available. (All prices include VAT).

Ammeter	£22.00
Voltmeter	£30.00
Inclinometer	£44.00
Locking handbrake	£19.00
Standard carpet set	£42.00
Rear bench seat (SJ410Q only)	£150.00
Sports steering wheel	£30.00
Roll bar guard	£12.00
Sill guards	£11.00
Hardtop	£660.00
Free wheeling hub set	£70.00
Bull bar	£110.00
Headlight guards	£11.00
Tow bar	£60.00
Surfing side stripe	£110.00
Surf bar set	£150.00
Roofrack for surf bar set	£55.00
Side sill bars	£35.00
Tonneau cover	£168.00

Much of the success of the Suzuki SJ range has been due to the accessory package that is offered. The model we tested had a full range, the major item of which was a very sturdy roof rack. This certainly allowed for extra carrying capacity, while still being open-topped. Inside, and the most noticeable additional item is the sports steering wheel.

Technical Specification

Engine

Type	Four cylinder, water cooled Single OHC
Capacity	970 cc
Compression ratio	
Maximum power	45 bhp (33.5 Kw) at 5500 rpm
Maximum torque	54 lb ft (73.2 Nm) at 3000 rpm

Transmission

Type	Four speed all synchromesh via two speed constant mesh transfer box
Tyre size	195 SR 15
Steering	Recirculating ball and nut
Turning radius	4.9 m (16ft 1in)
Brakes	Front: Disc Rear: Self adjusting drums

Suspension

Front and rear	Live axles supported by semi-elliptic leaf springs and telescopic dampers

Capacities

Fuel	8.8 gallons (40 litres)
Towing	2204.6 lbs (1000 Kg)
Kerb weight	1874 lbs (850 Kg)
Gross vehicle wgt	2734 lbs (1240 Kg)
Max. trailer wgt	1653 lbs (750 Kg)

Dimensions

Lenght	135.0 in. (3430 mm)
Width	57.5 in. (1460 mm)
Height	66.1 in. (1680 mm)
Wheelbase	79.9 in. (2030 mm)
Ground clearance	9.1 in. (230 mm)

Load deck

Length	34.3 in. (870 mm)
Width	50.1 in. (1270 mm)
Height (tilt raised)	40.2 in. (1020 mm)

Official fuel consumption figures

Simulated urban driving	27.2 mpg
Constant 56 mph	33.2 mpg

Warranty

All vehicles have six year anti-corrosion treatment

Prices

Suzuki SJ410Q	£4899.00
SJ410 (Passenger car)	£4999.00
SJ413VX	£5885.00

The SJ410QB (Blind soft top) and the SJ410B (Blind van) are both commercial vehicles and exempt from Car Tax. Their prices are £4599.00 and £4699.00 respectively.

Suzuki Samurai

Look what followed you home.

• Are you a person who gets adopted by puppies? If you are, watch out for Suzuki. The Suzuki Motor Company, Ltd., a machinery manufacturer for 76 years (starting with textile looms), is a big name in motorcycles today, but this company also makes ATVs, motorized wheelchairs, outboard and multipurpose motors, mobile power generators, prefab housing, small trucks, four-wheel-drive vehicles—and automobiles.

Even though Suzuki is known here for its bikes, 61 percent of its 1983 fiscal-year income came from cars. Logically enough, the firm's next step will be the introduction of its name on four-wheeled machinery for the American market. The timetable for building a marketing, distribution, and dealership structure from scratch covers the next three years. At first, only one product will be sold in just a few areas; California, Florida, and Georgia are the initial targets. As for the product, GM is already selling the three-cylinder Suzuki mini in the U.S. as the Chevrolet Sprint, and that car (in an altered form) could have been available. But Suzuki chose another product to debut its nameplate: the stubby little SJ413, a sort of Jeeplet.

Its official name is Samurai. A trifle cute, perhaps, but this is precisely Suzuki's intention. The plan is to make this little puppy of a four-by-four so roly-poly cute—and cheap—you won't be able to resist bringing it home.

How cheap? Figure about $7500, fully equipped.

We're talking four-wheel drive, three transfer-case modes (2H, 4H, and 4L), beam axles and leaf springs at both ends, fifteen-inch wheels, a nine-inch ground clearance, a 32.2-foot turning circle, approach and departure angles of 48 and 39 degrees, respectively, and the ability to climb a 43-degree slope. Along with cute and cheap comes compactness: an 80-inch wheelbase, a 135-inch overall length, a 57.5-inch width, and a curb weight of 2150 pounds. The engine is proportionally small as well. It's a forward-mounted, 1325cc in-line four with an aluminum block, a single overhead cam, and a carburetor. Suzuki says the powerplant will deliver 63 hp through a five-speed transmission, though this figure is subject to adjustment for final U.S. specifications.

This is *not* a new puppy. The Suzuki SJ413 Samurai has actually been on sale in Canada and other places for over a year. In fact, as the SJ410 (970cc, 45-hp four-in-line with a four-speed transmission), it has been sold in over *one hundred* nations since its introduction in 1971. Suzuki even knows that some 3000 of the one-liters have followed various unofficial paths into service in the U.S. You see them here and there at beach and mountain resorts, often in rental fleets.

What we're getting in the U.S. market, starting November 1, is only a portion of the complete SJ range: just the comparatively new engine; just the short-wheelbase, four-seater chassis; and just two body styles. U.S. customers will be able to choose between an all-steel closed body and a convertible with a canvas top and a steel roll cage; we won't get the raised-roof, pickup-bed, and long-wheelbase six-seater models that are sold in other markets. There will be two grade levels, the higher of which includes sport seats, a tach, carpeting, and A/C.

C/D has had some casual experience with the small-engined SJ410 and found it an agreeable and capable little tool, providing the job at hand does not overtax its small engine or cargo rating. There are no excesses, either of performance or cargo volume. A brief run in an SJ413 development hack indicated that, even with 1325 screaming cc, it still won't light tires or eyes. There is a bright side, though: fuel mileage should be in the high twenties.

And that is why the Samurai is being positioned more as an economy car than a traditional off-road vehicle, less a serious dirt scratcher than a versatile auxiliary runabout for shoppers and students with a nose for fun.

The Samurai will probably suit the very people who find it appealing. It's easy to drive, and its street handling, though not advanced, is okay. The ride is stiff, and the steering (no power assist is available) may be a bit heavy for some. The interior room and the amenities are fine, given that this is a short-haul two-plus-two. A transcontinental trip would be a suitable feat for a young person; if that sounds attractive, rest assured that the Samurai could take some very interesting routes.

Sure, you can get more four-by-four, but this is a lot for the price. Watch out for doggie hairs on your doormat.—*Pete Lyons*

Vehicle type: front-engine, rear/4-wheel-drive, 4-passenger, 3-door wagon

Base price: $6200

Engine type: 4-in-line, aluminum block and head, 1x2-bbl carburetor

Displacement	81 cu in, 1325cc
Power (*C/D* estimate)	60 bhp @ 5000 rpm
Transmission	5-speed
Wheelbase	79.9 in
Length	135.0 in
Curb weight	2150 lb
EPA fuel economy, city driving	28 mpg

Suzuki Samurai JX

Our newest Japanese nameplate stakes its claim on the cheap-Jeep niche.

• There seems to be no end to the number of Far Eastern car manufacturers eager to hawk their wares in America. Mitsubishi and Isuzu joined the existing five Oriental exporters in the first half of this decade when they set up their own distribution networks here, and at least two more will attack our market before the decade is out. The first of these is Suzuki, the well-known motorcycle manufacturer.

Suzuki, which has been building cars since 1961, is a relatively small carmaker both in volume and in car size. Its production last year totaled only 647,000 units, and the biggest car it builds is powered by a 1.3-liter engine. The company's best-known car is the Cultus, which has been marketed here for the past two years as the Chevrolet Sprint. For its first venture into the American market under its own nameplate, Suzuki wanted a unique product, one that wouldn't tangle head-on with any established competitors. Fortunately, the perfect machine for the job was already in the company's lineup: a mini-Jeep called the Samurai.

The Samurai isn't a total stranger to America, for it's been sold in Canada, Hawaii, and Puerto Rico for several years. In fact, it has been sold in more than 100 countries since it was introduced fifteen years ago. If our experience with our test Samurai is any guide, America is ready and eager to be added to the list. Every time we stopped, people wanted to know what it was, how much it cost, and where they could get one.

What the Samurai is, in essence, is a pint-sized four-wheel-drive truck. Compared with the classic Jeep CJ-7, itself no giant, Suzuki's mini-Jeep is about twenty inches shorter overall, five inches narrower, five inches shorter in height, and, at 2100 pounds, about 900 pounds lighter. But even though it's been scaled down appreciably, the Samurai embodies most of the design features of the traditional Jeep. In normal driving, the rear wheels do the work. When the going gets rough, the part-time four-wheel drive can be engaged through a dual-range transfer case controlled by a floor-mounted lever. If the manually locking front hubs have been engaged, the high range of four-wheel drive can be selected on the fly, provided the Samurai is traveling in a straight line. To engage low range, it's necessary to come to a complete stop. Although not the most sophisticated four-wheel-drive system

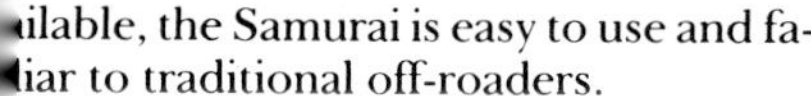

[av]ailable, the Samurai is easy to use and fa[mil]iar to traditional off-roaders.

[U]nderneath its skin, the Samurai is basi[cal]ly a compact copy of the Jeep. The front [and] rear suspensions each consist of a rig[id] [a]xle located by leaf springs. An anti-roll [bar] is used only in front. An unassisted re[cir]culating-ball steering gear directs the [fro]nt wheels. The major components are [bol]ted to a full-length ladder frame, which [als]o supports the steel body with rubber [mo]unts. All in all, the Samurai chassis [cou]ldn't be more conventional.

[U]nder the hood, however, the Samurai [de]parts from Jeep practice. Instead of a [lar]ge-displacement, slow-turning, cast-[iro]n pushrod engine, the Suzuki is [po]wered by an all-aluminum, 1.3-liter [fou]r-cylinder version of the Chevrolet [Spr]int's 1.0-liter triple, complete with a [bel]t-driven overhead camshaft. This mod-[est] engine develops 61 hp at 6000 rpm [and] 71 pounds-feet of torque at 3500 rpm, [and] it revs to a lofty 6500-rpm redline. The [out]put from this high-revving humming-[bir]d is converted to low-speed grunt by [wel]l-chosen gearing.

[W]e took the Samurai off-road and were [imp]ressed by its pulling power. On a dirt [roa]d, climbing a hill that got steeper as we [wen]t, the Samurai ran out of traction long [bef]ore it would have run out of power—

and it didn't lose its grip until we were so far up the grade that backing down was our only option. Going downhill, the low range provided a reassuring brake on the Samurai's speed. We wouldn't want to pull a heavy load up a loose-surfaced mountain with the little Suzuki, but it certainly has no problem hauling its own weight.

The Samurai also maneuvers well in the dirt. With its compact dimensions and short wheelbase, it can turn on a dime and slip through passes that would be too tight for larger vehicles. The short wheelbase also helps keep the chassis components from dragging over rough terrain.

Although its off-road capabilities prove that the Samurai is a real truck, not just a compact car in Jeep clothing, we suspect that most Samurais will turn most of their miles on paved roads. Unfortunately, the Samurai is no match for a normal car in civilized environments. On the other hand, it's not bad for a basic four-wheel-driver.

Performance is the Suzuki's weakest area, for there is no way that its small engine can cope with its parachutelike aero-

dynamic drag. Acceleration from rest is reasonable, but it tapers off quickly as speed rises. Reaching 60 mph requires 18.7 seconds, and the Samurai tops out at a mere 77 mph in fourth gear. Fifth gear, as

behind this main cage. We had no occasio[n] to test the structural integrity of the parts, but they certainly look reassuring.

They are also well padded, lest the Samurai's occupants bang themselves sens[e]less during rough going. Indeed, the Samurai's interior, at least in the deluxe [JX] model we tested, is quite nicely finishe[d] considering the vehicle's rustic natur[e]. The dashboard is a modern plastic mol[d]ing complete with full instrumentation a[nd] a well-designed heating system. The fro[nt] seats are comfortable enough for drive[s] several hours. The folding rear seat [is] more basic, but it does offer adequa[te] room for two. Our Samurai also had a[ir] conditioning, though it was taxed to [its] limits on a 95-degree sunny day.

Some of the blame for the margin[al] cooling ability of the A/C must go to t[he] Samurai's convertible top. A very crude [af]fair consisting of sewn white vinyl a[nd] transparent plastic panels, it is hardly a[ir]tight. It also admits a lot of noise, enou[gh] that the sound of surrounding vehicles c[an] easily drown out the Samurai's o[wn] rumblings.

The top at least provides excellent w[et] weather protection. We drove the Samu[rai] through a carwash, and afterward could[n't] find a single drop of water inside. T[he] credit goes to the top's elaborate attac[h]ment system. Its forward edge slides int[o a] groove on the top of the windshield fram[e]

indicated by the Samurai's 42.2-second top-gear time from 50 to 70 mph, is useful for little more than maintaining modest speeds on level roads. Hills require the use of lower ratios.

Fortunately, shifting the Samurai is a pleasure. The gearbox responds precisely to a light touch, and the engine gives its all freely, with minimal vibration and an eager surge to its redline. Naturally, we used the Samurai's powertrain to the max in our test driving, but we still managed a commendable 25 mpg. For use in town, we found the Samurai's performance quite acceptable, though it wouldn't be our first choice for the next One Lap of America marathon.

The Samurai's ride motions are another reason to avoid long highway trips. The combination of the short wheelbase and the firm leaf springs does little to smooth out freeway imperfections. Harsh pounding is not a problem, thanks to the large, low-pressure tires, but the Samurai's constant pitching and pogoing, although mi-

nor, quickly become tiresome. On secondary roads, the Samurai is more comfortable. There's enough suspension travel to deal with any rut or pothole, and the firm ride seems less intrusive when the bumps become less frequent.

The Samurai is also reasonably happy on winding roads. It has nicely responsive steering and can corner to the tune of 0.71 g, thanks to its all-weather tires and pleasantly neutral handling balance. It didn't even do a barrel roll on the skidpad, though the inside rear tire was barely in contact with the pavement during right-turning laps.

Mindful of the rollover problems associated with other vehicles of this type, the Suzuki engineers built extensive passenger protection into the convertible version of the Samurai. (A hardtop model is also available, for an extra $150.) Just behind the front seats is a stamped-steel structure that is connected to the top of the windshield frame by four longitudinal members. In addition, a tubular roll bar sits just

Vehicle type: front-engine, rear/4-wheel-drive, 4-passenger, 3-door convertible

Price as tested: $7650

Options on test car: base Suzuki Samurai JX convertible, $6950; air conditioning, $700

Sound system: Clarion AM/FM-stereo radio/cassette, 4 speakers

ENGINE

Type	turbocharged 4-in-line, aluminum block and head
Bore x stroke	2.91 x 3.03 in, 74.0 x 77.0mm
Displacement	81 cu in, 1325cc
Compression ratio	8.9:1
Carburetion	1x2-bbl
Emissions controls	3-way catalytic converter, feedback fuel-air-ratio control, EGR
Valve gear	belt-driven single overhead cam
Power (SAE net)	61 bhp @ 6000 rpm
Torque (SAE net)	71 lb-ft @ 3500 rpm
Redline	6500 rpm

DRIVETRAIN

Transmission	5-speed
Transfer-case ratio	1.61:1
Final-drive ratio	5.25:1

Gear	Ratio	Mph/1000 rpm	Max. test speed
IL	5.89	2.4	16 mph (6500 rpm)
IIL	3.13	4.6	30 mph (6500 rpm)
IIIL	2.29	6.2	40 mph (6500 rpm)
IVL	1.61	8.9	58 mph (6500 rpm)
VL	1.28	11.2	73 mph (6500 rpm)
IH	3.65	3.9	25 mph (6500 rpm)
IIH	1.95	7.3	47 mph (6500 rpm)
IIIH	1.42	10.1	66 mph (6500 rpm)
IVH	1.00	14.3	77 mph (5400 rpm)
VH	0.80	17.9	75 mph (4200 rpm)

DIMENSIONS AND CAPACITIES

Wheelbase	79.9 in
Track, F/R	51.2/51.6 in
Length	135.0 in
Width	60.2 in
Height	65.6 in
Ground clearance	8.1 in
Curb weight	2100 lb
Weight distribution, F/R	52.4/47.6%
Fuel capacity	10.6 gal
Oil capacity	3.7 qt
Water capacity	5.3 qt

CHASSIS/BODY

Type	full-length frame with rubber-isolated body
Body material	welded steel stampings

INTERIOR

SAE volume, front seat	44 cu ft
rear seat	34 cu ft
trunk space	3 cu ft
Front seats	bucket
Seat adjustments	fore and aft, seatback angle
General comfort	poor fair **good** excellent
Fore-and-aft support	poor fair **good** excellent
Lateral support	poor **fair** good excellent

SUSPENSION

F:	rigid axle, leaf springs, anti-roll bar
R:	rigid axle, leaf springs

STEERING

Type	recirculating ball
Turns lock-to-lock	4.0
Turning circle curb-to-curb	33.4 ft

BRAKES

F:	11.0 x 0.4-in disc
R:	8.7 x 1.5-in cast-iron drum
Power assist	vacuum

WHEELS AND TIRES

Wheel size	5.5 x 15 in
Wheel type	stamped steel
Tires	Bridgestone SF-405 Steel M+S, P205/70R-15
Test inflation pressures, F/R	20/20 psi

CAR AND DRIVER TEST RESULTS

ACCELERATION

	Seconds
Zero to 30 mph	4.5
40 mph	7.6
50 mph	12.0
60 mph	18.7
70 mph	33.5
Top-gear passing time, 30–50 mph	17.1
50–70 mph	42.2
Standing ¼-mile	20.5 sec @ 64 mph
Top speed	77 mph

HANDLING

Roadholding, 300-ft-dia skidpad	0.71 g
Understeer	**minimal** moderate excessive

BRAKING

70–0 mph @ impending lockup	219 ft
Modulation	poor **fair** good excellent

Fade	none **moderate** heavy
Front-rear balance	**poor** fair good

COAST-DOWN MEASUREMENTS

Road horsepower @ 30 mph	6 hp
50 mph	17 hp
70 mph	44 hp

FUEL ECONOMY

EPA city driving	**28 mpg**
EPA highway driving	**29 mpg**
C/D observed fuel economy	**25 mpg**

INTERIOR SOUND LEVEL

Idle	48 dBA
Full-throttle acceleration	85 dBA
70-mph cruising	83 dBA
70-mph coasting	82 dBA

and flaps on each side fit into vertical grooves in the main rollover structure. The bottom edges snap onto the body-work with plenty of overlap, the upper rear is supported by a folding frame, and other loose edges are attached by Velcro straps to various other tubes and frames. It takes nearly five minutes for one person to erect this roof, but it's worth the trouble.

The Samurai may be primitive in certain respects, and it's much less versatile than its competition, such as the Isuzu Trooper II, the Mitsubishi Montero, the Chevy S-10 Blazer, and the Ford Bronco II. The little Suzuki, however, has two aces in the hole: it's small enough to be cute, and it's cheap. The base Samurai convertible lists for $6550. A JX model like our test vehicle, with air conditioning and a stereo system, costs only $7650. That's at least $3000 less expensive than any of the competitors named above, and about $2000 less than a comparably equipped CJ-7. And none of the others except the CJ is available as a convertible. What we have here is your basic cheap Jeep.

In fact, if you want a rugged four-wheel-driver for the minimum amount of money, the Samurai is the only game in town. If you live in the right town, that is: the Samurai will be sold initially only in California, Florida, and Georgia. As the supply increases over the next couple of years, Suzuki plans to expand the dealer network to cover the rest of the country.

Our advice to Suzuki is to crank up the assembly plants and send Samurais by the boatload. A hungry market awaits.

—Csaba Csere

DIRTY WEEKEND

Below zero temperatures did not deter 50 enthusiastic Suzuki owners from gathering in a disused Essex quarry to sample the sport of off-roading. Michael Harvey donned his wellies to grab a piece of the action

All-Wheel-Drive Club members had advised owners to remove rear foglamps, for obvious reasons

The odd thing about Suzuki GB's first 'Action Weekend' for LJ and SJ410 owners was that the conversation had precious little to do with the off-road event itself. What seemed to be occupying the minds of drivers and marshals alike were two things; firstly the terrible cold, and secondly the maniac in the cut-down, coil-sprung, turbocharged LJ.

The funny thing about cold is that it affects everyone, no matter what sex, class, politics, or religion; when it is cold, it is unpleasant. Shoulders are hunched, feet are shuffled, and arms flapped. It really does make for quite a funny sight. That certain expression of half-concealed pain that lets everyone know you are suffering. You can't hide it, you want to be inside in the warm, and no matter what anybody does, nothing is going to make you feel better.

The Suzuki event took place on just such a day, and given that the chosen location for the event was Essex, the other-side-of-the-Dartford-tunnel Essex, way down the world's most horrible road, the A13, Suzuki must have been well pleased that as many as 50 LJs and SJs turned up.

The idea came from the success of Suzuki's Off-Road '85 driving event for the Press last year. That was such a success that it was felt the owners of these diminutive 'jeeps' should get a chance at proving their mettle under the safety of the watchful eyes of the All-Wheel Drive club of Great Britain, who spend every weekend trying to get their cars stuck as much as they possibly can, so they can then get them out again.

The AWDC had spent a whole day establishing a testing trial around the muddy environs of Arena Essex, an old open-cast mine now used mostly for motorcycle trials. The AWDC is expert in what an off-roader can and cannot do, and had established the course on the grounds that the novices would need to build up their confidence gradually. A four-mile loop, it became progressively more testing.

However, as is the way with the best-laid plans, it all went very wrong overnight — wrong to the tune of three inches of snow. Tests by the marshals to establish if the course could be used proved the point: the Club's Land Rover got stuck. Now, with all due respect to Suzuki, if the Land Rover got stuck . . .

After 1½ hours' wait, however, the green lights shone and we were off. The first car on the run proved the point of Suzuki's warning to remove number plates, towbars, and foglights. Scrambling away over the start, the little SJ sat on its rump and removed the foglamp. The first of many. A Suzuki official remarked, tongue in cheek: "Ah yes, the entire point of this weekend is to encourage sales of Suzuki replacement body panels."

A pragmatic insurance salesman had set himself up in the cold, offering extra off-road cover for a mere £5 for the day, which seemed very reasonable, except that among the items not covered was the foglamp.

PHIL RUDGE

Four-mile *course became progressively more testing for the novice off-roaders. Heavy overnight snow didn't help matters*

Following the trail of broken foglamps, we made our way around the course, and had our first experience of the cut-down, coil-sprung, turbocharged LJ. There I was, waiting my turn to slip down what seemed an almost vertical slope, listening carefully to the man from the AWDC, when half-way through his careful explanation ("Don't touch the brakes, the clutch or the . . .") he began to shout. I looked up and saw the LJ blasting around the queue and leaping over the hill like someone auditioning for *The Dukes of Hazard.*

"I don't know who on earth he is. Looks like an accident waiting to happen," said one of the marshals who, like everyone else, remained in the dark as to the driver's identity.

As he blasted off into the distance, jumping over the bumps the rest of us seemed to be absorbing through our stomachs, I slid my way down the slope without traumas, and bounced my way over to the hill. The hill didn't give anybody any trouble, except a couple of chaps that had turned out in full-face helmets and intercoms, clearly suffering from an overdose of Paris-Dakar fever, who got half-way up the slope and then promptly seemed to find reverse and slide right back down again.

One of my highlights of '86 so far was watchng the couple in the SJ at the bottom of the slope, right in the target line for the errant backwards LJ. Scrabbling to loosen their seatbelts, they dived out of the doors like The Professionals, climbed out of the mud and the snow in time to see that the pair of clowns in the helmets had stopped inches in front of their pride and joy. None too pleased, they climbed back in and pointed the little Suzuki towards Chelsea. The clowns then stuck the car back into first and, showing a complete inability to grasp the fundamentals of off-road work, they gave the car about a million revs and spent 10 minutes getting up the same hill that took the rest of us about 60 seconds flat. Still, they looked the part!

The next obstacle was very frightening indeed, and demonstrated the level of trust the drivers were prepared to put in the AWDC marshals. They were offered the chance of taking the easy route, but when convinced that their SJs and LJs could do it they all gave it a go, and none had mishaps. Which was very commendable indeed, when you consider that they were being faced with a very bumpy 40-foot drop with trees on either side and a sharp right turn at the bottom, and being warned that from the moment they left the level ground they had to trust the Suzuki to take them down.

That stage cleared it was uncomfortable but comparatively straightforward to get back to the start and go around again, the end of the course a spectacular affair with the little Suzukis fair flying through the air to arrive by a sign that said 'Slow . . . 5mph'. Not easy when your car is airborne . . .

Many of the owners then took the chance to go around again, as the four-mile loop was supposed to

Special stages *showed the superb capabilities of the Suzukis*

prepare people for the competitive event, which comprised six very twitchy stages marked out by posts. Posts you were supposed to avoid hitting, I was told after I had taken out a straight half dozen on the trot.

These stages really showed why the little Suzukis have to be taken seriously off-road. With a power-to-weight ratio second only to the Land Rover, and axle articulation on a par with the best, most of the novice drivers negotiated the posts superbly, and there was always a marshal on hand to give advice should it be needed. I tried to cover up and pretend I was just after tips for this report, but I don't think I convinced them too well. You see, I was always asking for advice when the car just happened to be stuck firm.

All the competitors were given score cards by the AWDC, which they proudly displayed on their windscreens. The enthusiastic LJ driver, although he was spotted on every section by at least one marshal, never had his card marked, and seemed to be going around again and again. He must have stopped at least once to make a call of nature, but no-one spotted him, and his mystery-man image stayed intact.

By five everybody was reaching down to the ratio box and putting their cars back into two-wheel drive, re-affixing their numberplates, and wondering what had happened to their foglamps. It had got very cold by this stage, and the AWDC was packing up to do the whole thing again the next day. ■

What is it that makes aficionados scoff, purists refuse to look, and buyers line up to buy? Samurai! In fact, Suzuki has been so overwhelmed with the success of its first-ever entry into the U.S. auto market, it has revamped its entire marketing scheme.

Initially, Suzuki had planned to introduce the Samurai in California in November 1985, in Florida and Georgia in December, and then expand the dealer network in appropriate areas over the next three years. Well, sales have been so brisk that dealerships are being set up in eight additional western states already.

The Samurai concept is by no means new. A smaller version has been selling in Third World countries for the last 15 years. In fact, the little Suzuki is a common sight in places like Sri Lanka and Puerto Rico, playing the role of motorized pack mule.

Suzuki has made good use of this experience and done its marketing research well, but even Suzuki is a bit surprised at the little generic 4-wheeler's immediate acceptance. Suzuki has planned for each new dealership to have a free-standing showroom and complete service facility. In doing its homework, Suzuki learned of the American thirst for individuality and/or aftermarket products. Not only will the dealers have parts departments, they will also have "personalization centers," with the available accessories on display so the buyer can mix and match as desired.

Even before the Samurai was introduced, a multi-page color accessory catalog was printed with everything from wheels to windows for the little truckster—these guys know what they're doing.

Admittedly, the big plus for the Samurai is its $6500 base price. That not only makes it one of the lowest-priced vehicles in the States, it's about half the cost of many 4-wheel drives on the market. Another plus is the fact that it's not locked into any one vehicle category. The Samurai could be considered a sport/utility, light pickup, or subcompact, and could be appealing as a second car or to a first-time buyer. And, this being the '80s, with so many image-conscious people, you can't deny that the 4-wheel-drive Samurai must be considered macho—if only quasi-macho. Definitely a market to consider.

For the image-conscious, the Suzuki's versatility is a boon. The Samurai has a myriad of uses, is economical, tough, and, most important, fun.

With all the fervor about the Samurai, it must have something going for it. And it does. Though lightweight, it seems very strong and almost impervious to the beating it takes off road. Granted, many U.S. buyers will never get off the black part, but if it holds up off the pavement, think how long it will last on the highway.

Speaking of off road, the main limiting factor is the tires: P205/70R15s are standard. They are fine on the highway and will go off road. But for serious off-roaders, there is plenty of room in the wheelwell for big, gnarly

Suzuki Samurai

The quasi-macho generic 4-wheeler

by Michael Brockman

PHOTOGRAPHY BY JIM BROWN

grippers to take them wherever they want to go.

Another limiting factor may be a blessing in disguise. The 1324cc overhead cam all-aluminum engine is a bit anemic, but in reality it allows you to use the ample suspension and 8½-in. ground clearance to the fullest extent without terrifying yourself. The high/low-range 4-wheel drive gives more than enough variance to pull through or climb just about anything you might need to or be brave enough to attempt. (Again, tires are a limiting factor.)

On the road, the demure motor has to work pretty hard to get up to cruising speed, but once there seems pretty happy until it's time to pass. Also on the highway, the short wheelbase tends to make for a choppy ride; this isn't a great problem unless you have to do a couple hundred miles every day.

The real sweetheart in the drivetrain is the 5-speed gearbox. It has a good, solid feel. The gears are nicely spaced, and on the highway it becomes your savior with the 1300cc engine.

No road test or off-road test would be complete without going to the

Even Suzuki is a bit surprised at the little generic 4wd's immediate acceptance

track and gathering performance data. The numbers we generated were a little bit surprising. Of course, when driving off road it's not a case of needing to go fast, but on the street the Samurai seems very quick. It puts you in the mood to play, so you're always darting in and out of traffic and sprinting from one light to the next. On the track, it was not so quick—0-60 in 16.9 sec and the quarter mile 64.5 mph in 20.47 sec. Stopping distance was an acceptable 35 ft from 30 mph and 151 ft from 60 mph. On the skidpad, the Samurai stood its ground, with a 0.77 g lateral acceleration. A very respectable number for a vehicle with 8½ in. of ground clearance. Not great performance figures overall, but the Samurai's so much fun it doesn't matter.

A big plus for the Samurai is its $6500 base price

If you have ever seen the interior of one of the Samurai's predecessors, you would not believe there was any blood between them. The new Suzuki's dash is simple, yet handsome and easy to read, the standard seats are good, and sport seats even better. The rear door opens wide for easy access, and the rear seat folds forward easily (it can be removed with four bolts). Also, the interior is simple, functional, and comfortable. The model we tested was equipped with the optional air conditioner that worked well, and the heater would melt an igloo.

The Samurai comes in two basic configurations: hardtop and convertible, or targa. The hardtop is a tad quieter and less breezy, but for this type of ride, the soft top seems to be in order. A targa-type hoop separates the front from the rear, and the vinyl top is a snap for two people to erect or stow. Additionally, an optional fiberglass cap and top are available to seal the Samurai during inclement weather.

This quasi-macho generic 4-wheeler might not be everyone's cup of tea, but in the short time it's been on the scene, notice has been given that it's not to be taken lightly. The Samurai is so versatile it's bound to take a nip out of several market segments. It's inexpensive, it's tough, and it's fun.

It could be beginner's luck that Suzuki is having such instant success with its new little Samurai. But it looks like the company has done its market research well, and come up with a winner. _{MT}

Inside and out, the little Samurai may be plain, but it's just plain fun to drive.

DATA

1986 Suzuki Samurai

POWERTRAIN

Vehicle configuration	Front engine, 4-wheel drive
Engine configuration	L-4, OHC, 2 valves/cylinder
Displacement	1324 cc (80.8 cu in.)
Max. power (SAE net)	46 hp @ 5000 rpm
Max. torque (SAE net)	57 lb-ft @ 2500 rpm
Transmission	5-sp. man.
Final drive ratio	3.91:1

CHASSIS

Suspension, f/r	Solid axle/solid axle
Brakes, f/r	Disc/drum
Steering	Recirculating ball
Wheels	15 x 7.0 in., steel
Tires	P205/70R15

DIMENSIONS

Wheelbase	2030 mm (79.9 in.)
Overall length	3430 mm (135.0 in.)
Curb weight	964.8 kg (2127 lb)
Fuel capacity	40.1 L (10.6 gal)

PERFORMANCE

Acceleration, 0-60	16.97 sec
Standing quarter mile	20.47 sec/64.5 mph
Lateral acceleration	0.77 g
Braking, 60-0	151 ft
BASE PRICE	$6550
PRICE AS TESTED	$8128

Faced with the current shortage of Suzuki SJ413s, Dave Cochrane set off to find one himself – in Holland. Ian Booth explains the ins and outs of Dave's personal import

The Cochrane SJ4013 fresh from Holland, complete with nudge bar

Dave and Maggie Cochrane who live in Kent are a typical couple who, having got the first child bit out of the way, wanted a second car – something a bit different. Maggie had wonderful ideas of an exotic sports car, but Dave was quick to point out the pitfalls of expensive insurance, only two seats, etc, and anyway – he couldn't quite run to a Turbo Porshe.

It was after a drive in a friend's Suzi SJ 410 that the idea hatched. Dave pointed out all the advantages to his wife – good views into neighbours gardens, being the only woman on the estate able to get up the hill to the shops in the snow, and the joys of open-top motoring. How could she refuse?

With the money in his bum pocket, Dave set off in search of a new Suzi only to discover there was a mile-long waiting list for such a wonderful vehicle. After a look in the *Exchange and Mart* he spotted an ad for importing your own Suzuki and rang a certain Charles Oakley in Brighton. It's worth pointing out here that only the 1300 Suzuki is available. If you want a 410 1000cc then join the queue

The SJ413 offers slightly better comfort than its smaller-engined brother, the SJ410

in Blighty. The 410's over here are around £5,200 at the moment and an imported 1300 with a far superior level of trim comes in at around £5,900.

With the SJ 413's bigger engine and fifth gear there was no choice, and Dave set off, as instructed, for Sheerness to import his own car. This is all a totally legal business and all the form filling is done for you where and when it becomes necessary. If you want to take a partner with you it will cost you an extra £43. In no time at all he was boarding at sunny Sheerness and heading for Vlissingen in Holland. A meal, a little pep talk and off to your cabin, or to the bar in our Editor's case! Off the boat at 7.30am and on a coach to Delft which is approximately halfway to Rotterdam. Here you're given time to look round Delft and also a break for some nosebag.

Onward they travelled to a rather uninspiring industrial unit closely resembling Arthur Daley's lock-up. It's an Alladin's Cave for the 4x4 freak, however, for here they lie waiting, some still in wax even! You now examine your vehicle for any dents or scratches, etc, and make sure it's what you ordered. The cars are registered with Dutch number plates and a company rep helps you with the paper work here, although it should really be no problem for us Brits, used as we are to filling in useless Government forms in triplicate . . .

Once you have the car you need to get some petrol and a receipt so the customs see you've actually driven the car in Holland. Off you go, heading towards the port again, and it's at Vlissingen that you retire to the nearest hostelry as a three-hour delay on the paperwork then

ensues. Fortunately these naughty boring bits are taken care of by the rep while you relax in the bar.

Onto the boat again and after more food and more drink which you, by the way, pay for, the rep briefs you again prior to your nights' kip. Driving off the boat you are then greeted by a now-smiling Customs and Excise man who wants you to part with your import tax and VAT. What's a grand amongst friends? Anyway once that's over you're free to go home once you've bunged on your English number plates. Dave also had some extras fitted like the bull bar and a

locking hand brake lever.

Is it all worth it? Yes – you're getting a vehicle that isn't available over here, which with a 1300 engine coupled with the five speed box makes all the difference and gives you a lot more umph! For more information phone Charles Oakley on Brighton (0273) 603322/3 and don't forget your passport!

Price Breakdown

Car Price	£4,654.73
Registration	£100.00
Import Taxes	£1130.00
Grand Total	£5884.73

A proud Cochrane at the wheel

SUZUKI SJ413K

WE EUROPEAN off-road vehicle enthusiasts have tended to look askance at some of the diminutive Japanese 4×4s that have recently shuffled on to the market. Open derision was not uncommon and a universal reluctance to take them seriously, at least initially, has cost our motor industry dear. The Japanese have a flair for identifying potential markets for their products and quietly getting on with meeting that requirement, whilst our people were still sitting on their backsides wondering how much the next pay rise was likely to be. Things have changed, but not very much, and now the Japanese are at it again.

Suzuki, having created a substantial sector of the 4×4 market that is all their own, are now aiming fairly and squarely at an area formerly dominated by Land Rover but now shared with most of the other manufacturers who have commercial derivatives of their off-roaders available. It could be argued that the current crop of machines in this bracket are over engineered and over priced for this task and this is why

Suzuki are likely to score again when the potential of their latest version of the SJ series is realised. The vehicle is the SJ413K, a light pick-up truck built on the long wheel based chassis of their mini 4×4. The declared market sector is that of the farmer, horticulturalist, builder, engineer, constructor, forester and any business man who may have essential goods to deliver or collect in adverse conditions.

For those of you who are not familiar with the Suzuki concept, and there can't be many now, a brief description is in order. The all steel body is mounted on a conventional box-section ladder chassis. Front and rear suspension is by means of live axles on semi-eliptic leaf springs with double acting hydraulic shock absorbers all round. The latest models include an anti-roll bar across the front springs which improves lateral stability when cornering, but can only limit axle articulation in off-road situations. Once again, compromise is the name of the game.

Servo assisted brakes, discs at the front and drums to the rear, provide excellent retardation under all conditions. The parking brake acts on the transmission by means of a drum mounted on the rear output of the transfer case – a sure sign that Suzuki, at least, take their off-road abilities seriously.

The 1.3litre power unit now available

SUZUKI SJ413K

offers vastly improved performance over its 970cc predecessor which is, however still fitted in the SJ410 series. In all, the extra 354cc bestows an approximate 40 per cent increase in power and torque, albeit at 6000rpm and 3500rpm respectively, some 500rpm up on both figures when compared with the smaller unit which was already quite a busy little motor. Obviously, for this sort of extra output, there is slightly more than just the greater capacity involved and in this case, features such as a twin-choke downdraught Aisan carburettor, a camshaft profiled for torque at low speeds, air injection and efficient combustion chambers all play their part in producing a very impressive little engine.

Power is delivered via a cable operated clutch to a five-speed primary transmission and a two-speed, part-time four-wheel drive, remotely mounted, transfer box; a short universally jointed shaft connects the two. Drive is then transmitted by conventional tubular propeller shafts to the two live axles. All components are light (the engine weighs in at only 172lbs) and compact, creating an impression of neatness and efficiency.

Underbonnet access for servicing and maintenance is superb with all areas of the engine within easy reach from the front of the vehicle and more manoeuvring space is quickly made available by ignoring the stay and opening the bonnet right back until it rests on the top of the windscreen, at which point a rubber block has thoughtfully been placed for the purpose. Just beware of a rising wind! The distributor is located well back and high up on the engine, keeping it immune from routine water ingress and enabling water fording up to a couple of feet in depth. Unfortunately the alternator is set rather low down, so spare a thought for it and its diodes before you take the plunge into the nearest slurry pit for your entertainment.

A certain amount of care should be taken when checking the oil level in the engine as the dipstick lurks right at the front of the block. When it is extracted, drops of oil can, and do, dribble onto the

anbelt. No immediate cause for concern, but it could lead to problems later.

From the front bumper to a point a few inches behind the doors the SJ413K is much like any other Suzuki 4×4. Thereafter though, it looks as if somebody took a buzz saw to the panels, neatly removing all bodywork from immediately behind the front seats. A glazed bulkhead is fitted neatly into the resulting hole, producing a cab that is snug. Perhaps a little too snug! There is no adjustment whatsoever available on either seat and, depending on the length of your legs, you may sit 'upright' or 'bolt upright'. Long legs would definitely be a problem with attempts to reach clutch or footbrake hindered by the knees striking the steering wheel; reminiscent of early Land Rovers that taller people had to drive with legs splayed on either side of the wheel. A shame, and a potential sales drawback.

The interior trim of the cab is very basic indeed with little or no sound insulation and a rather thin and slippery, but thoroughly practical, vinyl floor covering. The seats are also covered in vinyl which, in fact, isn't as unpleasant as it looks and is, of course once again, thoroughly practical for a working vehicle. Older readers will remember the legendary door seals of the VW Beetle which were so effective that a window had to be opened before the door could be slammed shut. The Suzuki Pick-up's door seals are a bit like that and it does help if you open a window slightly before pulling the door shut. Talking of the windows, the action of the winders is superb; only three full turns to open or shut, and light enough to be easy, even for the driver to reach across the cab (almost full stretch) to open the passenger's window too. There is a small lockable glove-box, but that is the only stowage available in the cab. No advantage has been taken of the limited space behind or under the seats and, in such a confined area, this is a sad waste. The inertia reel seat belts are of a fairly basic type and are really too sensitive for off-road work where each bounce causes them to progressively wind the seat's occupant tighter into the cushion, but occasionally releasing enough slack to

bring you back with a jerk at the next lurch. The trouble is, there is no way you can stay on your seat without them!

The business end of this vehicle is, of course, the pick-up body mounted on the rear of its lengthened chassis. The 93.5in wheelbase permits a bed length of 61 inches with a width of 52. There are no intruding wheelboxes, the flat deck being raised above the level of the tyres' maximum travel by a sub-frame between it and the chassis. This results in a very useful load area, but at an unfortunately high level, not far off 36 inches. A full dropside body is fitted, though on the test vehicle the benefit of this was lost to a certain extent by virtue of the optional ABS liner that was installed, restricting access to the rear tailgate only. The liner, nevertheless, is a good idea, protecting the floor and sides from potentially damaging cargoes and easing the unloading of sand, gravel etc. Pity about the drain holes in the forward corners which could allow all sorts of nasty fluids to find their way down to the steel deck, there to do their worst, unmolested and unobserved. Should it be necessary, removal of the liner is a straightforward enough job, involving a few nylon nuts and some rubber loops that engage on the tie-down hooks on the sides.

The payload of this diminutive workhorse is 883lbs or about 400kg. It does not sound a lot and, in the case of high density loads like animal food concentrates, fertilizers, sand and cement or bricks, you will need to be careful not to overload it. Even so, it is a useful capacity and ideally suited for many light tasks.

The spare wheel is always a problem on light 4×4s; it is invariably bulky and must be readily accessible even when the vehicle is laden and up to the hubs in mud. Suzuki's solution on the Pick-up is to tuck it up under the load deck where it fits, neatly cradled, between and slightly above the chassis side rails. The rear number plate hinges upwards to allow the unclamped spare to be slipped out horizontally from the back. An excellent location which, on most off-roaders, would be unsatisfactory due to their construction.

It took the Japanese manufacturers of off-road vehicles a long time to realise that bits and pieces that hang down from the rear of their vehicles need to be very carefully placed if they are not to be broken-off on the first cross-country skirmish. Preferably, they shouldn't hang down at all. With the last batch of models this lesson appeared to have sunk home, but, inexplicably, Suzuki have decided to locate the high density rear fog light, under the off-side rear bumper where it projects prominently below the line of departure. Yes, you've guessed! It was knocked off within about three minutes of taking to the hills. Silly, 'cos there are so many places it could

Mike Hallett takes a nasty fall at, what looks like, Beechers Brook but fully utilising the limited resources available, coupled with a lifetime's experience saw him drive the vehicle free in just one hour – and perhaps a little bit more. Left: The 1.3litre power unit in the SJ413 offers 63bhp, a 40per cent increase over the 1.0litre version.

Technical Specification

Suzuki SJ413K Pick-up

Engine

Type	All aluminium, OHC, four-cylinder, water cooled
Bore	2.91in (74mm)
Stroke	3.03in (77mm)
Capacity	1324cc (80.0cu.in.)
Compression	8.8:1
Maximum Power	63bhp (47kw)
Maximum Torque	74lb.ft. (100Nm)
Fuel System	Twin-choke Aisan downdraught carburettor
Tank capacity	8.8 gallons (2 star)

Transmission

Type	Five-speed, all synchro primary with two-speed, part-time transfer box
Ratios: First	3.650
Second	1.946
Third	1.422
Fourth	1.000
Fifth	0.793
Reverse	3.463
Transfer Ratios:	
High	1.409
Low	2.263
Final Drive:	3.909

Suspension

	Semi-elliptic leaf springs all round with live axles and telescopic dampers. Anti-roll bar at front

Brakes

	Hydraulically operated, servo-assisted system with floating caliper discs at the front and self-adjusting drums to the rear. Handbrake operates on transmission mounted drum

Wheels and Tyres

	8 spoke steel 15×5JJ shod with Dunlop 195.SR15 SP44 steel belted radials

Principal Dimensions

Length	153.4in (3896mm)
Width	57.5in (1460mm)
Height	66.1in (1680mm)
Wheelbase	93.5in (2375mm)
Track Front	47.6in (1210mm)
Rear	48.0in (1220mm)
Ground clearance	9.0in (230mm)
Approach Angle	48 Degrees
Departure Angle	39 Degrees
Turning Circle	37.5ft (11.4m)
Load Deck Length	61.0in (1550mm)
Width	52.0in (1270mm)
Fitted with 11in (280mm) deep tailgate and dropsides	
Kerb Weight	2017lbs (915kg)
Gross Vehicle Weight	3186lbs (1445kg)
Max Towing Weight	2420lbs (1100kg)

Fuel Consumption (Official)

Urban Cycle	31.7mpg
Constant 56mph	35.7mpg
Constant 75mph	33.6mph

Price

£4,521.74 plus £678.26 VAT

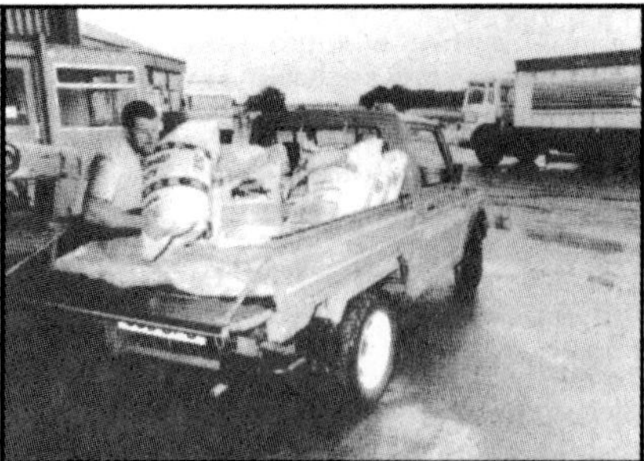

The new pick-up proved ideal for transporting relatively small quantities of high density materials, such as cattle feeds and fertilizers.

have been mounted right out of harm's way. They have also fitted long mud flaps which hang perilously close to the back wheels. Fine as long as you are going forward, but as soon as you back-up on rough going they are going to suffer. Many owners of older Land Rovers will have experienced this problem before now.

Driving the Suzuki Pick-up on the road is an interesting experience. In common with most vehicles of this type, load carriers, its suspension is firm, to say the least. Even the dual rate springs can't disguise this. With no load in the back, progress, along any but the smoothest surfaces, is a series of hops and lurches. It isn't necessarily just the fault of the springs. With two live axles, four hefty wheels and tyres and four leaf springs all pounding up and down under what is, relatively, a very light vehicle, the sprung to unsprung weight ratio leaves quite a lot to be desired. So, one should perhaps acknowledge that what the company has achieved on such a basic suspension system is quite remarkable. The fact remains, though, that driving any sort of distance is not a restful experience. The steering too was somewhat heavy, requiring some strenuous efforts in off-road conditions.

The criticism, often levelled at the SJ410 series, that it lacked poke can't be made of the SJ413. The larger and more powerful engine lays that bogey to rest. It's no Boy Racer's machine, but it will accelerate briskly enough up through its five-speed box to a happy cruising speed of 65–70mph. That's unladen, of course. You wouldn't want to press on so keenly with nearly half a tonne of cargo perched on the back, particularly as the Centre of Gravity is up there somewhere too. But, it can hold its own on the motorway quite happily and is not so prone to being blown about by anything larger than a passing malicious Range Rover. Obviously the extra 13 or so inches on the wheelbase have helped significantly to improve stability in these situations also allowing the vastly superior brakes to haul the thing rapidly to a halt without drama too.

The Pick-up's off-road performance is really quite good, though hardly the equal of its shorter stablemate. The longer wheelbase has led to a reduction of the ramp breakover angle, so it is more prone to getting high centred on humps and ridges. This we discovered the hard way when your roving reporter, who should have known better, failed to look before he leapt. The front wheels dropped neatly into a gulley while the chassis came to rest gently, but firmly, on top of the preceeding, soggy ridge.

With the rear suspension at maximum stretch, there was no way the back wheels had any part to play in the proceedings. It was at that point that the heavens opened, rent by thunder and lightning, saturating the unhappy scene below. It had never occurred to us that *He* might be an ardent off-roader and was obviously unimpressed by this reporter's crass stupidity. Eventually the downpour eased and steps were taken to extricate the Suzuki. With only the scissor jack supplied, the spare wheel and assorted pieces of debris found lying about the place, the front end of the vehicle was raised until the rear wheels could get some traction and the chassis was clear of the hump. And out she came. Sounds easy doesn't it? It took an hour and the photographer was beginning to wonder where his next meal was coming from. It just goes to show how even the simplest off-road jaunt can suddenly and unexpectedly go wrong. Had we planned it properly, taking various essential equipment or at least a second vehicle, the whole incident would have been unremarkable. Another lesson learnt (for about the third time) or, as Brian Hartley would say, 'Do as I say, not as I do!'

Generally the Suzuki did well, competently picking its way over most of the ascents, descents, ruts and mud with ample power to carry it through the stickier bits. For such a small engine the low speed torque is a pleasant surprise providing good traction as long as the tyres stay in contact with the ground which, in the unladen state, they sometimes had trouble doing; the hard suspension and limited axle travel conspiring to lift wheels clear on any terrain that was, in anyway, arduous. However, when fully loaded with ten 50kg bags of fertilizer (slightly overloaded actually, but probably realistic) its performance was impeccable, the extra weight endowing the tyres with a good solid bite at the ground. In this state it was taken all round the rougher tracks and areas of a local farm where we were able to satisfy ourselves that it could indeed cope, and with a useful payload. It was also found to be ideal for picking up small loads of animal feedstuffs for subsequent delivery to the fields. One rarely needs to take out much at one go and four tons of Massey-Ferguson tractor with trailer could be deemed overkill when the little Suzy can do it so easily.

It has frequently been said, by those in the know, that there is a hole in the 4×4 market for a small, light and simple utility that can cope with demanding off-road conditions. The Series I Land Rover filled the need for years, and many still do. But, as the British company's vehicles grew in stature and complexity, and the Series I's slowly died, the slot has re-appeared. Subaru moved into it with their very popular MV pick-up, but it's not the whole answer; it lacks the true off-road ability – excellent machine though it is. Suzuki have got a head start with the SJ413K. It is far from ideal, but it is a good attempt to meet the need and proves that they have, at least, got the courage of their convictions.

Sincere thanks to agricultural merchants, Shearing & Loader and farmers WC Totman & Son for the use of their facilities during the course of this Off-Road Test.

SUZUKI
SANTANA

When is a Japanese off-roader not Japanese? When it's built in Spain. Suzuki's new Santana is not just built in Spain, however, and there are some significant changes to the suspension. And some of those changes are not for the better

Suzuki made its four-wheel drive debut in the United Kingdom only eight years ago when they introduced the LJ80 model with its puny stature and tiny 797cc power unit. The butt of many jokes within the off-road fraternity, the vehicle nevertheless proved to be a competent performer in the rough, though somewhat lacking in the urge and comfort departments, and soon acquired a following amongst trials enthusiasts. A few years later, Suzuki, having 'felt the water' and found it to their liking, brought in the much more sophisticated, relatively speaking, SJ410 range with its modern lines, 'softer' interior and larger capacity engine; 970cc this time. The car was an instant success, attracting many customers who had never even considered a four-wheel drive machine before and establishing the little jeep as the cult car of the 1980s with sales figures that were second only to the home-brewed Land Rovers. To be perfectly fair, it is a completely different market with only a very small overlap into the 'workhorse' category. Even so, the comparison was made, many people commenting favourably on the Suzuki's lighter controls, sprightly off-road performance and greater fuel economy. Attributes that made it particularly attractive as a cheap second vehicle. Something for the wife to potter about in, and to act as 'essential' transport when winter occasionally did its worst.

At last year's International Motor Show in Birmingham came the first signs of a new development when Suzuki GB Cars announced that they were intending to import SJ410s from Spain. These were to be machines built under license by the Land Rover Santana

Second only to Land Rover

factory at Linares – Suzuki has acquired a 20 per cent interest – with a high degree of local content. The joint venture is now up and running, and the first vehicles are already with their owners. Two Spanish models are being brought in, one black one and one white one (quiet please) with exclusive side-stripe treatment and more luxurious interiors than perhaps Suzuki owners have been used to. Features include a five-speed main gearbox, colour co-ordinated trim, twin, folding, rear bucket seats, servo assisted brakes, Santana badging and colour keyed lamp guards, bumpers and wheel arches. Motive power is the tried and tested 1 litre unit (970cc) and not, surprisingly, the 1.3 engine. Santanas will be sold alongside the existing range of Suzuki 4×4s from Japan.

The fact that the model is now being produced within the Common Market, and meets the local content requirements, means that it is outside the so-called gentleman's agreement on import quotas for Japanese cars, hence, for the first time, Suzuki should be able to meet the demand for their diminutive off-roader.

Our test vehicle was a shining black example with all the usual decals and stick-on panels much beloved by Suzuki. At least it didn't have a full paragraph devoted to the technical specification as some of the SJ413s have. Even so, one was left in no doubt that this was a Suzuki Santana model Sport and that it had a five speed gearbox and four wheel drive. The black paint job was

SUZUKI SANTANA

immaculate with no runs or orange peel effect, but the contrasting grey panels with red stripes that adorn both sides of the vehicle are merely stuck-on plastic film, and one wonders how long it will be before the edges start to lift. The Santana badging on the rear was already beginning to peel.

The soft-top is a lightweight, lined, PVC affair, secured by press-studs and velcro tapes with exposed leading edges threaded into grooves, and supported by a single hoop and the built-in roll bar.

The interior is where the Santana differs most from the Japanese built models. The doors are trimmed neatly in grey plastic with colour co-ordinated cloth inserts, a theme which is picked up again on the seats, also in grey cloth, but with a touch of the red that boldly decorates the outside of the doors – diagonal stripes across the aforementioned grey plastic.

The vehicle is carpeted throughout, but it's a very thin material, not particularly well fitted and completely lacking any sound insulating qualities. Their only saving grace being that they are easily removed for cleaning the machine out with a hose, and look as if they could stand a thorough washing themselves. Actually quite a useful asset, considering the adverse conditions this vehicle is capable of operating in when it has to.

The two front bucket seats are fully reclinable, but only the driver's is endowed with any fore and aft adjustment. The passenger's hinges forward on its frame to give access to the rear, but is otherwise fixed. In the Santana, the rudimentary rear bench seat of old has been dispensed with. In its place are two individual bucket seats which are well padded and fitted with lap straps. Both may be folded forward

to increase cargo space, but this involves unscrewing butterfly nuts, two for each seat, from studs set in the floor. The front seat occupants are supplied with slightly over sensitive inertia reel safety belts and in off-road situations you are probably better off without them, unless you are actually doing something stupid.

The spare wheel is carried externally, mounted on the side hinged tailgate, and is secured by a neat locking device to deter the light-fingered types.

The main criticism levelled at the SJ Series in the past has concerned its taut, if not excessively hard, leaf spring suspension, and one has to admit that, in that respect, it displayed the true and established traditional characteristics of all the old 4×4s. A wheelbase of marginally under 80 inches doesn't help either, producing a degree of pitching that is only barely acceptable in this context. The on-road handling also left a great deal to be desired.

Part of the Santana project was to introduce an improved, softer suspension package, presumably to tie in with the popular road going image that was emerging for the vehicle. The design compromise, that is nearly all off-roaders, needed to be biased just a little more towards on-road use, to make it more agreeable for the majority who have no intention of giving it a hard time in the rough and tumble of cross-country motoring.

The developed suspension, it is true to say, behaves differently to the original set-up, though whether it is, in fact, an improvement is open to speculation. What the Spanish have done is to fit single leaf parabolic springs at the front with a similar arrangement at the rear, but in the latter's case, each spring has a secondary or helper leaf that is intended to come into play under heavy loads or

Its off-road ability has not been affected – it's still very good

SANTANA
OFF ROAD
4 WHEEL DRIVE
TESTED
OFF ROAD
4 WHEEL DRIVE
SUZUKI
SANTANA
D789 VUF
D789 VUF

SUZUKI SANTANA

extremes of axle travel. To a certain extent the design has made the car's ride on smooth main road and motorway surfaces marginally better, but on rural and urban roads which tend to be anything but smooth, it doesn't seem to be able to cope very well at all. Every pothole or surface irregularity makes it lurch and wallow; the pitching and twitching is such that your neck muscles are working overtime to keep your head upright and it's not long before the passengers start to complain of feeling nauseous. The steering is also noticeably

On rural or urban roads it doesn't seem to cope well at all

lighter and unresponsive when the rear seats are occupied. However, with only a driver on board, the situation improved to the point of being acceptable – having the steering wheel to hang on to must help – and longish journeys, though tiring and very tedious, were at least feasible.

In off-road conditions the Santana Suzuki is every bit as competent as its Japanese counterpart, though still a bit underpowered to cope with long stretches of heavy going, especially on a gradient. Nevertheless, it will scramble about quite happily, clambering over ruts, banks, ditches and other obstacles with an eagerness that earns immediate forgiveness for its road-going efforts. The willing little one litre unit with its ignition system mounted high-up and at the back of the engine bay performs well in water, provided that one is not too heavy handed. We spent an afternoon at the new off-road demonstration facility at Sweetwoods Farm near Cowden in West Kent where some very reasonable off-road sections have been carved into the hillside. Lots of lovely mud, water, humps and bumps, and not all of it

drivable, so you need to think about what you're doing. The little Santana behaved impeccably, always being able to find some traction, though helped considerably in this by the very effective Spanish made Michelin X M&S 195R15s which adorned its spoked steel wheels. The ride quality on the rough going was very similar to the Japanese model's and entirely acceptable for the conditions if you took it easy; press-on though, and things got much more lively and one got the distinct impression that the dampers couldn't control the springs. How we longed to try a set of those Monroe Gas-Magnum 4×4s on it!

From the driver's point of view the controls of the Suzuki are mostly light and responsive. The cable operated clutch, and the gearchange, are delightfully smooth and accurate. The steering, however, was heavier than expected and the rim of the steering wheel was thin, hard and unpleasant. The brakes, if anything, were too good, taking very little effort to lock-up the back wheels which is not surprising considering the massive servo that is fitted and the light overall weight of the vehicle. One soon gets used to them, but extra caution is required on damp, muddy roads.

Generally the Suzuki Santana model is an attractive little vehicle. A trifle over-decorated for some tastes perhaps, but there is no doubt that it is a competent off-roader, well able to take advantage of its lightweight and four-wheel drive to manoeuvre its way over some very difficult ground. Its on-road performance, however, precludes its use as a long distance tourer for any, but the most ardent (and long suffering) enthusiast.

It has to be said that although on paper the Spanish connection should have produced a higher specification vehicle, it is doubtful that this has in fact been achieved. It will be interesting to see in the ensuing months how the Santana is received. ■

All the ingredients are still evident for the Suzuki Santana to continue its growing appeal, but smart paintwork and neat interior trim cannot hide its on-road shortcomings

Technical Specification

Suzuki Santana Sport

Engine

	Water cooled, four cylinder, four stroke with single OHC, cast iron block and aluminium head
Capacity	970cc
Bore/Stroke	65.5mm/72.0mm
Max power	45bhp (33.5kw) @ 5500rpm
Max torque	54lbf.ft. (73.5Nm) @ 3000rpm
Compression	8.8:1
Fuel System	Single, side draught carburettor

Transmission

	Five-speed, all synchromesh primary gear box with remotely mounted, two-speed, part-time transfer case	
Primary Ratios	1st	3.138:1
	2nd	1.947:1
	3rd	1.423:1
	4th	1.000:1
	5th	0.790:1
	Reverse	3.466:1
Transfer Ratios	High	1.580:1
	Low	2.511:1
Final Drive Ratio		4.111:1

Suspension

Front	Live axle with single parabolic leaf springs and telescopic dampers
Rear	Live axle with two-stage parabolic leaf springs and telescopic dampers

Brakes

	Servo assisted hydraulically operated discs at the front with drums on the rear. Parking brake actuates independent drum on rear output of transfer case

Wheels

	5.5 × 15

Tyres

	195SR15 (Test car fitted with Michelin X M&S)

Steering

	Recirculating ball (manual)

Principle dimensions

Length	135.4in (3440mm)
Width	57.5in (1460mm)
Height	66.1in (1680mm)
Wheelbase	79.9in (2030mm)
Track Front	47.6in (1210mm)
Track Rear	48.0in (1220mm)
Ground clearance	9.0in (230mm)
Approach Angle	48 degrees
Departure Angle	39 degrees
Turning Circle	32.2ft (9.8m)
Kerb Weight	1958lb (890kg)
GVW	2750lb (1250kg)
Towing	Unbraked 980lb (445kg) Braked 2200lb (1000kg)
Fuel Tank Capacity	8.8 gallons (40 litres) 2 star
Fuel Consumption	Average for duration of test 24.9mpg
Price	£6,499 inclusive of Car Tax & VAT

FIRST OF ALL, it's cute, the Suzuki Samurai. Second, it's several thousand dollars cheaper than any other 4wd on the market. And third, it obviously fills some sort of need in the U.S. market. Why else would it be selling in such shockingly large numbers?

Actually, a good case can be made for it being a toy car, not a real sports utility at all. It has minimal highway performance, its ride and handling are primitive, and comfort isn't a word you need when you talk about it.

Now, with those unkind words plainly stated, we can go on to say that it's more fun to drive than many other sports utilities on the market. The problem with some vehicles is that they have more power than you dare use. With the Samurai, you can keep your foot to the firewall and use every ounce of power just about all the time and this is terrific fun.

The Samurai is small. The wheelbase is only 79.9 in.; length, a modest 135.4 in. It sits quite high, however, which combines with its narrow track to make it feel quite tippy if you don't moderate your exuberance.

Its design and construction are fundamental. It's built on a ladder-type frame, there's live axle with leaf spring suspension at both front and rear, there's a perfectly straightforward part-time 4-wheel-drive system and there are manually locking hubs.

The engine is a 1.3-liter rated at 63 bhp with 74 lb-ft of torque and that's not really enough to give a 2100-lb package more than minimal highway performance.

There are soft-top and hardtop versions and Standard and Deluxe trim grades. There's also a truck version with no rear seat. With the soft-top model, there's a Targa-style rollbar that is additionally braced to the windshield frame.

The top is a chore to erect but it rewards your patience by being snug, moderately flap-free and commendably weatherproof. Standard equipment is basic but with the uplevel Deluxe trim things get less Spartan and you also get additional instrumentation and a radio.

Unless you have a very high tolerance for discomfort you may find that after an hour behind the wheel you'll be shifting your body around, looking for a more comfortable position. This is partly a result of the cramped quarters but we also suspect it has something to do with the high-frequency vibrations that emanate from the busy, buzzy little engine.

But let's go back to the beginning and repeat what we believe is the reason for its sales success in this country. It's undeniably cute, it doesn't cost much and it obviously fills a need.

SPECIFICATIONS

Base price, base model	$6895	Fuel capacity, U.S. gal.	10.6	Transmission	5M
Country of origin	Japan	Fuel economy (EPA), mpg:		Final-drive ratio	3.73:1
Body/seats	2D*, conv/4	Federal	27	Suspension, f/r	solid/live
Layout	F/4wd	California	27	Brakes, f/r	disc/drum
Wheelbase, in.	79.9	Engine	sohc inline-4	Tires	P205/75R-15
Track, f/r	51.2/51.6	Bore x stroke, mm	73.9 x 77.0	Steering type	ball & nut
Length	135.4	Displacement, cc	1324	Turning circle, ft	33.4
Width	60.2	Compression ratio	na	Turns, lock-to-lock	na
Height	65.6	Bhp @ rpm, net	63 @ 6000		
Curb weight, lb	2095	Torque @ rpm, lb-ft	74 @ 3500		

*indicates model described in specifications; na means information not available

Being an ex-Suzuki Sierra owner, GEOFF MIDDLETON was the first to put his hand up when a test of Suzuki's LWB Resin Top Sierra was imminent. He set off with photographer HELMUT MUELLER into the Blue Mountains west of Sydney to get the lowdown on this top-of-the-range Suzi.

The last time I tested a Suzuki was on a test drive with the intention of buying one. I was therefore enthusiastic about doing this report. Apart from Production Editor Scott Kelleher, I'm probably the only person on the Overlander staff who actually likes Suzis. To be perfectly frank, I am quite enamoured of the little beasties.

This possibly stems from the fact that my first 4WD was an LJ50 which was a bit tricked up and could actually embarrass a lot of my mates who owned larger 4WDs. I suppose that left me with a spot for them somewhat softer than Suzuki suspension systems. They are also the most affordable 4WD on the market, with the possible exception of the Lada Niva, and Suzuki certainly has the reliability edge there. So, on with the test . . .

WHAT YOU GET

AT first glance the LWB Resin Top is a neat-looking package. The factory top fits the vehicle and its lines very well. Any person vaguely cognisant of the LWB soft top will know that there is a step in the roofline just behind the B-pillar. In the Resin Top this is taken into consideration through a gradual slope from the top of the windscreen to where the step would normally finish in the Softie. Because of this the exterior of the vehicle has a cleaner and more streamlined appearance and the interior becomes more spacious.

Incorporated in the sloping part of the roof is a small sunroof or 'moonroof'. This is of tinted glass construction and winds up slightly, supposedly to aid ventilation but neither Mueller nor myself could find any use for it bar lighting, or as a chimney for cigarette smoke.

HIGH SIERRA

The interior of the vehicle is extremely well lit, assisted by the long windows above the passengers' opening ones. These slide-opening windows in the rear of the Sierra are excellent. They provide a good view of the passing countryside while also being of good quality, wide opening and having secure locks. Headroom throughout the vehicle is very good.

Exit and entry though, is tight, and not assisted by the fact that the passenger's side door is the only one by which entry can be gained to the rear seat. This is because that seat is the only one with a slide-forward feature. The driver's seat only slides and tilts for adjustment. Granted, it is safer to enter and exit on the kerb-side of the vehicle, but it's not always practical.

The rear cargo door of the Resin Top is a beauty. It is a one-piece unit which utilises the existing hinges on the small metal door you get with a soft top. It's double-skinned (as is all the canopy) and the interior skin continues down to the bottom of the original tailgate. Very well thought out and very functional. The large rear window sports an electric demister which works well.

Inside the Resin Top Sierra you also get cloth seats for your money, but

Climbing ability of the Suzuki was good but could be improved with better tyres.

don't get too excited, they're the same ones you get in all JX-spec Sierras. They might not be sticky in summer, but the cloth doesn't mean you're not still going to suffer from a painful posterior and/or a sore back after a long trip. The folding rear seat is also cloth covered. It's a small two-person job suitable only for short trips for adults, but fine for a couple of kids. If you are paying top dollar for top spec, what's wrong with top seats?

The Resin Top also comes with carpets — in a Suzuki? Unheard of! They have such good drain plugs that I used to just hose mine out. Market appeal perhaps?

It also has a quite reasonable radio/cassette with two

sensibly-placed speakers. Quite an improvement on the radio in the standard LWB version.

The test vehicle was equipped with some aftermarket goodies (and baddies), such as bullbar and winch (goodies) and towbar (baddy due to clearance problems). I'm not sure if the headlight protectors were standard. They were functional-looking items nonetheless.

So that is about what you get for your money if you go from a standard LWB Sierra up to the Resin Top — that is, of course, if you never want to use the open-air aspect of the softie. Let's hit the road . . .

ON ROAD

FIRSTLY, let me get one thing off my chest. This vehicle was in poor tune and that is the nicest way I can put it. The little 1.3-litre donk was pinging its head off and the exhaust pipe looked as though it was running richer than J. Paul Getty. Perhaps the air-conditioning had something to do with it, but I know for a fact that 1.3s can run better and much faster than this one did.

Performance aside, the noise level in the Resin Top on the highway was pretty good. The double-skinned top

HIGH SIERRA

...id its job well, aided by the carpet. It also has very good waterproofing and dust-sealing qualities. Silicon sealing is evident between the body and canopy.

Handling wise, the steering is still a bit vague, turning circle is still a bother and suspension is still Suzuki. However, I can live with that if the vehicle goes well. I've owned one, remember. Things can't have been all that bad, as Helmut went to sleep on the run down from the mountains on the afternoon after the test (and he's the second *Overlander* photographer known to have slept in a Sierra).

OFF ROAD

WE traversed a fairly easy fire trail in the mountains with a few rocky climbs and a couple of water crossings. Road conditions ranged from fast dirt to sand and the Suzuki handled all of it as I thought it would, even the droopy tow bar.

On the fast dirt it was bumpy and bump-steered accordingly, but was handleable with throttle steering. On sand it was perfect. Water crossings were no problems due to well-mounted electrics and light weight, so that we didn't sink in the sandy bottom.

All was okay until we got to the rocky climbs and descents.

The canopy, as with most of this genre of coverings, was a whinger. By this I mean it creaked, groaned and complained as the vehicle flexed on irregularities. I mentioned to Helmut that I could almost hear the stress fractures coming into being. This may not present a problem in the short term, but I would think that in the long term it would weaken the canopy.

Speaking of weak canopies, where was the rear rollbar? Gone! I would hate to roll one.

Climbing ability and low-range stuff is still good in the Suzuki, though. Traction could be improved with a set of tyres different from those you get as standard, but giving it its due it was a cold, damp day that did not afford

Interior lighting was enhanced by wrap-over skylight windows in the rear and moonroof in the front.

perfect traction conditions. Suzuki has gone for an all-rounder rather than an off-roader with the Bridgestone Mud and Snow radials. Maybe they're better suited to the market at which they're aiming.

Ground clearance is pretty good at 225mm, taking into consideration that it is a long wheelbase version. We didn't bottom out very much and when we did it appeared to be the chassis rails.

SUMMARY

IT all boils down to the old question of value-for-money. Are you getting enough for your dollar to warrant buying this vehicle over the basic Softie LWB? Some people must think so, as I know that there aren't too many left in the country and there are no more being imported due to the new model release next year.

The price of the Resin Top LWB is a bit uncertain, as I was told that Ateco had dropped the price of some of them from $18,100 to $16,500. At the latter price it would seem like a good buy if you were in the market for a four-seater 4WD with a plastic top. As for the former price — it seems like too much cash for a Suzuki at this stage.

HIGH SIERRA

The front of the test vehicle featured bull bar and Warn winch (not standard).

Interior sported cloth seats and door trim as well as radio/cassette and carpets.

Large one-piece rear door was excellent and featured demister on the rear window. Droopy towbar was a worry.

The trick bits you get for the extra bucks you can obtain from any good aftermarket manufacturer — except the canopy. I've not seen a better one for a Suzy. You are therefore justifying your excess expenditure solely on the top. If you want or can handle the soft top, then get the basic LWB.

In a market where everything is over-priced, it is hard to conceive that a bottom-of-the-market vehicle can cost more than half the average yearly income of an Australian male, however, that's not going to change in the foreseeble future. As this model of Suzuki has, in effect, dropped in price nearly two grand (and I'm sure other models will drop a bit as well as the time for the new release approaches), they could well be one of the best buys in the 4WD market in the coming months.

As for the market of the Suzuki Sierra LWB Resin Top, well, in my mind it would be the young person who doesn't want to get into the more serious side of off-roading where he might damage his vehicle's looks, but more the bloke or girl who wants to get around in the snow or mud, or take the occasional foray down a fire trail. Fishermen also would love it, it has the best sand ability of any 4WD I know and (if in tune) has a bit of towing ability to boot.

I would give the air-conditioning a wide berth, as it's unsuited to this vehicle and, in my mind, almost unnecessary. Leave those sorts of things for the blokes whose bank balances and dyno figures can afford it.

*C*hic. Merriam-Webster defines it as *cleverly stylish: SMART; also currently fashionable.*

Manufacturers and advertisers have spent millions trying to capture its essence and failed; others have stumbled into its magic spell. In our culture, it can range from faded, torn 501s to Benetton, from Swatch to Movado, and from the venerable VW Bug to the Ferrari Testarossa. It's the VW Bug/Thing that the Samurai can perhaps be most closely identified with, from its utterly simple unchanging design and toughness to its ability to be comfortable in any environment or socioeconomic group. In any case, one only need drive along Pacific Coast Highway or cruise high school and college campuses across America to realize that, at least among the youth, the Suzuki Samurai is a *chic* ride.

In its launch year of 1986, Suzuki of America began importing a modest 1200 cars per month. By the end of that year, aided no doubt by an attractive base price of only $6500, it had sold over 47,000 Samurais. In doing so, it captured the best first-year sales record of any Japanese car company, plus the distinction of being named top-selling convertible in the U.S., outselling all competition, both foreign and domestic. Some 20 months after its introduction, Suzuki had sold over 100,000 cars and is now selling its hot little ticket at the rate of more than 8000 vehicles per month. Suzuki of America's dealer network has grown from 80 dealers in only 17 states to 170 dealers in 30 states, with plans to have dealerships operating throughout the continental United States by 1989.

Interestingly enough, the Samurai is not a new design concept from Suzuki. A version of this vehicle has been sold and tested in third-world countries for the past 18 years. The

'88½ Suzuki Samurai

An unconventional marketing strategy pays off

by D.R. Beckstead
PHOTOGRAPHY BY MIKE GASPAR

The new interior offers a higher degree of comfort and quality

Samurai was unveiled in the U.S. at a time when sport/utility vehicles were viewed and used primarily as weekend off-road vehicles for serious "4-wheeling" enthusiasts. But Suzuki of America didn't market its mini-4x4 in the traditional "macho" genre. It let consumers decide for themselves what this new vehicle was and how they would use it. They were encouraged to drive it just for fun (Beep-Beep, Hi!). This rather unconventional marketing strategy has obviously paid off.

Suzuki, perhaps caught a bit off guard by its success, is now concerned about preserving the image of the Samurai. Keeping in mind the success of the VW Bug, the manufacturer stresses that, in years to come, it will revise, not change, the vehicle, therefore retaining its style and simplicity. The '88½ incorporates the first "major" revisions since the Samurai was introduced into the U.S. in late 1985.

In an effort to tame the Samurai's less than pleasant ride characteristics, spring rates have been lowered front and rear. Along with this, shock absorber rates have been altered and a larger front stabilizer bar has been incorporated. To improve acceleration in 5th gear, the ratio has been lowered from 0.795 to 0.864. Also new in the '88½ is an aluminum radiator and a redesigned valve cover.

On the outside, the Samurai grille has undergone a subtle styling change that gives a smoother, integrated appearance to the front end. The wheels have been restyled and now feature a 10-hole design.

The interior has been refined with a more car-like instrument panel with legible gauges and a new four-spoke steering wheel. Seat material has been improved, and overall the Samurai's new interior offers a higher degree of comfort and quality. As in our '86 test model, we found the heating and optional air conditioning effective.

What has all this done for the vehicle? Well, the ride is definitely improved; however, a 2100-lb 4-wheel-drive vehicle with live axles at both ends sitting on an 80-in. wheelbase is still no highway cruiser. With a fuel tank capacity of 10.6 gal and average consumption of about 28 mpg, one could conceivably go over 280 miles between stops; but even with the "softened" suspension, we found ourselves much in need of R&R after 150 miles. Its shortcomings as a long-distance traveler are heightened by high noise levels (83 dBA at 60 mph in the convertible). Yet, when it comes to cruising around town or an off-road adventure, this vehicle is *fun!*

Redesigned wheels, refined instrument panel, and four-spoke steering wheel keep the 88½ Suzuki on top of the fun-to-drive 4x4 list.

The little 1.3-liter all-aluminum engine, although of modest power, is a willing performer. The 5-speed gearbox has nicely spaced ratios and is a real joy to use. Even with the lowered 5th gear, the engine is comfortable cruising in the 70-75-mph bracket. Overall handling is better than one would think from a 4wd vehicle with ground clearance of over 8 in. Surprisingly, the Samurai delivers a kind of fun reminiscent of mid-'60s sports cars such as the Midget, Sprite, and Spitfire, with a reliability record that's generations improved.

We were also impressed with its off-road capability. Whether it was roaring over the dunes at Pismo Beach or climbing and descending steep, rutted hills our better judgement told us to stay away from, the little Samurai always amazed us by making what looked difficult seem easy. No doubt its off-road ability could be further enhanced by larger tires.

Suzuki hopes to keep the base price of the '88½ at the same level as the '88—$7995 for the standard convertible—making it approximately $3000 less than a 4-cylinder Jeep Wrangler. However, because of the Samurai's huge sales success, many dealers actually get away with selling the vehicle above window sticker. In fact, Suzuki sales were so strong last year it was one of only two Japanese manufacturers not having to resort to factory sales incentives. Coupled with the fact that Suzuki has a list of over 90 accessories, we doubt that many Samurais will leave the lot for under $9000. Now brimming with confidence, Suzuki of America will be introducing several new vehicles over the next few years, starting with a slightly larger sport/utility vehicle now sold in Europe and Australia under the name Vitara. This vehicle will offer such amenities as automatic transmission and power door locks and windows. Expect to see it in the U.S. in late 1988. Also on the horizon is a car line that will, in all likelihood, be powered by exotic, high-performance engines and offer the option of 4wd.

Suzuki already has one definite winner on its hands by the name of Samurai, albeit in a field with no real competition. However, with mountains of technology gained through its motorcycle endeavors, it stands poised to compete with the other high-tech Japanese manufacturers and bring us some truly exciting vehicles. In the meantime: *Beep-Beep, Hi!*

TECH DATA
Suzuki Samurai

POWERTRAIN

Vehicle configuration	Front engine, 4wd
Engine configuration	Inline-4, OHC, 2 valves/cylinder
Displacement	1324 cc (81 cu in.)
Max. power (SAE net)	64 hp @ 5500 rpm
Max. torque (SAE net)	73 lb-ft @ 3500 rpm
Transmission	5-sp. man.
Final drive ratio	3.73:1

CHASSIS

Suspension, f/r	Solid axle/solid axle
Brakes, f/r	disc/drum
Steering	Recirculating ball
Wheels	15 x 7.0 in., steel
Tires	P205/70R15

DIMENSIONS

Wheelbase	2030 mm (79.9 in.)
Overall length	3430 mm (135 in.)
Curb weight	950 kg (2094 lb)
Fuel capacity	40.1 L (10.6 gal)
BASE PRICE	$7995
PRICE AS TESTED	$8945

Somehow, I can't quite see a Ranger setting out to war in the Suzuki SJ 410. A Sloane Ranger, perhaps: but not a US Ranger. And yet, there is a curious affinity between the diminutive 970 cc Japanese designed but Spanish-built Suzuki Santana SJ 410 and the original 2199 cc Willys Jeep MB in which soldiers of virtually all the WW2 Allied armies rode into battle.

Alone among present-day all-terrain 4wd cars, it is the little Suzuki that is commonly referred to as "a jeep", and you don't have to look far to spot the reason why. It is straight out of the same mould as its 1940s American forebear.

Both are no-nonsense vehicles that make little, if any, concessions to the ultimate in comfort. Both have half-elliptic leaf springs at front and rear. Both are high-built, the Suzuki possibly even a little more top-heavy than the Jeep. If the Jeep's big, lazy side-valve engine has the edge on power — 54 bhp net at 4000 rpm compared with the Suzuki's 44 bhp at 5500 rpm — it also has more to propel. Where the Suzuki weighs in at a sylph-like 17.5 cwt, the more heavily-built Willys turns the scales at 21.9 cwt. Where the old-stager gains, though, is in its sheer pulling power. A Jeep driver has 105 lb ft of torque on tap at just 2000 rpm. The Santana can boast only 54 lb ft at 3000 rpm, but evens up the score by possessing five forward gears against the Jeep's three. Both have "on-demand" 4wd, with high and low ratios in the transfer box.

On the road, there is little to choose between them. The Willys "Go Devil" engine was, in its military applications, governed to a speed of 65 mph, and on most Jeeps you'll find a painted reminder not to exceed 55 mph. But the Suzuki is no ball of fire on the tarmac either: it's actually faster in fourth gear than fifth, with maxima of 66 mph and 62 mph respectively.

Both cars are nominal four-seaters, but there the resemblance ends. The Suzuki is equipped with comfortable bucket front seats and small, but adequate, rear seating. The Jeep boasts only thin cushions and backrests (stuffed with horsehair in their original form) thinly covering solid metal seats at the front, and open benches at the rear. And the

driver's seat perches, menacingly, right on top of the fuel tank.

So, the Suzuki is the more comfortable? Well, yes — and no! So far as creature comforts are concerned there is more to recommend it. It has not only good seating, but modern heating and ventilation, and though its canvas hood is time-consuming to remove and re-install it is at least warm and weather-proof inside.

The Jeep, by contrast, is about as spartan as you can get. No heater. No sidescreens — at best, just a canvas hood to form a roof. No doors. Ventilation in plenty, of course, but completely uncontrolled. Of course, there are good historical precedents for making up your own sidescreens. Many units did just that, using anything from canvas or plywood to armour plating. Even so, the MB is never going to be snug.

On both cars, the windscreen can be folded flat on to the bonnet for the ultimate in airflow, but the Jeep has the added attraction of a hinge-open front screen. It may (or may not) also have windscreen wipers, but if they are original-equipment then they will be manually operated.

And yet, it is the Jeep that offers the better ride, both on the road and off. Its suspension has a suppleness that eludes the Suzuki, and though the modern car rides more evenly on the rough than it does on the road it is no match for the Jeep on either type of surface.

Even more surprisingly, the Jeep also wins hands down on actual handling. It shouldn't, because the driving position is daunting. Like all Jeeps, it offers only left-hand drive, and you sit with the large and solid-looking wheel caressing your midriff. You are acutely aware that the non-collapsible steering column is aimed, like a spear, right at your chest. And yet, on road and off, the Jeep responds to its controls easily and obediently.

By contrast, the Suzuki's handling has to be *learned*, and on tarmac it is anything but forgiving. A combination of light weight, stiff springing, and a necessarily sloppy recirculating ball steering system can make the Suzuki quite a handful on indifferent road surfaces, even at town speeds. On the rough, where speeds are low, the Suzuki improves to the point where there is little to choose between the two cars. The Jeep, though, still has the edge.

Not so with the transmission. Here, 40 years of progress cannot be denied. The Suzuki's gearchange is inclined to be notchy, but it is nonetheless light and precise. So, too, is the action of the separate stubby lever that controls the choice of ratios in the transfer box.

With the Jeep, there is usually play in the selectors which can make gear engagement a hit-and-miss affair, while the twin-lever 4wd selector system, with its interlock, can at times be hard to engage. The auxiliary lever next to the long, cranked gearstick engages the drive to the front axle. A second lever, alongside it, selects high or low ratios, and also has a neutral position for power take-off.

When the going gets really rough, which car wins? Though the Suzuki has an enviable reputation for coping with really tricky terrain, it is difficult to imagine it beating the Jeep, which must surely be the all-time champion where cross-country driving is concerned. Its record speaks for itself: from desert to jungle, from the Arctic to the Equator, the Jeep has been there and — what's more — has usually come back. Even 40 years on, it is hard to imagine that one could find any type of surface in Britain that would defeat a determinedly-driven Jeep.

What's more, it is not much given to suffering damage from a hostile environment. Stark it may be — but it is also strong. The body is mounted on a massive ladder-type chassis to form a structure so tough that the US Army actually had to issue detailed instructions on how to destroy a damaged Jeep that would otherwise fall into enemy hands. These involved the use of sledgehammers, axes, petrol, incendiary grenades, or TNT. Normal wear and tear is unlikely to have included any such hazards. . .

So, which to choose for duty as what will almost certainly be either a second car or a fun vehicle? Really, the deciding question is who is to drive it, and for what.

For all its excellence, the Jeep is obviously unsuited as a year-round means of family transport. One's wife could not use it to run the kids to school, on safety grounds alone. As a shopping runabout, it would be a daunting prospect in midwinter. Besides the bitter cold of wind-chill, anybody not dressed in full motorcycle riding kit would soon be soaked to the skin. All Jeeps have holes in the floor. They're there to let the water run out. So, practicality points to the modern Suzuki, at prices ranging from £5950 to £6499. A good Jeep should be about £1000 cheaper.

If, on the other hand, you are seeking a solid slice of history then the Jeep has no peer. It may not actually have won the war, but winning it without this tough and uncomplaining "go-anywhere, go-everywhere" vehicle would have been even harder than it was. It served in every theatre of operations, and everybody who was anybody rode in one. King George VI and Queen Elizabeth. Winston Churchill. Franklin Roosevelt. Every general from Eisenhower and Montgomery down. Even de Gaulle contrived to fold himself up sufficiently to wedge into its front passenger seat, while on the other side of the world Mao Tse-Tung reviewed his troops from the ubiquitous Jeep. It has (in a modified amphibious version) sailed across the Atlantic. It has been a weapon of war, and a potent weapon of peace.

Providing you have adequate alternative transport — the bigger engined Suzuki SJ 413, perhaps? — it's all those associations that could swing your vote in favour of the Jeep.

Our thanks to the National Motor Museum, Beaulieu, whose wartime Jeep is featured here, on location on the Beaulieu Estate.

FORM FOURS

A brand-new all-terrain Suzuki convertible? Or the car that started it all – the original 4wd Willys Jeep? If you've upwards of £5000 to spend you can make your choice. Both will go wherever you ask: but how do they compare? John Thorpe supplies the answers

Above: Civilised amenities in the cabin of the Suzuki, enhanced in the Santana version. Below: The tiny sohc 970 cc engine gives 44 bhp at 5500 rpm

Above: The Jeep makes no concession to creature comforts. Below: Offset to the left, the 2.2-litre Willys side-valve engine produces 54 bhp at 4000 rpm

SUZUKI SIERRA
soft top

TEXT/PICS: RAY BARKER

When BUSHDRIVER last tested the Suzuki Sierra, we reported that it was a great little four-by-four. However, it did have room for improvement in several areas: the seats were too thin, holes in the floor were covered by stick-on patches, and there was considerable engine transmission noise at speed.

Obviously, the Suzuki Motor Co read this magazine. The latest Sierras have more padding in the seats (although they are still low-backed), the stickers have been replaced by real plugs, and a lot of work has gone into eliminating the whine the transmission used to emit at 80 km/h and over. Some Sierras I have driven since the last test were particularly noisy — especially when you took your foot off the throttle at speed and let the vehicle slow without using the brakes. You would have sworn it was a Fokker Friendship taxiing down a runway.

1983 Sierras also get, as standard equipment, free-wheeling hubs and an AM/FM radio instead of the previous AM only unit. In New South Wales, all Suzuki 4WDs are rust-proofed prior to leaving the distributor's warehouse.

The Suzuki pictured here is the SJ410R or more commonly known as the "half-door soft top". There are two soft-top models — the "half-door" that has a waist-high steel door plus a clip-on side curtain, and the "full-door" which has a similar door to the hard-top and the wind-up windows. Sierra hard-tops and soft-tops are available with either 600 x 16 cross-ply bar tread tyres or steel radial multi-purpose tyres on 15" white spoke sports wheels. If you order the sports wheel model you also get very neat rubber guard extensions. You cannot order a new vehicle with bar tread tyres and flares. Remarkably, the guards on the sports wheel model are a different stamping from those on the narrow wheel model. Therefore, if you want the flares, it is not a simple job of ordering the parts and then screwing them straight on.

The Sierra engine is an enlarged version of the type used in Suzuki 4WDs since the introduction of the LJ80 model in 1977. However, the difference in performance between the old 797cc job and the Sierra's 997cc powerplant is significant, especially when you consider that the Sierra is also slightly larger overall than the model it replaces. Around town, the performance is brisk. The Suzuki accelerates in time with most suburban traffic, and seems happiest when spinning along at 80 km/h. Its perkiness and ability to weave in and out of heavy traffic provide probably the main reason why it has become a popular city commuter. A good percentage of sales appear to be to buyers who have no intention of taking them into the bush.

The Sierra's short overall length, economy, roomy cargo area and the visibility afforded by the high seating position have made it an attractive vehicle for city and suburban courier work and as a "shopping basket for mum".

The Sierra can also put up a surprisingly good highway average. Top is around 120 km/h, although the engine sounds much happier back at 100 km/h. In fact, it is the engine and drivetrain noise that trick the driver into believing that the motor is working hard — a legacy of not having any sound-proofing or floor-covering apart from the very thin vinyl mats.

At speed, the sound of the engine can also have the driver reaching for 4th gear when he's already in it. A five-speed overdrive box and sound-damp-ening material or carpet would trans-form the Sierra and make it a much more pleasant place on a long trip. Unfortunately, it appears that the Suzuki Motor Co do not have a five-speed on their priority list, and even the new, long-wheelbase version will come only as a four-speeder. Yet, I find it hard to believe that a company as progressive and "switched-on" as Suzuki does not have a new gearbox somewhere in the pipeline — especially when you consider that the majority of 4WD manufacturers have introduced five-speeders in the past year.

The ride is something that you must get used to in such a short-wheelbase, stiffly-sprung vehicle. Over corrugations, the Sierra bounces rather than bumps, and the driver and passenger must relax and go with the vehicle rather than fighting it. Tense up, and you tire very quickly and could end up with sore neck and back muscles.

Of course, the Suzuki doesn't pretend to be a limo. It is designed for short hauls and for serious off-road conditions. It is also the lowest-priced 4WD on the market.

In fact, because it is the lowest-priced four wheeler, it is surprising to find that standard equipment includes free-wheeling hubs, radio, rust-proofing, reclining bucket seats, tripmeter and the option of factory-fitted sports wheels, radials and flares.

From May '83, all Sierras will be fitted with disc brakes on the front axle, AM/FM radio, roll-bar-mounted interior light and (subject to ADR approval) an optional factory-built rear bench seat.

The soft-top vehicle used for the BUSHDRIVER test had the half-doors and clip-on side curtains. Apparently this is the least popular version of the Sierra, while the full-door soft-top is very much in demand. After living with the test car for two weeks, I can understand why, for, while the soft-top itself is great, those side curtains are a real pain. The clear vinyl windows warp and buckle, resulting in poor vision — especially at night. Add a drop of rain, and the situation is ten times worse. It is also difficult to get your hand out in a hurry to pay a toll or something similar. None of those problems would exist on the wind-up window version.

Where the half-door does score is the odd time you may want to rip the roof off and drop the windscreen. In this form, the half-door looks fantastic. If you lower the screen on the full-door, the door window frames stick up into the air like Mickey Mouse ears. And, if you intend running on dusty roads with the top off, it is far better to have the windscreen down. With the screen up, it sucks all the dust into the vehicle and over the occupants.

In the bush, the Sierra is in its element. It is easy to handle and very forgiving. Because of its compact size and excellent ground clearance it can weave its way in, out, over and under obstacles that would bring larger vehicles to a halt. I'm sure that, as a working vehicle on a property, the Sierra would make work feel like fun.

There are some areas that could do with improvement —

(a) The floor mats are a joke. They are too thin and come away from their clips at the slightest suggestion of usage. Even in a budget-priced passenger car they would be unacceptable.

(b) The soft-top can be removed and replaced quickly, but, if you want to lower the windscreen, you have to remove eight screws that hold the bars between the top of the screen and the roll-bar. It's time consuming and you run the risk of losing the bars or the screws. There must be a simpler way of holding the support bars in place.

(c) The big front bumper looks impressive but it could be a nuisance in country where mud sticks to everything. Mud caked inside the boxy bumper would be extremely difficult to remove.

The fuel-consumption check was carried out over 800 kms of metropolitan stop-start motoring — the worst conditions you could imagine for an economy check, yet the Sierra produced 9.2 l/100 km (30.9 mpg). It would be difficult to get a poorer figure unless you subjected the vehicle to extensive low-range work.

It is interesting to find that the Sierra with its "big" 970cc four-cylinder

SUZUKI SIERRA   SPECIFICATIONS

HALF METAL DOOR TYPE

DIMENSIONS			ENGINE	
			Type	Four-stroke cycle, water-cooled, OHC
Overall length	3410 mm (134.3 in)		Number of cylinders	Four
	(6.00-16-4PR)		Lubrication system	Wet sump
	3430 mm (135.0 in)		Bore	65.5 mm (2.58 in)
	(FR78-15, F78-15)		Stroke	72.0 mm (2.83 in)
Overall width	1395 mm (54.9 in)		Piston displacement	970 cm^3 (970 cc, 59.2 cu. in)
	(6.00-16-4PR)			
	1460 mm (57.5 in)		**POWER TRANSMISSION**	
	(FR78-15, F78-15)		Transmission type	4-forward all synchromesh, 1 reverse
Overall height	1690 mm (66.5 in)			
	(6.00-16-4PR)			
	1680 mm (66.1 in)		Transfer gearbox type	2-speed constant mesh
	(FR78-15, F78-15)		**WHEEL &**	
Wheelbase	2030 mm (79.9 in)		**SUSPENSION**	
Load deck size:			Tyre size	
Length	870 mm (34.3 in)		Front & Rear	6.00-16-4PR or
Width	1270 mm (50.0 in)			(FR78-15, F78-15)
Height	1020 mm (40.2 in)		Suspension type	
Ground clearance	240 mm (9.4 in)		Front & Rear	Leaf spring with double action damper
	(6.00-16-4PR)			
	230 mm (9.1 in)		**STEERING**	
	(FR78-15, F78-15)		Turning radius	4.9 m (16.1 ft)
WEIGHT			Steering gearbox	Ball nut
Curb weight	800 kg (1764 lbs)		**BRAKE SYSTEM**	
Gross vehicle weight	1250 kg (2756 lbs)		Type	4-wheel, hydraulic
Seating capacity	Two persons		Wheel brake,	
PERFORMANCE			Front	Two-leading
Maximum horsepower	33.5 kW (45.0 HP)		Rear	Leading and trailing
	at 5500 r/min.		**CAPACITIES**	
	(SAE net)		Fuel tank	40 L
Maximum torque	73.5 Nm (7.5 kg.m,			(10.6/8.8
	54.2 lb-ft)			US/Imp gal)
	at 3000 r/min		Engine oil	3.0 L (6.3/5.3
	(SAE net)			US/Imp pt)

engine is more economical than the original Suzuki 540cc two-stroke that was introduced way back in 1974. Years ago I did a check on an LJ50 in similar conditions and found that it returned 10.6 l/100 km (27 mpg). With the LJ50 you also have to add the cost of the two-stroke oil it burns continuously. Who says they don't build 'em like they used to?

The secret to the Suzuki's combination of performance and economy is its modern, highly-developed engine. It incorporates the latest thinking in the form of an overhead cam, cross-flow head, hemispherical combustion chambers and typical Japanese thoroughness in layout and finish.

Also well thought out is the ancillary equipment. The electrics are high and back near the firewall away from dirt and water. The air inlet for the air-cleaner is also right up near the firewall. There is plenty of room between the radiator core and the grille so that a slight impact at the front should not mean costly damage.

The Suzuki Sierra may be basic transportation to some, but for many it is a superb little runabout that can double as a fun car or a work-horse. And it has one feature that many vehicles cannot offer, regardless of price: The Sierra looks and feels like a friend.

STABLE PROPOSITION

The latest model Suzuki jeep, the SJ413 JX, known as the Samurai, boasts some major changes in the suspension and dimension departments. **Paul Chudecki** tests a Janspeed turbocharged version

There might be some people in the United States and the UK who would like to see Suzuki's Samurai given the chop, but if the version imported to the UK is anything to go by, it seems a case of much ado about nothing. The main difference between the Samurai, the name given to the new SJ413V JX, and the previous 413 Suzukis lies in the suspension, the track having been widened by 3.5 inches front and rear, the springs softened and the anti-roll bar stiffened, together with revised damper settings and lower profile tyres. The idea is to improve the Suzuki's on-road ride as well as reducing excessive body-roll. Unfortunately 79 US Samurais are claimed to have suffered roll-overs, resulting in 16 deaths, with the vehicle's

as such had received the Wiltshire company's excellent engine package which increases power by no less than 40 per cent. The off-roader was thus capable of greater speeds than standard, but still the package gave absolutely no cause for concern at any time – of course increased power can give more advantages than simply increasing speed, particularly in off-road machinery.

In standard form, Suzuki's 1324 cc four-cylinder produces 63 bhp at 6000 rpm with peak torque of 74 lbs/ft realised at 3500 rpm. As anyone who has driven a 413 – or the 410, where this is even more evident – will know, the popular 4×4's biggest handicap is poor acceleration and lack of low down torque. True, this may be of less consequence for those who use their SJs purely on the road, but for those who regularly go off-road, it is a definite shortcoming and one which Suzuki seems unwilling to overcome. What the simple Janspeed Stage 1 conversion does is to supply those missing horses in such a way that both on and off-road capabilities are enhanced. Unlike the Stage 1 conversion for the SJ410, where the 970 cc engine's

● **The track is 3.5 inches wider front and rear**

high centre of gravity and wheelbase dimensions cited as the probable causes. Having spent a week with the latest UK Samurai, all I can say is it's extremely difficult to believe that these figures relate to excessively bad handling. You would need to be driving extremely badly to turn one of these vehicles over.

It is significant that the Samurai tested belonged to Janspeed Engineering and

● **The Janspeed conversion produces an extra 24 bhp**

power is pushed to 70 bhp, an increase of over 50 per cent, on the 413's alloy motor the cylinder head is left completely standard, the 87 bhp being produced courtesy of a Weber 32/34 DMTL carburettor, extractor exhaust manifold and freeflow exhaust system – indeed it thus produces 63 bhp at the wheels rather than at the flywheel. The 24 bhp increase is produced at 5000 rpm, a useful 1000 rpm lower than the normal engine's peak while torque is upped to 97 lbs/ft at the same rpm as the standard engine's peak torque. More importantly, the Janspeed version produces a useful

● **Revised dashboard**

● **8.1 inches ground clearance**

91 lbs/ft at 3000 rpm (and at 5000 rpm where the standard engine starts to tail off with 66 lbs/ft) while the figure of 79 lbs/ft at 2000 rpm is still five pounds greater than the standard engine's figure at this speed. Equally, at 5500 rpm torque is 81 lbs/ft compared to 57.

The complete Stage 1 package, inclusive of £160 for fitting, costs £683 though its components can be fitted separately, offering varying degrees of improved performance. For example, the exhaust manifold and system alone cost £94 and £95 respectively and are said to give a 21 per cent increase, the remaining increase coming from the Weber kit costing £294.

On the road, it is immediately evident that acceleration is improved over standard – revised gear ratios compensate for the lower profile tyres – with much-improved low down response, causing more than a few people to be startled at the Suzuki's uncharacteristic pace. When I last drove a Janspeed converted SJ 413 I commented that the extra power highlighted the otherwise standard vehicle's chassis shortcomings such as excessive body-roll thanks to the long vertical wheel movement. This time there was no such complaint, the combination of increased track and a stiffer anti-roll bar reducing body-roll to a marked extent. The ride has also been improved on the Samurai, the softer springs and the road-type tyres without chunky sidewalls and with greater grip noticeably lessening the tendency of other SJ variants to bounce around. At high speed, however, there is still the problem of stability, the slab-sided little Suzuki being severely affected by cross winds and the turbulence of large commercial vehicles.

Turning to the controls, the faster setting of the two-speed wipers was not able to cope with heavy rain. This standard fitment on the Samurai also has an intermittent setting and the indicator stalk on this 2000-mile old vehicle would only self-cancel on one side and the washers would not work due to a pinched pipe behind the revised

dashboard. The latter is another of the other interior differences of the Samurai together with a new four-spoke steering wheel, though our example had Janspeed's own leather-covered item (£115) which obscured the all important 20 to 60 mph segment of the speedometer. The seats have pleasant new trim colour options, with the rears now split so that they can be individually folded, and a heated rear window is standard. The heater itself is also said to be improved though we had little cause to use it, unlike the sunroof which was opened on several occasions. Strangely, although equipped with a tow-hitch, a nearside door mirror does not appear to be a standard fitment. Externally, the Samurai is distinguishable by colour co-ordinated wheel arch extensions, which with the wider track give it a chunkier look, and body side protection mouldings (shared with the new SJ 410 Sport).

The opening of the heavens during our typically British summer had turned our photographic location of the Sweetwoods off-road centre in Kent into a quagmire. Once photographer Hodson realised it was not such a good idea to photograph the Suzuki standing next to the muddy puddle I was driving through, we ventured into the fields of this off-road haven, reached via steep and rutted paths. It was clear the boulevardier-oriented 205/70 R15 Dunlops were not up to much in these sort of conditions, the narrow tread pattern quickly clogging with mud. However, we never got stuck, now with four-wheel drive and low ratio engaged on the transfer box – the optional free-wheeling hubs were not fitted. Despite the lower profile tyres the Samurai still retains over eight inches of ground clearance and, as with other SJs, the semi-elliptic springs combined with plenty of vertical wheel movement make for unfussed progress over deep ruts and steep banks, delayed only by the inadequate tyres.

Progress was also enhanced by the greater torque of the modified engine and its wide, flat curve, the improvement

low down the rev range not only helping to pull the Samurai through axle-deep sludge, but also increasing the effectiveness of engine braking down the steep slippery slopes. As with on-road performance with high ratio engaged, In low ratio there is less need to use the gears themselves and the extra acceleration here also ensures noticeably faster progress across rough terrain.

Back on the road, this latest SJ 413 certainly seems a more driveable vehicle, less of a compromise and more civilised in its road manners. The brakes – disc front, drum rear and with the handbrake now operative on the rear wheels rather than the transfer gearbox – are very effective and with noticeably less body-roll and the wider track, road-holding and handling are much improved. The vague steering, while still a little slow, has a steering, while still a little slow, has a better feel due to the stickier low profile better feel due to the stickier low profile tyres. With the harder springing of previous models and knobbly tyres, there was a tendency for the back end to break away quite suddenly when cornering at speed, though it was always easily recoverable. Now the breakaway is less sudden, again helped also by better tyre grip, and I found the Samurai could be cornered at speed pretty hard without drama, though still the trait of lifting the inside rear wheel remains, albeit at higher cornering speeds than before. In normal road driving, of course, one is unlikely to push the little Samurai so hard, but it does suggest that to turn one of these vehicles over when in normal road use, one would have to be driving recklessly. Any problems encountered on the road will no doubt be when those in supposed control expect the chassis to respond like that of a standard road car. As we have said before, the increased performance of the Janspeed package could increase such a person's chances of becoming unstuck, but such a person is unlikely to be interested in conversions or even have heard of Janspeed Engineering, let alone *Off Road and 4 Wheel Drive*!

As for the Samurai itself, it seems a worthy addition to the SJ line-up with better road manners, improved looks and levels of trim, great value for money, though like other 413 versions it is still a little too underpowered in standard guise. The simple Janspeed conversion adequately makes up for that deficit.

● **The combination of increased track and stiffened anti-roll bar improves handling**

Technical Specification

Suzuki SJ413 JX Samurai

Engine	
	Water-cooled, four cylinder, four stroke with single OHC, cast iron block and aluminium head
Capacity	1324 cc
Bore/Stroke	74.0 mm × 77.0 mm
Max power	(Standard form) 63 bhp at 6000 rpm (Janspeed conversion) 87 bhp at 5000 rpm
Max torque	(Standard) 73.7 lbf.ft. at 3500 rpm
Fuel System	(Standard) Single, side draught carburettor

Transmission	
	Five-speed, all synchromesh primary gear box with remotely mounted, two-speed, part-time transfer case
1st	3.562:1
2nd	1.947:1
3rd	1.423:1
4th	1.000:1
5th	0.795:1
Reverse	3.466:1
Transfer Ratios	
High	1.409:1
Low	2.268:1
Final Drive	3.909:1

Suspension	
Front	Live axle with single parabolic leaf springs and telescopic dampers
Rear	Live axle with two-stage parabolic leaf springs and telescopic dampers incorporating anti-roll bar

Brakes	
	Servo-assisted hydraulically operated discs at the front with drums on the rear. Parking brake actuates independent drum on rear output of transfer case

Wheels	
	5.5 × 15

Tyres	
	195SR15

Steering	
	Recirculating ball (manual)

Principal dimensions	
Length	135.4 in (3440 mm)
Width	60.2 in (1530 mm)
Height	65.9 in (1675 mm)
Wheelbase	79.9 in (2030 mm)
Track Front	51.2 in (1300 mm)
Track Rear	51.6 in (1310 mm)
Ground clearance	8.1 in (205 mm)
Approach Angle	48 degrees
Departure Angle	39 degrees
Turning Circle	5.1 m (16.7 ft)
Kerb Weight	1958 lb (890 kg)
GVW	2750 lb (1250 kg)
Towing	Unbraked 980 lb (445 kg) Braked 2200 lb (1000 kg)
Fuel Tank Capacity	8.8 gallons (40 litres) 2 star
Fuel Consumption	Average for duration of test 24.9 mpg
Price	£7399 inclusive of Car Tax & VAT

SHARPER

SAMURAI

Suzuki's little off-roaders have been much in the news recently, standing accused of a distressing tendency to fall over if driven incorrectly. Surely that makes them one of the last vehicles suitable for tuning for extra power and performance? Well it's true that the SJs have toppled from time to time but that's a reflection more on their drivers than the machine itself; the only inherent fault (if indeed you can call it that) the little jeep has is one shared by all relatively tall narrow-tracked off-roaders. So if the Suzuki is flawed so are the rest of its kind. You simply can't drive them the same way as a Lotus.

The SJ has only a very small engine, so it could do with some more power right? That was a view we were guilty of, assuming that it was still pushed along by an engine of under one litre. The first SJs sold here over ten eyars ago did have just 970 cc to power them but the vehicle has rather grown up since then, to the extent that, as we noted in Focus last month, there's now a 1.6-litre engine in the Suzuki line up. The SJ413 we drove fell between the two extremes, being powered by a 1.3-litre all-alloy overhead-cam four with a bore of 74mm and a stroke of 77mm giving a displacement of 1324cc. There's the standard two valves per cylinder and a compression ratio of 8.8:1.

As you can see, there's nothing really fancy about the engine and hence nothing spectacular about its power output of 63bhp at 5000rpm. That's reasonable but hardly outstanding in these days of small multi-valve Japanese screamers, Suzuki themselves providing a good example of those with the 1.3-litre 6-valve four from the Swift GT which cranks out 101 bhp. But you need less outrageous engines for off-road use and Janspeed's conversion is a sensible conversion of a sensible engine. There's no justification or place for high-lift cams or fancy reworked cylinder heads and Janspeed have concentrated on the basics of getting more air and fuel into the engine and more exhaust out of it. The standard carburettor is discarded in favour of a single twin-choke downdraught Weber 32/34 DMTL. The second part of the exercise is Janspeed's speciality — the incorporation of an extractor exhaust manifold and free flowing exhaust system. As with most production cars, the Suzuki's cast-iron manifold is no great shakes, although not as poor as some. The real restriction, however, comes in the rest of the system, for example in the particularly large silencer box.

The tuned replacement consists of tubular four-into-two-into one extractor manifold attached to a far less restrictive system with a really miniscule front expansion box which is more of a bulge in the pipe than a box proper. The rearmost box is a substantial size but of course it's a straight-through affair.

Four-into-two-into-one manifolds, as we've discovered with the TR7

Distinguishing marks on the Janspeed conversion include alloy Compomotive wheels, a leather rimmed Janspeed steering wheel *(middle)* and the four-branch exhaust manifold *(above)*. With just a manifold, exhaust and carb change, the engine output rises from 63 to 87bhp – an excellent improvement. The plane *(left)* incidentally is courtesy of the Museum of Army Flying at Middle Wallop

(p63) increase torque significantly whereas for outright top-end power a four-into-one arrangement is the one to go for. A glance at the power and torque curves on p47 shows clearly that extra torque; from 3000rpm up there's very significant increase of the order of 20lb ft. What's more, it doesn't tail off at higher engine speeds, being more or less the same shape as the standard curve, just a little flatter.

Increasing maximum torque from 76lb at 4000rpm to 97lb at the same rpm is very impressive, as is the increase in outright power, from 63bhp at 5000rpm to 87bhp, also at 5000rpm. That's rather more like the output appropriate to a modern 1.3-litre four. It's been done with no penalty at low engine speeds either as both power and torque are up from 2000rpm.

Any self-respecting off-roader has simple rugged suspension and the SJ413 is no exception with live axles front and rear, suspended and located by semi-elliptic leaf springs which are still deservedly in use off-road where inter-leaf friction provides some useful extra damping. The front features two long leaves on top of one shorter and more substantial leaf. The rear is a variation on the same theme, having three leaves per side on top of a very short stiff leaf. It still sounds crude but in practice it's far superior to the early SJs which were set up tremendously stiff with virtually zero compliance, making them almost undriveable on anything but an ordinary metaled road. These days the suspension actually moves . . . .

Janspeed haven't had to do much to it, keeping the same sprint rates, merely switching to adjustable Spax gas dampers front and rear. You could argue the new wheels — 7 x 15in alloy Compomotives — are a suspension change too, reducing unsprung weight. Unfortunately the Compomotives are shod with Japanese Dunlop SP Qualifiers of 205/70 R15 section. They did not seem to be the right tyres to bring out the best in Suzuki's simple chassis.

The other Janspeed modifications are mostly cosmetic — the thick leather-bound Janspeed steering wheel is very nice indeed . . . and so it should be at £115. A nudge bar (£110) livens up the front of the SJ, the sunroof (£260) was hardly relevant on a day when the cloud was at rooftop level and as we drove only in the daylight (what there was of it) the driving lights (£48) were left unused. A tow bar (£155) was also fitted, presumably making the point about the SJ's extra torque.

All of those bits are incidental really, what of the cost of those mods that really count? Fitted, the manifold, exhaust and carb (along with gaskets and new plugs) comes to £683. That climbs to £785 when VAT is taken into account. That's not bad at all for a power increase of 40 per cent. Is it noticeable on the road? In relatively low-powered cars such as the SJ such a percentage increase is bound to be felt. The engine note gives the game away immediately; it's deeper, far more purposeful and it doesn't mislead as the SJ413 is now quite a brisk performer. A 0-60 time of just under 15 secs doesn't sound much to shout about, until you recall that the standard jeep is taking almost 20 seconds to reach the same speed. The in-gear times have been absolutely transformed; the eternity the standard car takes to travel from 50-70 in top (26 secs . . .) has been shortened by over 10 secs while the Janspeed tweaks mean that the SJ really can sprint effectively — 30-50 in third taking a mere 6.7 seconds compared with 8.4 secs for the standard car which is an excellent improvement — the SJ is only supposed to be a utility vehicle after all. Of course its four-wheel drive helps give excellent off-the-line traction; it may not look as spectacular as a front-drive hatchback in full wheelspin mode but it's very effective and the Suzuki gets going with no fuss at all.

Maximum speed has been greatly improved too; there was plenty of scope for that it's true with the best that the standard SJ could manage being a rousing 75mph. Janspeed maintain that a top speed of over 100mph is now a reality and they are right as it proved possible to wind the speedo well past its 95mph limit. That really is an academic exercise, however; Janspeed don't recommend it and nor do we . . . . But the fact that it can get over 100 means that its realistic cruising speed has been upped considerably. You can now trip (sorry . . .) happily along at 85mph or so without feeling that you are guilty of cruelty to inanimate objects. It's not all that noisy either as the gearing is reasonably high at 18mph per 1000rpm in 4H or 2H and at 80mph the SJ is ticking along at very near peak power rpm.

You can't pretend that the Suzuki is in its element at speed on the motorway but the main culprit for the noise is not the engine or those large tyres but the optional fabric sunroof which makes the same irritating and depressing noise as torrential rain beating against the car, so we would give that a miss.

Driving this SJ is no problem, the fairly simple modifications have not made the engine in the least intractable — in fact they have improved it in every aspect. Flooring the throttle at almost any speed in any gear produces no fluffing or hesitation, merely a nice smooth increase in power.

The long gearlever operates a precise change which is heavier than most slick Japanese car changes but is easy and quick enough to use while feeling robust enough for an off-road vehicle. The action of the transfer lever, which is mounted to the rear of the gearlever, is rather more awkward but then it doesn't have to be moved with anything like the same frequency.

Normal drive is 2H, in other words high-ratio two-wheel drive. 4H gives the same ratios but to all four

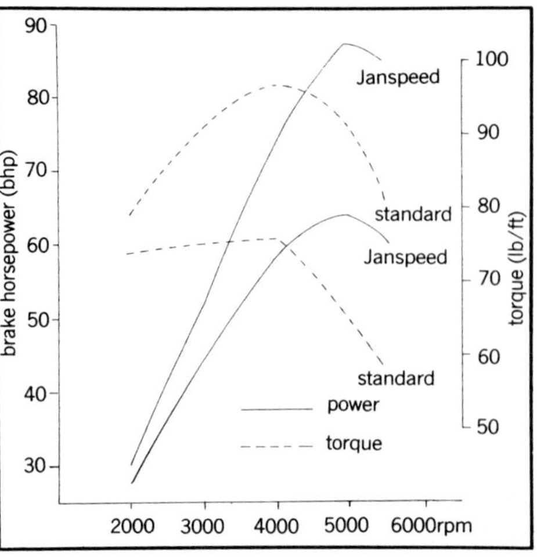

Changes such as the Compomotive alloys and the Janspeed nudge bar (middle) show that this SJ is out of the ordinary and the graph (left) proves the point conclusively

wheels although, unlike more exotic 4WD macines, its four-wheel drive is reserved for off-road or wet and slippery conditions on ordinary roads and there it makes a tremendous difference, making the SJ feel far more stable and secure. There's a list of dos and don'ts for the 4WD which is one of the penalties of simple systms. You have to be at a standstill to shift from 4H to 4L (not that that's usually a problem) and the handbook advises you that you must have the front wheels pointing straight ahead and the front hubs locked when changing from 2H to 4H but these are merely things to bear in mind rather than criticisms.

In 4L the ratios really *are* low, and the extra power now available allows you to play an amusing game with them. Find a distinct slope to climb, put the SJ in 4L first gear, take your feet off the pedals and sit back while the Suzuki climbs away just on tickover . . . . A neat trick but really 4L is designed just for awkward off-road conditions and thanks to reasonable compliance in the long-travel suspension and the extra power the SJ can be considered a proper off-roader; it isn't a Range- or Land Rover it's true but it certainly isn't the toy it used to be. The chassis and suspension are both tough enough to ensure a good working life; you re not bounced all over the place on broken surfaces and the power allied to a wide set of gear ratios means its climbing ability is high, as is its ability to extricate itself from sticky situations. It would be higher with proper off-road tyres of course; it didn't take long at all for the Dunlops fitted to be packed with mud during our off-road experiments.

But not many SJs *are* used as serious off-road vehicles; it's become a minior cult vehicle, a sort of poor man's Range Rover and hence the cabin is quite nicely appointed with comfortable, if small, front seats, proper trim and a surprising amount of room in the rear. Instrumentation is clear and adequate with a speedo showing up to 95mph, a tach reading to 8000rpm, red-lined at 6500, and between the two a water temperature and fuel gauge. Missing is the little gimmick present in the last SJ we drove, the inclinometer — a device that showed how far you had tilted the car and how far there was to go. Suzuki would presumably rather not draw attention to such things these days. It bears repeating that this isn't a problem for the sensible driver; swing the SJ hard into a corner under heavy braking and you may well go over (particularly as this SJ's brakes are very fierce and the rears can easily be locked) but in general you get enough feedback from the chassis to be well aware of its limits and adjusting to the handling of a high live-axled vehicle doesn't take long.

So the Janspeed conversion works very well but surely the Suzuki is an odd choice for the treatment? Odd yes, but it was also right as there's been great demand from Suzuki owners worldwide much to Janspeed's delight. ∎

BIG BROTHER
1300cc MUSCLE

The 413 offers a far bigger engine, and some trim changes, but does that make it better than the Santana?

The SJ413 has been around since 1985, and immediately proved popular with the Suzuki driver wanting a little more punch under his right foot. Despite the extra ccs, however, the 413 isn't really the vast improvement over the 410 everyone thought it would be. It also gave away Suzuki's subtle, but noticable (to those who took the 413 off-road) concessions to on-road users.

That was basically that the ratios in the transfer box, unique to the 413 were far higher than those used for the 410, and suddenly controlled downhill descents become a thing of the past.

On-road of course this didn't really matter, and the extra power provided by the 1324cc engine (63 bhp@6000rpm and 73.7lb ft torque@3500 rpm) gave the 413 substantially more 'driveability' than before. Linked to a five speed gearbox, with the same overdrive fifth gear ratio as the Santana, high speed driving became a relaxed matter, with the 413 pulling just over 4000 rpm at 70 mph. Even so, fifth gear was still too high for the 413 to cruise at a constant speed, and drive's found that frequent downchanges to fourth were required to keep up with the traffic.

Visually, the 413 was distinguished by a stylish bonnet bulge to cover the taller engine, a new all-plastic front grille, and black plastic hub covers at the centre of the familiar spoked wheels.

Inside, the dashboard was graced by a rev counter, and Recaro-style fabric seating gave the front seat occupants more comfort. Available in this country in hard top form only (the SJF413V JX), you could also im-port (via dealers) a soft top version, the SJ413 JX. The latter has proved to be immensely popular.

Nothing much has changed with the advent of the Samurai, except detail alterations covered in our new model preview.

A better driver's car

As a driver's car, the 413 is better than the 410 and Santana, of that there is no mistake. The 1324cc engine features a hollow crankshaft to keep weight to a minimum, but with that Suzuki has lost the sweet scream of the 970cc unit. Instead, the crankshaft echoes all manner of grumbles from the bottom end, making the engine rough and 'clapped' sounding! At the top of the rev range, things get even louder, and it's an unpleasant engine to work hard. Even so, the extra power is most evident.

The ride quality, however, is a vast improvement, with multi-leaf elliptic springs smoothing out the ride noticeably. Better aftermarket shock absorbers make the 413 almost as smooth riding as a conventional saloon. Braking performance is excellent too, with a nicely weighted servo to add plenty of bite.

Off-road, the 413 is as agile as the Santana, but only just. Its higher gearing, even in low ratio, makes a meal of hill climbing, whereas a Santana will scamble up just about anything. Coming down, it's a matter of gently applying the handbrake to make up for the loss in engine braking — a bit radical, but it works if you're careful!

On level ground, low ratio work is still limited to first gear, and the 413 is more susceptible to irritating geartrain shunt than its smaller engined brother. Every other characteristic is as per the Santana.

1300cc might give the little SJ more muscle, but at a cost, in overall performance terms, that is hard to justify. ●

ON THE LIMIT

What every good Suzuki jeep needs is 150bhp, so thought Terry Fry and Andrew Pettitt, and with the help of Alan Allard achieved just that . . . with a stunning appearance to match

There's a lot of interest in tuning Suzuki jeeps, so said Janspeed when we tried their relatively mildly tweaked Samurai (*Performance Tuning*, January '89). Well they would say that wouldn't they? In fact they were right and just to show you how much here's an example of the most radically altered Suzuki SJ413 you are likely to come across on the road. You might encounter it at Santa Pod or perhaps the Chelsea Cruise but you won't find it in the jeep's supposed normal off-road habitat. This Suzuki is designed to look good . . . and go even better, rather than wallow in glorious mud and in fact it does not even operate in four-wheel drive format any longer.

The main man behind the project is Terry Fry from Leighton Buzzard and the most obvious first question to him was 'why a Suzuki'? Simply to prove that anything can be made to go fast and the results must have surpassed his wildest dreams and along the way have vastly increased his respect for Japanese engineering in general and Suzuki engineering in particular.

The latest SJ413 secured, Terry started looking around for some way to make it go faster; the man to provide the answer was Alan Allard, son of the famous Sydney, but a super- and turbocharging expert of long standing and some renown in his own right (and author of *Turbocharging and Supercharging*). Where Sydney's route to power was via enormous Mercury and Cadillac V8s shoehorned into some fearsome roadsters, Alan's is clearly different and his current interest is in giving some extra sparkle to a variety of off-road 4x4s.

In this case the extra sparkle consisted primarily of a Garrett AiResearch T2. That's the small one which lacks the water cooled centre bearing of its bigger brothers and so requires drivers to treat it sensibly, idling the engine for a few moments rather than shutting it down while still stinking hot, thus allowing the oil to cook. Terry does that, and uses Amsoil synthetic oil into the bargain for some extra protection.

Fuel is fed from a Weber DHTT down-draught carburettor and the exhaust system is a 2in bore stainless steel affair. The free-flow four-branch exhaust manifold itself, of course, has to be specially fabricated to take the turbo while the

Weber fits onto an adaptor allowing the original inlet manifold to be retained. Over the carb fits a cast alloy plenum chamber, connected to the air filter via a rubber hose.

But surely you cannot simply bolt-on a turbo to a modern high-compression engine and get away with it? In this case, apparently you can .... The engine concerned is Suzuki's all-alloy overhead cam four of 1341cc, a displacement given by the bore of 74mm and stroke of 77mm. With a compression ratio of 8.8:1 a fairly ordinary 63bhp is generated at 5000rpm; as we'll see shortly, that figure is left so far behind after these and the next set of modifications that you might be tempted to think it's a misprint (it isn't).

Allard claim another 25 per cent power from this, their Stage 2 conversion, as the power graph demonstrates. Their performance figures show the SJ413's 0-60 time falling from 15.8 secs to 13.6, the 0-70 time dropping from 23.6 to 19.8 and significant improvements being shown in the in-gear times — 40-60mph in fourth for example being improved by a second and a half, from 12.7 to 11.2.

The only problem encountered with this first stage of the conversion was some pre-ignition and detonation on 7.5 to 8.5psi boost, a problem Terry Fry solved by fitting an EMS 6 automatic ignition retard device. Retarding the ignition is literally a retrograde step and obviously not the ideal solution. Clearly the intake charge had to be kept colder, requiring an intercooler. With no off-the-shelf intercooler available it was a matter of having one made specially, by Turbo Technics who certainly know what they are doing.

Allard themselves now offer an intercooled conversion in the form of their Turbospeed kit, from £1045 plus VAT which increases power a full 50 per cent and the performance difference is dramatic — according to Allard's figures on the Samurai the reduction in 0-60mph times is almost 7 seconds, down from 17.5 to 10.7secs while the 50-70 time is slaughtered; from 17 secs it plummets to 8.6.

With the intercooler fitted and the car set-up on Autocraft of Houghton Regis's rolling road the Suzuki proved to be respectably rapid at Santa Pod, which was particularly satisfying given the doubting looks that had been cast towards that most unusual of vehicles, a performance jeep ....

On the basis that you can never have too much performance, Terry took another look at Alan Allard's performance menu and selected a head modification which lowered the compression ratio to allow even more boost, up to 10.5psi in this instance. This changed the Suzuki from being respectably quick to 'very, very fast' in Terry's words, and although detonation was still a problem to begin with, that was sorted out sufficiently for the SJ to return some outstanding standing quarter mile times, with a best of 17.55secs and a terminal speed of 74.23mph. To shove as unaerodynamic a shape as a jeep through air at those speeds, or rather with that acceleration, requires a considerable amount of power and the rolling road reveals that 118bhp is produced from Andrew Pettitt's example (the two jeeps are essentially the same, with variations such as Terry's having the bigger intercooler).

To show 118bhp at the wheels is actually more impressive than you might at first think in that the intercooler really isn't doing its job when the vehicle is standing still because although most rolling roads have large fans to pump cold air over the engine they can't match the wind generated by the car concerned driving along the road. Secondly, the transmission losses must be far greater with the Suzuki (or any 4wd vehicle) because the drive is going through the transfer

The two SJ413s *(above left)* make almost a matched pair but they do differ in detail, as do the two engines with Terry's *(left)* having the larger intercooler

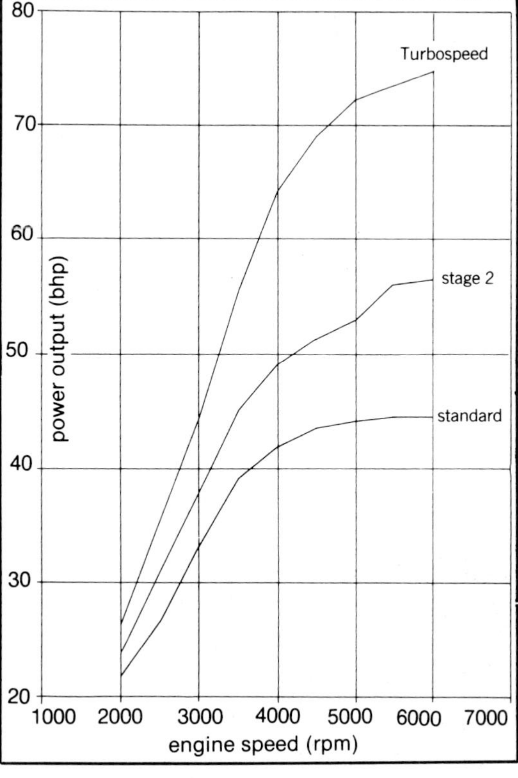

The truly enormous tyres are clearly apparent from the rear view *(above)*; if anything the tyres are too big, but they certainly look the part. Air brushed graphics are not to everyone's taste but these are done superbly *(left & below left)*.

The graph *(far left)* shows the considerable improvement over standard of the Allard conversions. The figures are for the 'standard' conversion; these two jeeps have had a little extra over that, in lowering the compression yet further to allow a higher boost pressure. The American-style number plates' illegality has been kindly overlooked by the local constabulary *(top right)*. The interiors of both are finished with leather trim to an extremely high standard *(right)*. The various component parts of the Allard conversion are laid out *(bottom right)* 'box as well as the gearbox so we can assume there's rather more than the usual 25 per cent or so loss to take into account. That, with the intercooler aspect just mentioned, means that flywheel output should be around the 150bhp mark — or, in other words, over twice as much as standard. Not only is that an impressive bit of tuning but it says a great deal for the Suzuki engine as the bottom end has been left totally untouched. Not only does the engine take what's dished out to it in its stride but then neither the gearbox nor the transfer box have protested and the halfshafts have stayed in one piece. It's not as though the two jeeps are pampered; both drivers are keen to see just what sort of acceleration and performance they can achieve and there has consequently been a lot of the dropping of clutches at high rpm that's required for performance figures and in over 17,000 miles there's been no trouble from Terry's machine while Andrew's has covered 6500 without incident. That's not strictly speaking true as both did develop hairline cracks in the exhaust manifolds due to the weight of the turbo being supported. The fabrication of proper brackets solved that.

Aerodynamic inefficiency is a serious limiting factor to top speed of course but even so the pair can approach 115mph which is very impressive. If you have driven an ordinary SJ413 you would not fancy doing that sort of speed and naturally both thses machines have been modified appropriately, Terry's more than Andrew's, having American Rancho reworked lower leaf springs and Rancho off-road shocks while Andrew's features adjustable Spax gas dampers all round. The American theme is continued with General tyres with Terry Fry's jeep having massive 275/60 15s on the back and slightly smaller 255/60s on the front — a selection the owner admits is a mite excessive and will be changed to a slightly more conservative choice, in all probability Pirelli P700s of 245/60 15 profile on some 7in rims currently winging their way from California.

That doesn't imply there's anything wrong with the Generals (apart from their size . . .) and Terry was full of effusive praise for the way they hang on in all conditions. Similar praise was lavished on the brakes too, our man claiming never to have come across stopping power like it. With such a tremendous build up having been given the jeep it was obviously time to try it . . . .

The first thing that strikes you on getting into either of the two machines is just how superbly they have been finished, with full leather interiors trimmed to the finest standard. But then these are showcase vehicles with even such luxuries as a CD player . . . .

With such a radical increase in power you might expect an engine with some funny quirks or foibles but this installation does just what it should . . . make the SJ's little ohc four feel like a much bigger engine, almost a naturally aspirated engine because it certainly doesn't suffer the horrendous turbo lag given by some conversions (or some factory installations come to that). There's no temperamental behaviour but there is a lot more power. Terry's engine was, by his own admission, not set up correctly and it obviously wasn't producing anywhere near 150bhp. Nevertheless the performance was still impressive, both from a standstill and, surprisingly, in the higher gears. This engine would still work 'off the boil' without complaint but obviously preferred to be used in turbo mode.

Switching to Andrew's showed what happens when everything is working as intended and it immediately felt faster in every respect, although still not, in truth, 150bhp worth. The noise from the side pipes perfectly matched the car's performance; deep and purposeful it urges the driver to get on with it. Terry could get on with it better than this driver, having had long enough

to get used to SJs in general and ones with truly enormous tyres in particular. It was soon clear why he's decided to go down a size in tyres; they make the steering heavy at slow speeds and actually make the vehicle more of a handful to drive quickly than would smaller ones. But to a large extent it's simply a matter of getting used to it. The suspension modifications are about right and again I suspect they would feel more impressive on slimmer rubber.

So is this as far as you can possibly take on SJ? Of course not; the next step Terry had been toying with was to indulge in a little injection of nitrous oxide which, in case you've forgotten, is an oxygen liberating agent and by generating more oxygen enables more fuel to be burned and more power to be generated. That, unfortunately, would require robust forged

pistons and they would cost £200 apiece from Cosworth so that idea got knocked on the head . . . in favour of dropping in a Cosworth or perhaps a radically tuned Pinto engine. Apparently there's sufficient room for engine and gearbox alike so if one day you are overtaken by a really fast Suzuki you might have some idea of what's motivating it . . . .

As for Andrew Pettitt, his interest will be diversifying to another interesting machine we hope to feature in a future issue . . . .

If you fancy modifying your Suzuki the Allard way, the company's address is PO Box 2, Lampeter, Dyfed SA48 7HA (0570) 470957. In addition to the engine and suspension mods mentioned here, Allard also cater for other 4x4s, and even diesel motorhomes, not to mention on-off turbo conversions. ■

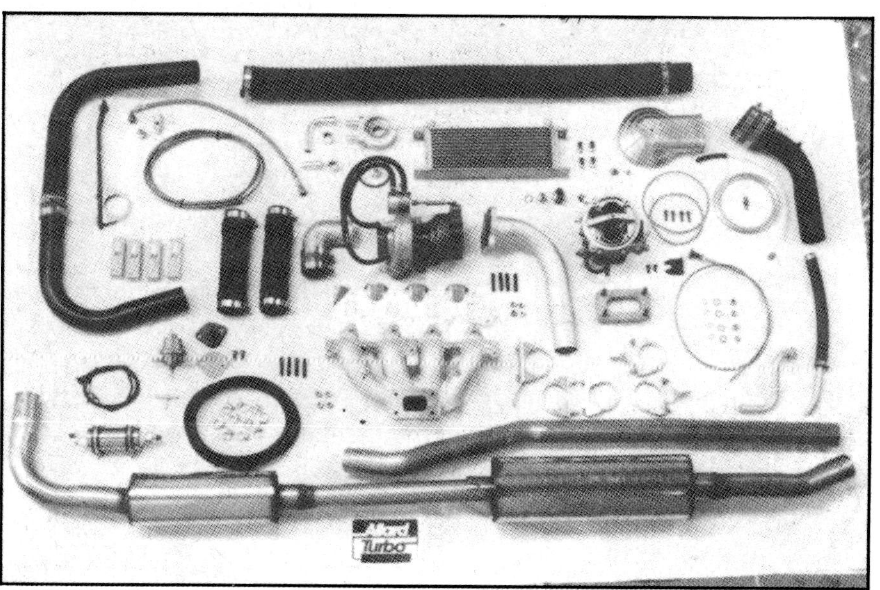

WAKE UP LITTLE SUZI

The Suzuki SJs have been described as unpredictable, unforgiving — or even dangerous — depending on whose views you are hearing. So, how can a taller, more compliantly sprung vehicle handle better than the standard version? Test editor Ian Shaw drives the Trans-Atlantic 4x4 UK demonstrator complete with Rancho handling kit and discovers a remarkable transformation

The diminutive 1,000cc engine screams as second is engaged, under braking through the downhill right-hander; a not inconsiderable amount of weight transfer can be felt as an armful of left-lock and full-throttle is applied. The Santana neatly brushes the apex of the uphill left-hander and I have to grab 3rd gear as it drifts out to the full width of the tarmac and flicks up the gravel beyond, on the exit.

Can this really be a Suzuki SJ410 Santana: the communication through the steering, the predictable slightly understeering stance and the sheer magnitude of the lateral acceleration as the cornering force is taken squarely front and rear?

They are somewhat unpredictable, you will be told, unforgiving, or even dangerous depending on who is informing you and the level of their personal values on what is or is not predictable or safe.

Not this one. Even sitting as it does on oversized five-spokes and 255/60x15 BF Goodrich Comp T/A performance radials, suspended albeit higher than standard on Rancho leaf springs and Rancho road-wheel and steering dampers. As you turn the key, in preparation to getting serious with the vehicle far from congested roads, put out of your mind the unfortunate publicity the marque has attracted and for that matter any previous recollections of how these little machines conduct themselves at speed.

The night before, however, things were very different. Driving the Suzuki home from the premises of Trans-Atlantic 4x4 UK, the company responsible for this transformation (and I do not use the term lightly) in Sutton-in-Ashfield, Notts, in a downpour I found it hard to imagine a more nervous vehicle. I'm convinced the behaviour was 90 per cent as a result of the tyres. When you consider that they are the same width as those fitted as an option on wide alloy wheels on a Mercedes G series and 40mm wider than those on a Range Rover you'll understand why the vehicle's reactions were somewhat less than pin-sharp.

Trans-Atlantic imports all manner of accessories from the practical such as tyres and wheels, springs and dampers, to interior and exterior trim and bull and roll (truck) bars, some of which are purely for cosmetic purposes, not that there's much wrong with that – their demonstrator SJ410 looks pretty serious in the flesh.

But, I can hear you asking, how can a taller, more compliantly sprung vehicle handle better than the standard version? Good question; I asked myself the same thing before I got my hands on the vehicle.

The increase in the height of the centre of gravity is just about offset by the increase in track generated by the greater wheel offset and wider tyres. The

Body roll is minimal, grip tenacious and Shaw impressed. **Right:** Ridin' high: the Rancho springs give an increase in ride height. Limit of suspension travel is shown here

add-on arches being packed to the edges in American rubber is testimony that.

The claimed increase in suspension articulation is a little harder to reconcile with an increase in cornering ability. After driving the vehicle, however, it seems that we're talking about ultimate travel only.

The Rancho springs seem to offer greater vertical wheel travel but stiffen considerably towards the limit, moreover they seem to be slightly – and it is only slight difference – softer in the initial stages than a standard Suzuki spring. This progression effectively means that there is greater initial cornering roll and more compliance to undulating surfaces yet the total amount of roll is not particularly any higher than with a standard vehicle.

That in itself would not produce the sort of reactions we were encountering

competition tyre or at the very least an all-terrain type would have been more suitable.

But even on its tarmac high-performance tyres the vehicle put up a good show. The ultimate posture is that of gentle understeer building to more terminal proportions as the speed is increased, yet just when you think the limit is reached and by persisting with the throttle, it starts to go at the back; but even then it's not so quick that the well-geared steering can't catch it.

Then comes the experience on tarmac as described in the opening paragraph. The neutral stance can give way to understeer on the limit and only by trail braking a long way into the corner could I bring about any change in attitude, the rear starting to go light and hinting at coming round on me, which is obviously the technique required in these contrived "J-turn" tests.

Within the confines of our facilities, and certainly never on trafficked roads, could we find a situation to cause any concern. The very fact that the roadholding levels are so high will mean that when the thing does relinquish its grip on the tarmac it will go a long way in a very short time. The key is that such high limits should never need to be broached.

We did some off roading, even though the tyres could not have been less suited to the task. As regards suspension travel, it seems the Rancho springs provide a little more, only a little, and the increased ride height gives better ground clearance. The steering damper's weight comes into play off road and kick-back through the steering is reduced.

The tyres seemed less able to wander than I had expected, but their wide high-resistance profile and almost wet-tarmac-racing pattern nearly brought about a very embarrassing incident in a couple of inches of mud: "I think you'll have to use four-wheel-drive," my passenger commented.

"This IS in four wheel drive," was the reply he received.

Overall the Trans-Atlantic conversion makes for a very interesting modification – if that's the right term for it. The ride is marginally better than that of a standard SJ, the steering is more communicative and the road holding in the dry is a revelation.

I'd be prepared to sacrifice a little in the way of ultimate dry-road adhesion in the interests of an increase in wet-road grip and improvement in behaviour by fitting a slightly narrower tyre, say a 225. To keep the same gearing this would of course require a taller aspect ratio, a 225/70 perhaps, which would also give a little more wall flexibility with benefits in ride, albeit very slight, and initial cornering feel.

I haven't enjoyed myself as much with a Suzi for a long time! **4x4**

ere the credit has to go to the dampers. Good dampers can go only some way to offsetting any inherent deficiencies in the springs, but can make a reasonable sprung ride better. They seem pretty well suited to the initial compression characteristics of the springs but moreover are particularly impressive in bound.

The steering also has a Rancho damper fitted, for my money it's still rather vague about the straight-ahead position and this isn't helped by the very wide low-profile Goodriches following every undulation and ripple in the road's surface like some giant record player stylus. Once this initial quarter-turn of lock has been dispensed with the steering is pleasant; it's positive, a little heavy even, but without requiring a sufficiently high input to deny feel to the driver, it loads up to some degree in hard cornering but no more so than plenty of front-wheel-drive cars I could mention.

We also had the opportunity to drive it on some loose but smooth surfaced tracks, where its ultimate behaviour could be broached at a lower speed. The tyres were hardly the most suitable pattern for such an exercise, a "forest"

Nimble, easy on gas, cute as kittens, eminently refreshable, the ultimate micro

By Dave Epperson

Samurais are ubiquitous, willing, nimble, cute as kittens, easy on gas, fun transport, the ultimate among micro sport/utility vehicles.

Once, the noun "Samurai" brought to mind a muscular fighting man with a topknot hairdo, wearing a kimono and swinging a long, sharp blade. Now, a Samurai conjures up thoughts of well-filled bikinis, jams, boogie boards, desert dunes, pine trees, running shoes, windborne kites, and all manner of fun in the sun.

A LOVE/HATE RELATIONSHIP

We experienced an almost year-long affiliation with a 1988½ Suzuki Samurai convertible in top-of-the-line JX trim. For most of us, this association was a love/hate relationship. Staffers really used the little vehicle hard for demanding nose-to-the-grindstone kinds of things—and plenty of R & R, too.

At lunchtime, the Samurai often would buzz off with two or three staff members

SUN, FUN, SAMURAI

bound for local fast-food gastro-emporia. Weekdays, it might haul cameras to a photo shoot. On weekends, whoever had the Samurai in hand would find it just right for running to the mini-mart for a quart of milk, or for a picnic, or for lugging a surfboard down to Big Corona to catch an early few. The Suzuki might be found on a fast, wild, skittering tour of nearby mountain fire roads just for fun, or ripping a few dunes in California's vast Mojave Desert playground. Maybe the Suzuki would give the dog a ride to the vet, or shuttle the kids to school. Perhaps it would go to the library for a quiet evening's study. Maybe it would snort a little and head out to the Crazy Horse for some fast Friday night Texas two-steppin'. At times like these, everybody loved the Samurai.

Some staff members, from time to time, used the Suzuki to commute, from home to office, for distances up to 70 freeway miles or more in each direction. Fast freeway running at a high-rpm whine over cracked concrete slabs, tar-strip expansion joints, and potholes in early-morning darkness is no fun. Neither is rowing along with a five-speed gearbox in a sea of wall-to-wall afternoon gridlock. Either way, it was a rough ride. Big people found their knees hard against the Samurai's dash panel. Their shoulders were cramped by the vehicle's rollbar/doorframe. For the tall ones, the Samurai just didn't provide adequate pedal-to-seatback distance for fast footwork on brake and clutch pedals. On hot days, the 'Zuki's air conditioning generated a lot of fan noise but couldn't move enough cool to cope. These were the times when everybody (who commuted with it in summertime) hated the Samurai.

The Samurai's steering proved quick—almost too quick—precise and positive. Drivers could put the vehicle where it was supposed to go. And in spite of unfavorable publicity generated by a consumer magazine, it seems to us that the light vehicle braked easily and handled as well as others in its class, remaining relatively aligned with the with roads and freeway lanes in all-out stopping efforts, although pedal feel was slightly spongy.

OFF-PAVEMENT

Off the pavement, the little Suzuki's four-wheel-drive system, operating in its 2.27:1 low-range, managed to go where all the big ones went, and often where the fat ones couldn't go at all. Most of the time, the sure-footed, agile Samurai traveled with great ease and facility over off-road impediments—and without panting. The live axles, with their newly rated leaf springs and hydraulic shocks, proved the worth of the redesign, soaking up the lumps in the rough stuff better than the original Suzukis and without bending or breaking. Except for diehard Jeep fanatics on the staff, everybody loved the Samurai in the outback.

Off-road at high altitude, the Samurai's two-barrel downdraft carburetor performed with surges, huffing and puffing and unable to provide a steady burnable mix to the cylinders. At elevations above 5,000 feet, everyone hated the Samurai.

The Samurai's convertible soft top came down easily on warm, sunny days, and went up with difficulty on cold evenings when dropping temperatures chilled the fabric, causing it to stiffen. There it is again: love/hate.

If every day could be a warm, sunny, sea-level short run to the big surf, everyone would love the Samurai all of the time. It doesn't work out that way. In the real world, what the Samurai does best is to provide economy and reliability. Somewhere along the line, it got all kinds of transportation chores for all sorts of people involved in a vast variety of work and play pursuits. This transport may not be as comfortable or as easy on the human body in all circumstances as a vehicle costing three times as much, but Suzuki transport is there, all day, reliably, at modest cost.

The vehicular Samurai may not be the master swordsman of its namesake, but nonetheless it is cheap and versatile. At a base price of $8,495, it is a serviceable package deliverer, outback runner, pizza rustler, schoolbook hauler, seashore transporter, mallmobile, motorhome-towed auxiliary, first-time 4x4, and . . .

BASICS PLUS

When the Samurai first arrived in the U.S., it was heralded as sort of a neo-Jeep. It was to fill a perceived niche in American tastes and sporting uses of motor vehicles. In a way, it did. In other ways, it didn't.

When our '88½ Samurai arrived for long-term testing, it displayed upgraded interior appointments and upholstery, and some newly available factory options. Inside, the new Sam' showed a revised instrument panel, along with a redesigned center console to house the AM/FM/cassette stereo, heater, and vent controls. The sides and corners of the new center console extend farther into passenger space, thus further limiting driver and passenger kneeroom. The '88½ also showed a new four-spoke steer-

The '88½ Samurai's instrumentation and controls are basic, functional, and easily accessed by the driver.

SUN, FUN, SAMURAI

ing wheel to replace the earlier three-spoke design.

New paint colors, new graphics, and some revised trim aimed to give the half-year vehicle a more youthful, sporting look. Obviously, the projected appeal was to teenage America, a marketplace where the Samurai is a solid favorite and remains eminently affordable.

The revised Samurai retains its short wheelbase, at 79.9 inches, which continues to force restricted front and rear seating arrangements. The Samurai 81cid four-cylinder engine still needs to be operated at high rpm, well toward the six-grand redline, to produce its peak horsepower.

Our '88½ Samurai arrived in the U.S. with some well-considered mechanical revisions: The transmission's Fifth gear was enlarged to improve acceleration performance and reduce gear-whine noise; the suspension was softened by reducing the number of front leaves from four to three, and decreasing the thickness of the rear leaves; the rear suspension was revised by reducing spring thickness; front and rear shock absorber rates were altered to compensate for changes in the springs; and the front stabilizer bar was increased in diameter to compensate for softer springs. The new suspension softness eliminates much of the earlier Samurai's harsh rocking-horse ride characteristics, but increased the vehicle's tendency for body roll in turns.

During its tenure with *Four Wheeler*, in all kinds of running, off-pavement and on, the Samurai delivered an average of 24.8 mpg, with a one-tank low of 21.8 and a one-tank best of nearly 34 mpg, another kind of worthwhile economy in this era of $1.25-plus-per-gallon gas.

Probably the greatest influence on '88½ Samurai sales was the nearly simultaneous advent of the Suzuki Sidekick. The less-boxy-looking vehicle is smoother than its elder brother, and roomier, too. The Sidekick seems more like, well, a small passenger car than a two-fisted, off-roading micro-4x4. However, the Sidekick, much like the Samurai, is a reliable, practical, economical micro, with a base price of $8,995.

FUN RUN

It's safe to predict that Suzuki eventually will phase out the Samurai, as Henry Ford did when he switched from years of making Model T's to manufacturing Model A's. The Sidekick likely will be Suzuki's Model A in the never-ending cycle of automotive evolution dictated by changing consumer tastes. If this happens, upwards of 200,000 naturalized-American Samurais will remain, like military Jeeps after World War II. As used-Samurai prices decline, the vehicles will become more readily available as hands-on learning experiences for teenage home craftsmen, much as Model T's and Model A's were for earlier generations of hot-rodding amateur mechanics. These Samurais will continue to be easy on gas, nimble, cute, and fun. They'll be kept running, some with bailing wire and some with precision-machined aftermarket parts. They'll serve their consecutive owners as cut-down roadsters, as jacked-up off-roaders, as senior-citizen econocars, and as economical second and third cars for working families who play a little, too. After-market entrepreneurs, it can be anticipated, will for a lengthy future time perpetuate the manufacture of performance components, accessories, and replacement parts for Samurais, as they now continue to do for Volkswagen Beetles. Plenty of aftermarket replacement parts, trim items, and other accessories are available for Suzuki Samurais today. This situation will likely prevail for a long time to come.

Halfway through its long hard-driven run with us, the little 4x4 became the centerpiece of a major renewal project (see "The Neat-Seat Trick-Top Fix," March '89.) Refreshing the 'Zuki were all-new front seats, a rear folding seat, top, door-panel and rollbar cover trim kit, new carpet, and a spare-tire cover, all for a total price of $1,526.49. The bright, new, color-coordinated trim, upholstery, and top package seemed to reenergize the Samurai, making it a more acceptable vehicle in which to be seen at dawn with surfboards at the beach or at midday with friends at a shopping mall. There's a lot to be said for the psychology of cosmetics.

Samurais may continue to do these things for a long time for their U.S. owners, well after the manufacturer also has phased out the Sidekick in favor of an as yet-unnamed Suzuki Model B. This Model B in all probability is on the company's engineering drawing boards right now: the next ultimate micro. □

Our Samurai JX received a new aftermarket soft-top/interior-trim/seating combo. The canvas top detaches with relative ease, allowing enhanced enjoyment of the great outdoors.

WILD TURKEY

'Few visitors make it to Divrigi — not that many try. But it's well worth a bit of tyre wear'. Chris Hellier takes a Suzuki on a trip through eastern Turkey

Above: Towering cliffs confront the Suzuki in the Oltu valley, north-east Turkey

Sivas, they say, is the gateway to eastern Turkey. And so it seemed, as, having looked round the city's impressive Ottoman mosques and minarets, we drove deeper into Asia Minor.

First destination was Divrigi, a small town hidden in a fertile valley 100km (62 miles) from the nearest decent road. Driving there was the first major test for the Suzuki's new suspension and, as it turned out, the only place we were unable to buy "super" petrol.

Few visitors make it to Divrigi, not that many try. For tour operators it's a little remote and most independents must be put off by an inconvenient trip by public transport and a lack of accommodation. But it's well worth a bit of tyre wear.

From Kangal, a scruffy town famous for its dogs, the pitted road stretched into the distance across the elevated steppe. Barren rocky land was interspersed with fields of wheat where peasants, surprised by a red Suzuki SJ410 weaving its way between the larger potholes, took a break from the hand harvesting, to wave or simply stare.

After a slow, dusty journey, the isolated Divrigi valley, nourished by the headwaters of the Euphrates, appeared like a green mirage. If visitors to Divrigi are few and far between, visitors in Suzukis are an even rarer sight.

"Ah," gasped an elderly Turk with a

The Keban reservoir: Donkeys only, said the garage owner

flowing patriarchal beard as we parked in the narrow main street, "Suzuki, very good." It was probably the only one he'd ever seen.

Divrigi has a historic core of fine timber mansions with balconies and shady courtyards, but the real interest lies in its 13th century Seljuk mosque and hospital. Turkey has so many old mosques vying for attention that it's easy to become blasé, but the elaborate originality of Divrigi's Ulu Cami, the old mosque, is astonishing. Its rich geometric patterns derived from Arab and Indian motifs, its stone foliage and inscriptions, make for an extravagant building. Its siting, miles out in the sticks, increases the sense of aberration.

From Divrigi we'd planned to cut along to the Keban reservoir. But, said the man at the garage – the one with no "super" petrol – "Even a 'jeep' won't get down there. Donkeys only." We took his word for it and, retracing our steps, took the long way round.

As we followed the Euphrates towards the Keban dam the landscape became stark, moon-like, with sand-coloured hillocks devoid of vegetation. Startling blue rollers darted from one telegraph pole to another; occasional eagles hovered overhead.

We spent several days in the Keban reservoir area finally crossing its blue expanse on an old ferry boat at Pertek. From there, we side-tracked into the spectacular Munzur Valley National Park where red-brown slopes tower above ash, oak and maple forests.

Apart from the Munzur mountains, much of east central Turkey is undulating plateau-land and while the roads we'd used were often dusty and unsurfaced they hadn't really been a trial for the Suzuki. Fancying a greater test of its mountain goat attributes we headed for the mountainous north-east, to the little-known Kackar range or Pontic Alps.

On a previous trip to the Kaçkar I'd travelled by minibus but poor roads and bad weather sometimes prevented the bus from reaching its destination. After one summer downpour had turned the road near Savsat (not far from the Russian border) into a mud-bath, the Bedford, wheels spinning furiously, refused to go any further. With the Suzuki I looked forward to overcoming any problems summer rains were to bring this year.

The Kaçkar mountains, particularly the landward side, include some of the most dramatic scenery in Turkey. The chocolate-coloured Coruh river gouges out a deep, rocky gorge which cuts around the main range to find an outlet to

Driving in the Nemrut crater: shimmering lakes and igneous debris

the Black Sea on the Soviet side of the border. Its tributaries, too, the Oltu, Berta, and Parhal rivers, run through striking glens. From the bottom of these deep valleys hair-raising tracks wind their way up the mountainside to scattered hamlets and the region's most interesting historic remains: its medieval Georgian churches.

Long before the Turks conquered Anatolia the upper reaches of the Coruh formed part of the medieval kingdom of Georgia. It was a prosperous state which, under succesive kings, built numerous churches south and east of the Kaçkar. Using Artvin, the district capital, and later Yusufeli, as a base, we aimed to reach at least some of these Middle Age monuments.

The 10th century church at Dolishane, now converted into a mosque, is decorated with the oldest figure carving in the region. It seemed a good place to start but the journey proved to be the most nerve-racking of the entire trip. The track was steep and bumpy and, as we snaked our way up the narrow byway, the mountain slope dropped almost sheer, invisible at the side. As pearls of sweat began to drip from my forehead we finally, and thankfully, arrived.

Dolishane is a pleasant mosque and having had a brief look around we sat by the village fountain eating plums with a few of the friendly locals. But the silence of the mountain village was soon broken by the roar of an engine and a white Range Rover, over-revving, came to a sudden halt a few yards away. Two white-faced Europeans slowly climbed out of the car.

"God!" cried the Austrian woman, that was awful." She glanced over to our car. "It must be all right in a Suzuki though. It's so much smaller."

At least we made it to Dolishane. Yeni Rabat, another cruciform church beyond Ardanuç, once capital of medieval Georgia, had other surprises in store. Having carefully negotiated a rough track, fit for little more than a donkey, a soldier flagged us down at the side of the road.

"Road closed," he bluntly informed us.

"Kaput." And with that an earth-shaking explosion rent the air and resonated down the valley. See," said the soldier gleefully. Kaput. You try again tomorrow."

As well as the lesser-visited areas around the Kaçkar and the isolated mosque at Divrigi, eastern Turkey has its share of major sites which are justifiably on the package tour itineraries, but, as yet, are mercifully uncrowded. Within the shadow of Mount Ararat, legendary resting place of Noah's Ark, stands one of the most striking and magnificently sited palaces in the whole of Anatolia, Isak and Pasa Sarayi, or Isaac's Palace, at Dogubeyazit. The palace, built in the 17th century and completed a hundred years later in a mix of styles, commands a memorable view over the dusty plain.

Until we reached Dogubeyazit the weather had been clear and bright. But as we dropped south towards Lake Van, the largest lake in Turkey, dark rain clouds obscured the higher peaks of the eastern Taurus Mountains. While there had been no sign of rain in the Coruh here it fell overnight with a vengeance. At seven the next morning the heavy clouds were beginning to lift as we climbed a track to the rim of the extinct Nemrut volcano. Several kilometres from the main road a battered truck, painted in naive pastoral scenes, blocked the way. Four mustachioed men stood around smoking.

"Is there a problem?" I called out as one of them approached.

"Evet," he replied, "Cok çamur." ("Yes, there's a lot of mud.") "But," he said, nonchalantly, "it's no problem for you. Four-wheel-drive, isn't it?"

One of the others jumped up into the lorry's cab and pulled over to let us pass. The four of them waved us on.

"Devam et! Devam et!" ("Go on!") they yelled, urging us to plunge into the mire. As we sank 6in into the mud I wondered whether the middle wasn't deeper than the truckers seemed to believe. Maintaining a steady snail's pace, despite our audience's encouragement to "step on the gas", we inched forward, sank deeper and, just as the wheels began to skid, we hit solid ground the other side. Apart from the local nomads, we'd be the only people on Nemrut Dagi that morning.

The view from the rim down into the Nemrut crater was stunning, particularly when the sun finally broke through the clouds. Two shimmering lakes reflected the mountain's volcanic lip. Igneous debris glinted black as it caught the sun's rays and basalt rocks lay in disorderly heaps where they were spewed out and cooled centuries ago.

There is another, better known, Nemrut mountain in eastern Turkey. This isn't a volcano but the site of one of the country's most curious archaeological remains. It, too, sounded a challenge. According to a three-year-old edition of one of the weightier travel guides we were carrying: "The best way to reach Nemrut Dagi is to rent an all-terrain vehicle. You'll climb the stony track trailing a cloud of dust. At a pinch, you could use your own vehicle . . . with all its risks and dangers!"

But things are changing fast in Turkey and the "stony track" had since been surfaced. It still wasn't an easy drive though. For nearly 70km (43 miles) the serpentine road climbed up steeply from Kahta, the nearest town, to within a kilometre or two of the 2,150 metre (7,050ft) peak. Although surfaced, the incline is still too much for today's luxury coaches and after 5,000km (3,100 miles) on Turkey's dusty roads the Suzuki was also beginning to complain. We made it at the second attempt.

Postcards of the gigantic stone heads scattered on the summit of Nemrut Dagi are on sale throughout Turkey. But little can prepare you for the grandeur of the sight. During the 1st century BC, Antiochos the First, King of Commagene, ordered the construction of a mammoth sanctuary on this barren mountain top. His supposed tomb – archaeologists are still searching for it – lies hidden beneath a mammoth artificial peak of crushed stone, while to east and west, giant statues of Antiochos; his father, Mithridates; and Persian and Hellenistic gods including Apollo, Zeus and Hercules, were built on raised platforms. Earthquakes have since toppled the statues but this only adds to the mystery of this awesome peak.

The minibus drivers at Kahta offer trips to Nemrut at sunset and sunrise, when the changing light and shadow catch the statues at their best. We, too, reached the summit before dawn after walking the final stretch and, with 50 other visitors, watched the sun lighten the eastern sky. But, however impressive the sunrise I preferred the lonely silence of the place an hour later when the others had returned to their minibuses. I was glad even 4x4s couldn't make it all the way to the top.

USEFUL TIPS

FLY-DRIVE. For those who don't fancy the long overland trip across Europe, or don't have the time, it's possible to hire Suzukis locally. Samurais can be hired through Hertz or Europcar and collected in Ankara or Trabzon in the north-east, as well as in many western towns.

OFF ROADING. East Turkey has innumerable dirt tracks for the off-road enthusiast but I've found the most rewarding area to be the north-east – north of Erzurum and west of Kars. Anyone venturing into the extreme south-east of the country, to Hakkari and the border area around Cizre should beware. While you can visit the towns, heading off into the wilds is not recommended. Kurdish insurgency

Crossing the Devil's Bridge at Muradiye, east Turkey

means that this is a very unsettled area.

ACCOMMODATION. Good accommodation can be found in the main towns but elsewhere you'll have to make do with very basic accommodation. This need cost no more than £3 a night for a double room. Camping is possible in some places including the southern shore of Lake Van and both Nemruts.

PETROL. Turkish petrol comes in two grades: "super" and "normal" which corresponds roughly with four- and two-star in Britain. "Super" might be difficult to get in some of the more remote areas. In this case try to get hold of a bottle of "Benzin Katigi", upper-cylinder lubricant. One small bottle added to 40 litres (9 gals) of "normal" gives a "super" equivalent.

THEFT. Theft is rarely a problem in Turkey, even with soft-tops, although particular care needs to be taken with some of the nomadic and poorer communities around Lake Van. The only time I've had something pinched was outside a mosque in Divrigi. Some mischievous kids unzipped the soft-top and walked off with a history book. The learned tome was on loan from the British Council Library in Ankara!

SERVICING/BREAKDOWNS. There's a Suzuki garage in Ankara: "Garanti Oto", Bahçelievler 2, Cad No 64, Ankara. Tel: (04) 2226492-2123235. **4x4**

STRETCHER CASE

John Beese assesses the potential of one of the first Suzuki Samurai long wheelbase models to arrive on these shores

● *Muddy boots and wet dogs aren't going to spoil the interior*

● *The LWB Samurai is an agile off-roader*

The long wheelbase version of Suzuki's popular Samurai SJ413 4x4 is now available in the UK. The vehicle has been sold in many other areas of the world for over 17 months and we can only assume the reason the vehicle didn't reach these shores sooner was a problem of supply. Especially when you consider that two of the main criticisms directed towards the Suzuki SJ were that its short wheelbase helped create an uncomfortably pitching ride on-road and also limited the interior storage space, making it less practical as a family car.

The ride on-road is certainly smoother, but the firm leaf-sprung chassis still gives imprecise handling – certainly when compared to conventional cars. The overall width and front and rear track of the vehicle are the same as the short wheelbase version and rapid cornering is not a relaxed affair. Apart from the body roll (inherent in all utility 4x4s due to their relatively high centre of gravity), the longer version Samurai seems to have more of a tendency to understeer. For those used to the cosy confines of a modern estate car with power-assisted everything, the Samurai would be something of a culture shock, but it's

certainly more interesting to drive in many respects.

Off-road driving is what this vehicle is all about. It would be absurd to talk much about performance characteristics if it weren't for the fact that the majority of these vehicles are purchased for road use. The long wheelbase model was almost as nippy as the short wheelbase version around town and great fun to drive on country lanes, with excellent visibility, ideal gear ratios and light steering. But if you need to do much long distance motorway driving buy something else.

The long wheelbase Samurai is fine if you're not in a hurry. The 1.3-litre engine remains unchanged for this model and, although the acceleration on-road is lack-lustre, the 63bhp unit is comfortably powerful enough to propel the vehicle through the most difficult off-road situations.

We drove the vehicle down to Nick Silwood's off-road centre, now open to the public, near East Grinstead. The muddy ground was saturated and the vehicle was fitted with Dunlop SP Qualifiers, definitely a compromise on-off road fitment, so it was with considerable trepidation that we began to pick our way around the site. The more difficult

S T R E T C H E R
C A S E

sections were inspected on foot and the heavy, clay soil clung with the tenacity of an angry octopus in large quantities to our boots. The same happened to the tyres of the Suzuki when driving off-road but the relatively light vehicle weight coupled with careful gear selection and economic use of the throttle made slow, steady progress possible.

Although described as long wheelbase, the new Suzuki is still an extremely manoeuvrable vehicle. With an overall length of 158 inches it's only five inches longer than the Defender Ninety. The wheelbase has been increased by nearly 14 inches, retaining the good appraoch angle of the short wheelbase, but reducing the departure angle because of the greater rear overhang. However, the price to pay for the improved storage capacity is a reduced ramp breakover angle. The underbelly of the vehicle grounded in several situations that would have been easily negotiated by the shorter version Samurai. However, this is only likely to prove a disadvantage in extreme off-road conditions.

The Suzuki showed its true off-road colours when driving on the rough, hardcore-prepared surfaces leading into the site. This kind of surface can be driven quite comfortably at reasonable speed with the suspension, including leafsprings, chassis and chassis mounts flexing to absorb the shocks. It's not

● *Good head room but limited leg space*

● *Ample room for luggage*

until you hit a larger hole or mound that the desirability of leaf springing is called into question. Although not ideal the ageing design provides a tough, economical off-road package. All the long wheelbase models imported into the UK will come from the Spanish factory Santana, who build the SJ range of vehicles under licence from the Japanese manufacturer. This is a shame as the build quality is certainly inferior to the Suzuki products coming direct from Japan. Several items of trim were already showing signs of wear, including the glovebox lock which in the best tradition 'came orf in me hand guv'.

The extra load space should give the vehicle wider appeal. With the rear seats in position there is 35cu.ft of storage; in the short wheelbase model there is just about room for a pair of wellingtons. The rear seats can be folded down individually and with both seats folded fully forward the storage is increased to 50cu. ft. Leg room for rear passengers is limited, and only the front passenger seat slides forward to allow easy access to the rear seats.

The nearest market competitor to this version of the Suzuki Samurai is probably the Lada Niva, which at £8395 is only £355 more expensive. Apart from the suspension, the design of the Suzuki is considerably more modern and the mechanical components are undoubtedly superior with a smooth-running, reliable engine and slick transmission. Resale values of the SJ range are good despite the adverse publicity regularly meted out by the Consumers' Association regarding the short wheelbase vehicle's stability.

Apparently around a quarter of the Samurai range constructed are long wheelbase models, which is quite a lot when you consider that between 40 and 50,000 units are expected to be sold worldwide this year. Suzuki GB was not willing to divulge how many long wheelbase models it would be importing, but as there are rumoured to be a lot of short wheelbase models in stock at the moment, presumably it won't be a great many.

The vehicle is fitted with a functional white resin hard-top. This is relatively easy to remove and has large sliding windows. The design of this could be more appealing and the various levers, handles and catches built into it lack the stamp of Japanese quality. A heated rear window and rear wash-wipe are fitted, but both smack of nasty aftermarket additions, particularly the unusual siting of the rear wiper switch on the outer side of the front instrument panel. There is also a removable panel above the front seats that has some pretensions to being a sunroof.

The vehicle is unlikely to hold the same appeal to the poser market – the trim and overall appearance simply aren't as good as the short wheelbase Samurai. Fuel consumption figures round the 30mpg mark are certainly favourable for a 4x4 vehicle and this coupled with the extra storage space could well attract families hoping to economise by simply running one economical, versatile car. ■

Technical Specification Suzuki Samurai LWB

Engine
Water-cooled, four cylinder in-line, four stroke with single OHC, cast iron block and aluminium head and single, side draught carburettor

Capacity	1324cc
Bore	74mm
Stroke	77mm
Max power	63bhp @ 6000rpm
Max torque	74lbf.ft @ 3600rpm

Transmission
Five-speed, all synchromesh primary gear box with remotely mounted, two-speed, part-time transfer case

Ratios:	
1st	3.562:1
2nd	1.947:1
3rd	1,432:1
4th	1.000:1
Transfer ratios:	
High	1.409:1
Low	2 268:1
Final drive	3.909:1

Suspension
Front – live axle with single parabolic leaf springs and telescopic dampers
Rear – Live axle with two-stage parabolic leaf springs and telescopic dampers incorporating anti-roll bar

Brakes
Servo-assisted hydraulically-operated discs at the front with drums on the rear. Parking brake actuates independent drum on rear output of transfer case

Wheels and tyres
205/70R15 Dunlop SP Qualifiers on 5.5x15 rims

Steering
Manually-operated recirculating ball

Principal dimensions

Length	4010mm (157.9in)
Width	1530mm (60.2in)
Wheelbase	2375mm (93.5in)
Track front	1300mm (51.2in)
Track rear	1310mm (51.6in)
Towing	Unbraked 980lb (445Kg)
	Braked 2200lb (1000kg)

Price as tested
£8750 inclusive of Car Tax and VAT

- *Far right: the longer wheelbase has caused some reduction in the vehicle's ramp breakover angle*
- *Right: the demountable hard-top will not be to everyone's taste, but it is strongly built and features opening rear windows*
- *Below: the spare wheel is asymmetrically mounted to reduce the loading on the rear hinges and the heated rear window features a wash/wipe mechanism*
- *Bottom: approach and departure angles are still good in this longer version Samurai*

LONG ON CHARACTER BUT WITH SHORTCOMINGS

Despite ground clearance and overhang problems, the stretched SJ413 has ability. Peter Phillpotts tests the long-wheelbase Suzuki Santana

Because I've not yet had the opportunity to drive the shorter Suzuki SJ variants, this test had to be treated as would that of a new vehicle. Owners of short-wheelbase SJs may therefore find some of the criticisms cover familiar ground.

However, my normal approach is to try to assess vehicles both against some imaginary yardstick of what a serious off-road vehicle *ought* to be able to do, and in the context of what the manufacturer seems to be attempting, for the price.

I've always preferred light vehicles so at 970kg this Suzuki comes much nearer my ideal than any other currently available make. Although 1,324cc sounds rather a puny capacity to haul more than a tonne (with driver), in practice its 75lb/ft of torque seems well spread and quite adequate. I was reminded of other small Japanese engines I've experienced, with similar surprising performances.

The dreaded roll-ability so much discussed in the past year did not stand out as a possibility, but perhaps long experience with off-road vehicles has adapted me. Whatever; it was quickly apparent why Suzukis have become so popular. The low inertia of a light vehicle, with consequent nimbleness of response, make it attractive in urban situations. This coupled with a slightly higher seating position and good all-road vision assists driveability in traffic.

Off-road use does not enter the minds of many purchasers, and one wonders whether a cheaper, two-wheel-drive version with better-steering independent front suspension might appeal to many of these buyers.

The steering is Suzuki's worst feature. A simple cross-axle link from the steering box tends to push the axle sideways, and with the very soft leaf springs used, along with rather compliant rubber bushes, a bit too much free play at the steering wheel is the result. Despite a beefy anti-roll bar on the front axle, the high narrow body lurches and rocks from side to side quite easily, so that small steering movements can produce exaggerated directional changes.

Right: *Axle articulation isn't wonderful: traction stopped here. Blame anti-roll bar and short-stroke dampers.* ***Far right:*** *Mild ruts had diff scraping. Very tame, but this is the limit*

Right: *40 deg-plus slope is climbable but needs 2,000rpm minimum, in 1st-low. With lower gearing, this would have been an idle-speed job*

Right: *Tidy and sensible dash. Plastic steering wheel can be slippery with cold hands. In the back, rear seats fold forward individually, leaving a generous load area. Rear side windows slide open, giving plenty of ventilation*

TEST
SUZUKI SANTANA
G103 UNJ

Above: *Uphill wheels still firmly planted, the Suzuki is more stable than many believe. The extra wheelbase helps.* **Below:** *Accessible engine bay with good protection for deep water wading: distributor up high at rear; air cleaner snorkel around back of battery; coil high on bulkhead. Note lightened jack on right*

This nervousness is then exacerbated by the heaviness of further lock application, owing to a greater than usual 3½deg castor angle. This marked unevenness of effort/result is very uncomfortable to live with, and gives concern over the ability to steer accurately. Strong winds add severely to the problem, whether from front, side or rear. It's all very reminiscent of the sort of handling I experienced learning to drive on small pre-war leaf sprung cars in the late '50s.

Although Suzukis are among the cheapest 4x4s available, the SJ413 has grown to the point where handling which was acceptable on the original 550cc two-stroke LJ50 is no longer acceptable. At the very least, proper Silentbloc type bushings and a simple Panhard rod to take the reaction from the steering should be added; ideally, a coil-sprung set up would be preferable.

Not that the leaf springs are uncomfortable; far from it. Despite there being no more than 20mm between the axle and the front bump rubbers, I found the Santana could be "Banzai'd" along my bumpy daily route just as quickly as the Land Rover Defender Ninety recently tested! This amazing performance must be credited to the light aluminium engine: there is no sensation of any mass jumping about up front, just a homogeneous lump of vehicle bounding along unperturbed. Such ability further adds to the necessity for more precise steering.

There is another reason for the call for coil springs though. The soft leaves wind

cruising speed up hills or against headwinds, especially when laden.

Considering this, the performance is not bad, and it's easy to see the engineers being tempted by this kind of final drive ratio. Even in 5th the engine will haul from 2,000rpm very readily, with no obvious point where power starts to increase.

The cam is well chosen for an off-road vehicle, pulling right from idle in the low gears, yet still able to rev right out to the red line when the need arises.

You need a little patience, mind: no zinging motorcycle engine this, but the ability is there, and as I say, for an off-road power unit, that lugging capacity is vital.

I liked this engine except for one thing:

being similar to an old three-speed Jeep; 2nd to 3rd then goes to the other extreme, with 1.37 – very nice, but misplaced on its own. Then the transfer shows a step down into low of only 1.6, making 2nd-low higher than 1st-high. In other words, you get only one ratio lower than 1st, making a two-speed transfer something of a waste in my view. It would be simpler to have a six-speed main box.

The shift lever, sprouting directly from the selectors, is as positive as anyone could ask for, although the side step to 5th is a little wide and the centre weighting springs a touch heavy. With reverse opposite 5th, again as on other vehicles tested, quickly shifting from forwards to backwards for rocking out of holes is rather awkward.

The controls felt well positioned though, including the steering wheel. No complaints there save for two small points: the rear wash/wipe switch is on the *end* of the dash and not at all obvious. The instrument panel reminds you of a typical motorcycle set up, and its illumination is a bit over zealous, almost dazzling the driver at night. By contrast the row of warning lamps beneath is too dim.

The long-body model uses very nearly the same wheelbase as the Land Rover Ninety, with 93½in, so the choppiness reported for ride in the SWB models is absent. At only 40kg heavier, it's a tidy stretch, with greater cargo bed length than the Ninety, as well. The two rear seats are clearly only for children, though, with adults being forced to sit with legs well doubled up.

The roof is in two parts: the forward section clips in with four strong over-centre catches and can be removed for open-top motoring. The rear combines one piece down to the waist and detaches via six over-centre catches, and is quickly removed. All the catches are covered by thick rubber protection caps, to avoid passenger injury. These panels are glassfibre mouldings and deeply ribbed, with special roof rack supports left in. Very practical and stiff, but also very un-streamlined, and wind noise is bad.

Vision is, as mentioned, very good all round, although the rear screen demist heater elements are so thick that they can obscure rear view at times. As on other vehicles of this style, the windscreen pillars must come very close to failing the angle-of-vision tests, but don't cause any real problems.

When starting from cold the twin-choke Aisan carb with automatic choke does its job well, but I must say the fuel consumption during the test left me disappointed. Probably heavy-footed driving, thanks to the tall gearing, had much to do with this figure. Whatever the case, if this is the level of economy to be expected then there seems little point in owning a small-capacity engine.

In the quaint Japanese-English

Stump cut down almost to ground is still a hazard; forward end shackles beg for trouble

up with axle torque far too easily, inhibiting use of the power of first gear, and causing drive-line vibrations in a variety of braking and accelerating situations because of the occurrance of universal joint angle mismatch. There must also be some risk of axle tramp under panic-stop conditions. At least the steering damper does its job well, with no shimmy whatsoever.

The gearing is another subject for discussion. Overall gearing would seem ridiculously high, with 5th gear showing only 3,500rpm at 70mph, according to the gauges. With an engine red-lined at 6,500 this gives an impossible maximum of 130mph! A vehicle like this is unlikely to see a lot of motorway work: it's too noisy, underpowered and unstreamlined for this sort of use, so "restful" low revs at speed is not a realistic requirement. Much more important to be able to hold

it's noisy. Man, is it noisy, once past 3,000rpm. This factor, along with fuel consumption, has probably much more to do with the gearing used. In practice the gearing *seems* sensible: with the engine being operated in the 2,000-3,000rpm band, where it's happiest, you quickly run through the box as though it were lower geared.

Note I said *seems*: any hills soon show up the shortcomings. For example, 3rd gear shows about 12mph per 1,000rpm, which means shifting up at about 35mph – quite normal. However, peak torque coming at around 40mph means that, on the type of twisty hilly bits that keep speeds down to around 30, the engine is struggling when it ought not to be. And this with only the driver on board.

The ratios in the boxes are a bit odd as well: 1st to 2nd takes a jump of almost 1.9:1. This is too much for any five-speed,

Lengthened rear of chassis retains crossmember in standard short-wheelbase position; fuel tank is accordingly standard 40-litre. Note curious spring curvatures, suggesting collapse

handbook much is made of the fact that this is an off-road vehicle. Competition results everywhere seem to support that claim, yet when you examine the layout underneath it is hard to credit this. Ground clearance is probably no more than an inch or two greater than some cars, and on a par with the 2CVs. The transfer box adds less than an inch to the diff head clearances, and the reverse cambered-springs put the shackles perilously low.

Part of the problem is due to the use of 70 series 15in tyres, but because the gearing is so high – at least 20 per cent over in my judgement – the use of even 6.00 x 16 tyres is ruled out. As it is, off-road work calls for much use of 1st-low with a deal of clutch slipping from time to time.

It's very irritating to be presented with vehicles claiming to have such great off-road performance when in reality they are severely handicapped like this. So far this seems to be a typically Japanese fault, but low-hanging appendages each end, lamps set in bumpers and unprotected exhausts are all too common. Just what all these makers think is an "off-road" situation is hard to fathom. It would seem they've never been there.

So once more I found myself attempting to drive around in the dirt without snagging or breaking something, and without getting instantly grounded on all the low points underneath. The shallowest ruts can cause problems, and the limited axle articulation coupled with the high, narrow body plus heavy anti-roll bar, means that opposite corner wheelspin is a constant hazard.

Yet for all that it *does* have ability, even with the extra foot or so in the wheelbase. Attribute it to low weight. Time and again I've seen this demonstrated, in so many different ways, so much so that it's hard for me to comprehend how one or two people could want to use, say, a ton and three quarters of vehicle to go off-road. Talk about making things difficult for yourself.

Returning to the Suzuki: with the Dunlops' pressures well lowered to compensate for their almost on-road-only tread pattern, the Suzuki proved able to claw its way up and down anything that did not present clearance or overhang problems. It dragged itself through thick mud and out of mucky holes. Even side slopes caused less anxiety than I'd been led to expect, helped by a comparatively low seating position, by 4x4 standards.

Some sensible mods such as re-arched springs and 16in wheels, along with revised gearing in the transfer box, and suitable tyres, would make this the formidable contender that others have demonstrated it to be. Going further, with a serious weight reduction programme and some engine blueprinting, the long-wheelbase model becomes a viable off-road racer. Make no mistake, this machine has potential.

As for the everyday user: does he or she get value for money? Of course. The question as to why Land Rover never attempted to compete at this level in the market is comprehensively answered by the price. Less material does not automatically mean less work: it would take Land Rover nearly as long to build something this size as it would the larger models.

The Santana has shortcomings, yes. Ground clearance and overhang problems mean that your off-roading must be kept to carefully selected trails, and overgearing means that, used laden, driving will be hard work – and thirsty. But otherwise this machine has character and, especially, potential. **4x4**

TECH SPEC

Suzuki SJ 413 Samurai LWB

ENGINE

4-cyl, 4-stroke petrol, SOHC, all aluminium castings: 1,324cc
Bore: 74mm
Stroke: 77mm
Compression ratio: 8.9:1
Maximum power: 63hp at 6,000rpm
Maximum torque: 75lb/ft at 3,500rpm

GEARBOX

5-speed all-synchro
1st: 3.652
2nd: 1.947
3rd: 1.423
4th: 1.00
5th: 0.795
Rev: 3.466

TRANSFER BOX

Low: 2.268
High: 1.409
Final Drive: 3.727 (overall: 5.25)
NOTE: Figures quoted from handbook. Test results disagreed

SUSPENSION

Live axles on leaf springs, front & rear, double-acting tubular dampers

STEERING

Ball nut, 3¼ turns lock-to-lock
Turning Circle: unspecified (poor)

BRAKES

Front: 285mm discs
Rear: 230mm drums: servo assisted hydr
Handbrake – mechanical on rear drums

WHEELS/TYRES

5½ J15; 205-70 R15 M&S Dunlop SP

DIMENSIONS

Length: 4.010m
Width: 1.530m
Height: 1.815m
Wheelbase: 2.375m
Track, Front: 1.3m
Rear: 1.31m
Ground clearance: 205mm
Kerb wt: 970kg
GVW: 1,400kg
Max trailer wt: 1,110kg
Fuel Tank: 40 litres (8.8gals)
Fuel Consumption: 27mpg (on test overall)

PRICE

£8,999 including car tax and VAT

Despite the effects of the recession and some unjustified bad publicity, the Suzuki SJ still commands good residual values.

David Sutherland examines the vehicle's market potential

Stand it alongside the off-road big guns, and it's perhaps hard to take the diminutive Suzuki SJ seriously. With meagre power and Matchbox dimensions, it is distinctly short on Land Rover macho and seems little more than a frivolous plaything.

That, of course, is not quite the case, but whatever its pedigree the SJ has made the 'micro' leisure market its own. For almost a decade the little off-roader has been in great demand; Suzuki GB has for the most part been able to sit back and sell all its limited import quota with ease.

It's easy to see why the SJ has proved so popular. It's cheap – new, it always cost about the same as a mid-range Fiesta – and modest running costs make it a perfect second vehicle if there's an off-road enthusiast in the house. And of course it looks the part; its Jeep-like styling is good for both Tesco's car park and the windsurfing club. It seems odd that no other manufacturer has ever tried to muscle in.

Though Suzuki's quota is among the smallest of the Japanese importers, there are reasonable numbers of used SJs for sale. Last year, for example, sales of the Samurai – in practice the swansong version of the SJ – totalled 1349 compared to 1554 Vitaras.

SPECIFICATION & MODEL DEVELOPMENT

The SJ410 appeared in September 1982, succeeding the LJ range. Measuring just 135 inches in length, its all-steel body was mounted on a box-section chassis. It looked square and boxy compared to its more traditionally styled predecessor. It was offered with one engine, a four-cylinder overhead cam unit of just 970cc. This gave 45bhp, accompanied by 54lbf.ft of torque at 3000rpm.

The transmission was four-speed manual, with selectable four-wheel drive and a two-speed transfer box. Freewheeling front hubs were a cheaply-priced dealer option. Live axles at each end were supported by simple leaf springs and telescopic dampers. Steering was unassisted worm and ball,

brakes were drums all round.

Commercial versions apart, there were three models. The SJ410 was the estate-style four-seater, the SJ410Q was the two-seater canvas-topped model, and the SJ410V the two-seater hard-top. All three were featherweights, tipping the scales at 850-900kg.

The first milestone came in October 1983, when front disc brakes were fitted. At the same time the interior trim was upgraded slightly. In March 1985 Suzuki introduced the SJ413, powered by a 1324cc engine. This gave 64bhp and 74lbf.ft of torque at 3500rpm. It was available as a hard-top only.

In early 1987 Suzuki introduced the SJ Santana Sport. It took that name because production had been transferred from Japan to the Santana plant in Spain. The 'regular' SJ models continued to be sold.

The Santana Sport was basically a high-specification SJ410 with a five-speed gearbox. It was based on the soft-top body, and featured a white hood along with

Suzuki SJ

colour-keyed external trim. Inside, there was more extensive carpeting, head-restraints on the front seats, and a 50/50 split-fold rear seat. In August 1989 a version of the Santana Sport with a detachable resin hard-top was introduced. The Santana and SJ413 were given softer suspension.

By this stage the SJ410 hard and soft-tops had been dropped, though two limited editions had appeared. The SJ410 Style, introduced in July 1988, was basically a hard-top estate version of the Santana, and continued until 1990 when the Vitara arrived.

The SJ410 Rhino was a run of 175 vehicles, introduced in August 1989. This was effectively the Santana hard-top (the detachable version) with special white paintwork and Rhino graphics on the body. The SJ lives on under the Samurai name. It is basically the SJ413, but is also offered with a long wheelbase and 1.6-litre engine.

SUZUKI SJ ON THE ROAD
Off-road, the Suzuki gives a good account of itself considering its limited power. But because it is set up for off-road use it is seriously flawed on the tarmac. The first problem is the engine: both units are willing, but very noisy indeed when cruising. The noise levels on five-speed models are only slightly less distressing. To get adequate performance from the one-litre, it has to be thrashed. The 1.3-litre has more in reserve but still needs to be worked hard.

The transmission doesn't make for relaxed driving, either. The gearshift – which has a direct linkage to the box – has a slow movement, and the drive always takes up jerkily. As in all off-roaders the driver sits high up, and through the flat screen enjoys good road vision. But the seats are small and unsupportive.

As far as on-road driving is concerned, undoubtedly the SJ's worst feature is the steering. The worm and nut steering is hopelessly vague, with zero feedback from the road. The driver must constantly correct to keep the Suzuki in a straight line; this aggravates the vehicle's already poor high-speed stability. On most road surfaces the SJ's cart-spring suspension gives a jarring, bouncy ride, and the 195SP15 tyres generate much road roar.

But if the SJ is a mobile torture chamber at high speed, at least it's practical as a mini load carrier. The interior features a sparse, no-nonsense trim that doesn't easily get messed up. The load bay is small, but the side-hinged rear door and exterior-mounted spare allow the space to be exploited to the full. The payload is quoted at 462lb, the towing weight 2420lb.

Given the SJ's strong leisure sector appeal, not surprisingly the soft-top models have been the most popular. The canvas isn't the snug-fitting hood you see on modern convertibles; lowering and raising it is quite a performance. But at least the sight of the substantial centre roll-hoop is reassuring.

The SJ's equipment specification has always been basic, but dealers offered a wide choice of extras. A tow kit, bull bars, indicator guards, rear bench seat for two-seater vehicles, spare-wheel cover and many other items were listed. Most should still be available through dealers.

HOW MUCH?
During the heady 1980s the little SJs enjoyed excellent resale value. This was due to the limited supply and the modest new price. But two things affected resale values. A couple of years ago publicity over the alleged instability problem weakened residuals, which have never fully recovered. And the recession has, of course, reduced demand for good-time vehicles like the Suzuki.

But SJs still command relatively high prices. For example a 1990 H-registered Samurai hard-top, costing £7990 new, would be offered by a dealer for just £7000. By today's standards of depreciation that's good going.

What's the rock-bottom price for an SJ? In theory, the early models ('82, X-registration) are worth less than £1000, but you don't see many of these for sale. Many of this age will be scrapped. To get something in a reasonable state a budget of around £3000 is advisable; this would allow you to purchase a 1986/87 vehicle privately, or a slightly older one from a dealer. Spend £5000 and you'd be looking at 1988/89 models.

Because the soft-top models are more sought-after they are worth slightly more. However, in absolute terms the difference in values between the various models is not great.

One of the early Spanish-built Suzuki SJ Santanas

BUYING SECOND-HAND

WHAT GOES WRONG?

For the first couple of years of life, virtually nothing. Like all Japanese vehicles the SJ runs like clockwork. But don't be fooled by the rugged-looking style of the SJ. It's not toughly built; look around the body and you'll see some flimsy-looking joints and seams.

At best, serious off-roading will very quickly render an SJ rattly at the joints, and at worst will ruin it. The paintwork appears to be no deeper or longer-lasting than a road car, so dents and scratches collected off-road soon turn into ugly rust patches. You see some relatively young SJs that are badly rusted.

Ground clearance is a healthy nine inches, but the front and rear leaf spring carriers are low-mounted, and hence vulnerable. There is no sump guard to protect the bottom of the engine and gearbox.

The SJ is a popular choice for small businesses looking for a working vehicle. Builders tend to go for the commercial versions, but operators who want an all-purpose vehicle often buy the estate model. Check who has owned an SJ previously as businesses are, largely, bad news. But there are plenty of SJs that live in towns and never put a wheel off-road – these are the safest ones to buy.

The one-litre engine suffers at the hands of drivers who expect 1.6-litre performance on road, and V8 performance off-road. Check for oil-burning and sounds of general wear. The transmission is tough enough if treated with respect, but again drivers who place unreasonable loads on it will wear it out.

The SJ is a simple vehicle, but think carefully before buying a cheap basket case with a view to rebuilding. Replacement engines and gearboxes for pre-1985 SJs are not available through Suzuki dealers; a rebuild using spare parts is necessary, which will be very expensive. Otherwise parts are freely available, even if the Suzuki dealer network is limited in size. Parts specialists and breakers' yards are alternative sources which are worth investigating.

Accessories are reasonable. For instance a complete new hood can be bought for under £200, a carpet set for under £100, and a rear seat for £150 (belts extra).

SERVICING

The SJ's simplicity is not reflected in servicing costs at Suzuki dealers. In London a typical price for a 6000-mile service is £120 minimum, with the full 12,000-mile service likely to be over £150. There is no difference in servicing costs between the SJ410 and 413. Much of the cost is made up by the sky-high labour rates charged by all dealers. Non-franchised specialists will undoubtedly be able to do the job equally well at a much lower price.

PARTS PRICES (supplied by Suzuki dealer, inc VAT. Hood price from non-franchised specialist)

Engine (short,exchange)	
SJ410	£646
SJ413	£568
Gearbox (exchange)	
SJ410	£623
SJ413	£693
Front brake disc	£52
Exhaust (full)	£130
Front shock absorber	£55
Front wing	£120
Hood	£195

SECOND-HAND PRICES

Under £1000	'82/'83 SJ410, rough condition
£1000–£2000	'84/'85 models, well used, not many for sale at this price
£2000–£3000	'85/'86 models, soft/hard-top
£3000–£4000	'86/'87 SJs, Santanas, avoid rusty or worn-out examples. First of 413 models ('86)
£4000–£5000	'87/'88 SJs, Santanas
£5000–£6000	'88/'89 SJs, Santanas, also Samurais
£6000–£7000	1990/'91 H-registered Samurais

SJ413 for photography loaned by 4x4 specialists Walton Motors, 26 Sandy Lane, Walton-on-Thames, Surrey. Tel: 0932 247176.

VERDICT

With its cute styling and low purchase cost, the SJ is appealing. But will it really suit your needs? If you do heavy off-roading forget it, because you'll break it very quickly. If you do long journeys, also forget it, or at least consider only the SJ413.

But if you want a little runaround that is good in town and can tackle – with care – off-road conditions, then the Suzuki makes sense. It's a particularly good choice of second car – and if you decide you've made the wrong choice, re-selling it shouldn't be hard even in today's depressed market.

The interior is basic but reasonably durable

The SJ is a versatile leisure vehicle

Technical Specification

Engines

One-litre petrol, four-cylinder in-line, ohc, carburettor (SJ410/Santana)

Displacement (cc)	970
Power (bhp/rpm)	45/5500
Torque (lbf.ft/rpm)	54/3000

1.3-litre petrol, four-cylinder in-line, ohc, carburettor (SJ413)

Displacement (cc)	1324
Power (bhp/rpm)	64/6000
Torque (lbf.ft/rpm)	74/3500

Transmission

Selectable four-wheel drive, high/low ratio, 4/5-speed manual, freewheeling front hubs optional (can be retro-fitted)

Brakes (front/rear)

Disc/disc (pre-October '83 front drums)

Tyres

195SR15

Dimensions

Length (in)	135
Height (in)	66
Width (in)	58
Ground clearance (in)	9
Weight (kg) soft/hard-top	850–900
Towing weight (kg)	1100
Fuel tank (gall)	8.8

POCKET-SIZED OFF-ROADER

Finding a four-wheel-drive recreational vehicle for less than £5000 is no easy task. Serious bog-trotters could opt for a beat-up Land Rover — but a more popular choice for the rest is the Suzuki SJ410, which has limited off-road ability but plenty of style. By David Sutherland

SECONDHAND *spotlight*

Model: *Suzuki SJ410 Santana Style*

Date Registered: *24/4/89*

Asking price: *£4495*

Mileage: *17,688*

Colour: *blue*

Service history: *none documented*

Warranty: *12 months parts/labour*

Number of owners: *2*

Dealer: *Walton Motors, 26 Sandy Lane, Walton on Thames, Surrey. Telephone 0932 247176*

Extra equipment in limited-edition Style

THE FOUR-WHEEL DRIVE 'LEISURE' market has boomed in recent years — but steady price increases have made off-roaders that once looked reasonably priced now seem decidedly expensive. You now need a budget of at least £7000 to buy a new off-roader, and that only gets you the capable but elderly Lada Niva or the slightly frivolous Fiat Panda 4x4. The trendiest small off-roaders around — the Daihatsu Sportrak and Suzuki Vitara — are knocking on £10,000, and that's only for the cheapest versions.

We set out to see what sort of off-roader we could get secondhand for less than £5000. A limited budget like this prompts the question: do you go for a serious off-road vehicle (and accept that five grand will only buy a fairly dilapidated Range Rover or slightly less scruffy Land Rover), or do you choose something newer but with less ultimate off-road ability, such as Suzuki's diminutive, Jeep-like SJ410?

If common sense comes into the equation, it's hard to argue in favour of the thirsty, potentially troublesome Land Rover and Range Rover. So it had to be a Suzuki.

The SJ was introduced in 1982, powered by a 970cc four-cylinder engine good for 45bhp. Drive was to the rear wheels, but four-wheel drive and a low range of gear ratios were selectable by means of an extra lever on the transmission tunnel.

Near the beginning of 1987 it was replaced by the SJ410 Santana, which used the same square-rigged shell but had front disc brakes instead of drums and a plusher interior. It was built in Spain at the Santana plant rather than in Japan, hence the name.

The SJ413 version is the same vehicle except that it uses a 64bhp 1.3-litre engine. The Santana is offered with either hard or soft tops; not surprisingly, the soft-top is more popular.

A year ago it was hard to find used SJs, but with the used car trade in the doldrums they are now more common on dealers' forecourts. We tracked down a 1989, F-registered Santana SJ410 hard-top that was for sale at non-franchised 4x4 specialist Walton Motors, in Walton on Thames, Surrey.

The blue Santana was a limited-edition Style model, fitted with 'Style' body decals, a tachometer, heated rear window and rear screen wash/wipe. It was a two-owner vehicle with 17,688 miles on the clock, and was fitted with an ultrasonic alarm. The knobbly tyres

appeared to be in nearly-new condition, while the tailgate-mounted spare was unused.

The service book carried no stamps apart from the pre-delivery inspection, but Walton Motors proprietor Charles Loveridge assured us that the Suzuki had been fully serviced from new.

It was priced at £4495 — £500 below book value — and the price included a 12-month, insurance-backed parts and labour warranty. It seemed sensible money to pay, given that the Santana's current equivalent, the Samurai, costs £9000 new.

The Santana appeared to be in good all-round condition. Unblemished bodywork and dent-free wheel rims suggested it had never

---

SUZUKI SJ410 SANTANA STYLE

LAYOUT
Longitudinal, front engine, rear/four-wheel-drive

ENGINE
Capacity 970cc, 4 cylinders in line
Bore 66mm
Stroke 72mm
Compression ratio 8.8:1
Head/block alloy/iron
Max power 45bhp (34Kw ISO) at 5500rpm
Max torque 54lb ft (74Nm) at 3000rpm

GEARBOX
Five-speed manual, selectable four-wheel drive, two-speed transfer box
Ratios 5th 0.79, 4th 1.00, 3rd 1.42, 2nd 1.95, 1st 3.14
Final drive ratio 4.11

SUSPENSION
Front Live axle, leaf springs, telescopic dampers
Rear Live axle, leaf springs, telescopic dampers

STEERING
Recirculating ball

BRAKES
Front discs
Rear drums

WHEELS AND TYRES
Pressed steel wheels, 195 SR15 tyres

DIMENSIONS
Length	135ins (3440mm)
Width	58ins (1460mm)
Height	66ins (1680mm)
Wheelbase	80ins (2030mm)
Weight	1958lb (890kg)

FUEL CONSUMPTION (claimed)
Urban 30.4mpg; steady 56mph 32.8mpg; steady 75mph not tested

been used off road, or if it had the driver had taken care not to brush tree branches or hit rocks. But then conditions are rarely that treacherous in London SW1, where the Santana's first owner lived. The second owner, who lived in Surrey, kept the Santana for just a few months before selling it to Walton Motors.

Inside, the Santana was in equally good condition. The seats were still supportive and the trim undamaged. Whoever valeted the cabin had been over-enthusiastic with the cleaning fluid, though; the overwhelming smell of detergent wasn't pleasant. But thankfully there was nothing to indicate that any foul loads had been carried in the rear — a common task for 4x4s.

The Santana's engine was responsive and the transmission was in good shape. The five-speed gearbox shifted slickly enough and the low range engaged correctly. The bodywork was rattle-free.

In general, little goes wrong with a Santana if it is treated with respect, but abuse can shorten its life significantly. The one-litre engine struggles if the driver expects 1.6-litre performance from it. If a Santana has been used enthusiastically off road there will almost certainly be dents and scratches on the body-work, floor and chassis, which can lead to premature rusting. Neglected, rusty SJs are not uncommon.

Some Santanas are bought as work/leisure vehicles and might have been used as delivery vans — the wide-opening tailgate and tall load area encourage this type of use. It is advisable to check for damage caused by messy or heavy loads.

However, Loveridge believes there's a good chance of finding a Santana that has been well cared for. "Not many are taken off road," he says. "Most are bought purely as fun vehicles — we have a lady interested in this particular one."

If we were in the market for a Santana we would have been happy to part with £4495 for this example. It looked smart in its blue paintwork and contrasting white wheels, and the general condition suggested that it had plenty of life left in it.

However, potential buyers should take a Santana for a thorough test drive to establish whether it is really the vehicle they want. It looks chic, but its performance is limited. Handling is very vague and stability is poor. It is deafeningly noisy at speed and is a useless vehicle for a long journey. Apart from that, it's a lot of fun. ■

What the trade says

PRIOR TO THE widely publicised instability scare of a couple of years ago, these little fun vehicles were in high demand with young drivers and those in search of a second car with image. Residual values were badly affected for a short period as a result of the publicity and have never fully returned to the heady levels they were at previously.

The recession has affected off-roaders more than most types of vehicle and the little Suzuki as badly as any. The tiny engine and flimsy construction make them unsuitable for heavy work and they must pick up their buyers from the leisure vehicle market and those who require only occasional off-road ability. The Suzuki does, in fact, perform quite well off road in a limited way, but the small engine size and bouncy, uneven ride make the experience a frenetic one. On road they are noisy and harsh with handling that can be described as delicate at best. Over-exuberance can result in the car falling over, but driven with respect the Suzuki is safe and secure.

A comparatively low price when new and good image have ensured low initial depreciation, and this is still the case despite recent setbacks. One-year-old examples will have lost 29 or 30 per cent of the price new, given low mileage, which is pretty good by today's standards. Long-term values are less certain because of the likely onset of corrosion after about three years. Bodywork is not robust and build quality only average, so prices for examples that are in any way inferior or have high mileages are much less than those for the best examples.

Depreciation accelerates after the second year; from around 17.5 per cent at this point it will be at something like 20 to 25 per cent by the fifth year. Most are a touch moth-eaten and mechanically tired at this age. £4495 is plenty to pay for a car with no history and two previous owners, and better examples can be had for less money privately. It would also pay to seek out a 1.3-litre version because these are superior in refinement, performance and durability.

John Coates

Don't expect much from one-litre engine

SUZUKI SAMURAI

Fun on a shoestring

PHOTOS BY RON PERRY

Suzuki's mighty-mite 4-wheel-drive Samurai is joined for 1991 by two new models: The 2-wheel-drive JA, which has no top or rear seat, and the standard JS version, which has a canvas top and a rear seat—also 2-wheel drive.

This is the first year for a 2-wheel-drive-only Samurai, and it's built on the same 79.9-in. wheelbase as the original and present 4-wheel-drive off-roadster. Offering a more basic vehicle has enabled Suzuki to trim the price of the base Samurai to $5999.

Wheelbase, overall length, track, overall width and height, are the same for 2- or 4-wheel-drive Samurais. Weight is slightly higher for the 4-wheel-drive model.

All Suzuki Samurais are powered by a 4-cylinder, aluminum-block, water-cooled sohc engine with 1298 cc, putting out 66 bhp at 6000 rpm. It has a 9.5:1 compression ratio and electronic fuel injection.

Drive goes through a single-disc, dry plate clutch and 5-speed all-synchromesh transmission to a live rear axle positioned by semi-elliptic leaf springs.

A 2-speed transfer case takes power to the front wheels on the 4wd version. The front hubs are manually

engaged. The adventurous owner who decides actually to go off road might want to know that ground clearance is 8.1 in., and the front approach angle is 43 degrees, the rear departure angle is 38 degrees.

Because of the Samurai's diminutive dimensions, it can go through spaces that other 4-wheel-drive vehicles couldn't squeeze through, but this narrow track and overall width make it mandatory that the driver use common sense.

The Samurai is particularly well suited for off-road work—if the driver is careful (advice that applies to *any* off road activity in *any* vehicle). My experience is that the Samurai is dangerous only in the hands of a nitwit—who would probably do dumb things in any vehicle he drives.

If I had to complain about the Samurai, it would be for its choppy ride. The short wheelbase, which makes it so maneuverable, also gives it a pitching motion that is uncomfortable for many passengers.

One of Suzuki's criteria for the Samurai is the lowest possible price. Simplification of production is a great way to accomplish that goal, and everything about the Samurai is predicated on that premise. The base 2-wheel-drive JA model comes only in white, for 1991, and the standard 2-wheel-drive JS can be obtained only in red or white. The standard 4-wheel-drive Samurai JL is available in white, red or black.

The basic Samurai can be improved with optional factory- or dealer-installed accessories, including air conditioning, stereo/cassette radio and a bikini top covering only the front passenger compartment.

A $200 modular roof rack system will carry a variety of things that outdoors people want to carry—bicycles, skis, surfboards, hunting gear or items from the hardware store that won't fit inside. A trailer hitch can also be fitted.

There have been sport-utility vehicles built before the Samurai, others are being built now and will be built in the future that will carry more, do more, and go faster, but it is unlikely that any will do it for so little, or will become the younger driver's cult car as the Samurai has.

When the Samurai made its U.S. debut in late 1985, it redefined the

Tiny 1.3-liter engine is the smallest of all the sport utilities.

entry-level sport-utility market. Prior to that time this category of transportation was mainly truck-like and rather homely. They may have had character, but they sure didn't have panache. The Samurai isn't much for acceleration, top speed, or towing capacity (1000 lb), but what it does offer is a whole lot of fun for a minimum of money.

I don't know how many Samurais are used for traveling or off-road expeditions, but I see a lot of them (particularly in Southern California) in urban use such as shopping, running errands, going to class at a high school or college, or hauling surfers and boards to the beach.

—*Dean Batchelor*

SPECIFICATIONS

Base price, base model	$5999
Base price, premium model	$6999
Country of origin	Japan
Body/seats	2D, conv*/4
Layout	F/2wd*, 4wd
Wheelbase	79.9 in.
Track, f/r	51.2 in./51.6 in.
Length	135.0 in.
Width	60.6 in.
Height	65.6 in.
Minimum ground clearance	8.1 in.
Curb weight	2125 lb
Maximum towing capacity	1000 lb
Gross Vehicle Weight Rating	2932
Cargo capacity	31.9 cu ft
Fuel capacity	10.6 U.S. gal.
Fuel economy (EPA city)	28, 29 mpg
Engine	1.3L 66-bhp sohc inline-4
Bore x stroke	74.0 x 75.5 mm
Displacement	1298 cc
Compression ratio	9.5:1
Horsepower, SAE net	66 bhp @ 6000 rpm
Torque	76 lb-ft @ 3500 rpm
Transmission	5M
Final-drive ratio	3.73:1
Suspension, f/r	live/live
Brakes, f/r	disc/drum
Base tires	P205/70R-15
Steering type	ball and nut
Turning circle	33.4 ft
Warranty, years/miles	
Bumper-to-bumper	2/24,000
Powertrain	2/24,000
Rust-through	3/unlimited

*indicates model described in specifications.

IT'S SMALL, IT'S CONVENTIONAL.
IS THE SAMURAI COMMERCIAL PROVEN,
OR JUST A LITTLE OLD FASHIONED?
LIGHT WORK

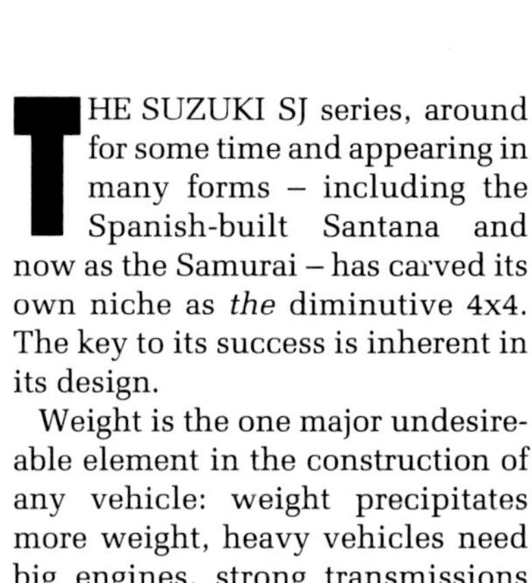

THE SUZUKI SJ series, around for some time and appearing in many forms – including the Spanish-built Santana and now as the Samurai – has carved its own niche as *the* diminutive 4x4. The key to its success is inherent in its design.

Weight is the one major undesireable element in the construction of any vehicle: weight precipitates more weight, heavy vehicles need big engines, strong transmissions large wheel and tyre combinations, all of which make them even heavier. The weight-strength-weight relationship spirals and efficiency goes out of the window.

The Suzuki has never fallen into that trap. Apply such thinking to a small commercial vehicle, and it looks promising.

OVERVIEW

There is nothing to set the pulse racing about the specification of the Samurai Commercial. A traditional ladder frame chassis is employed along with leaf-sprung live axles, a part-time four-wheel-drive system, disappointingly devoid of freewheeling hubs, and a four-cylinder petrol engine. Like so many commercial 4x4s, it owes more to the Willys Jeep than the Range Rover for its inspiration.

However, this simple thinking gives it two great benefits, which go hand-in-hand. Simplicity and competitive cost. The Samurai Commercial draws its features from a couple of existing Suzuki models. The cab area is identical to a soft-top SJ's (or Samurai's) forward portions, while the loadbed is that of the relatively rare long-wheelbase pick-up (no longer imported into the UK), although Suzuki has resisted the temptation merely to add a hard top, giving a split-tailgate arrangement and has instead fitted the side-hinged station-wagon rear door, with removable glass upper when running topless.

BEHIND THE WHEEL

To be polite, the Samurai's driving position was less than impressive. To be blunt, it was probably the worst I've encountered thus far for INATERNATIONAL OFF-ROADER. It begins with the seats. They are won-

derfully shaped, with big bucket-style side bolsters, very reminiscent of the Renault Fuego's, for those of you with long memories or strange tastes in coupes.

The seats are comfortable enough, they even have reasonable lumber support, which is increasingly rare in non-adjustable types. But they simply cannot be positioned accurately enough. The most upright position is about equal to 30 per cent reclined in all other vehicles

Report and pictures by test editor Ian Shaw

I've come across. Try to achieve a relatively upright posture and you find the seat is past its last position and on disengaged tilt.

Couple this to the need for good wheel leverage required for the unassisted steering once off-road, pedals which must be attacked from above like those of a truck, and the narrow '5-gallon-can' footwells, and the laid-back, straight-arm, knees-hitting-the-facia picture is complete.

The controls themselves are quite good. The gearchange is light if a little notchy, the transfer selector has swiss-watch movements, the brakes have feel and the steering does its best to communicate, although around the straight-ahead it's as vague as a politician's intentions.

The clutch is the worst area. The pedal loads are light, but the bite point is vague and inconsistent, and the take-up loads non-linear.

The instrumentation is clear if somewhat basic and the switchgear is, in the main, well placed. The column stalks, unusually for a Japanese vehicle, follow Euro-convention with the lighting controls on the left-hand and windscreen wash and wipe to the right.

The rear wash/wiper switch is exactly where you'd expect it. Out of sight, around the corner of the facia, just ahead of the driver's side window demist outlet; and with all that space *beneath the passenger seat* going to waste!

ON THE ROAD

Under the influence of the autochoke, the 1.3-litre four-potter starts instantly but is reluctant to pull immediately. This probably could be attributed to our particular vehicle having a suspect choke since a couple of hundred metres further on, it would idle at 2,000 rpm.

Performance is actually quite good, with a power-to-weight ratio of 65bhp/tonne, superior to that of, say, a Tdi Discovery. It'll win no drag races but it is quick in traffic.

It needs revs, however. That 63bhp is developed at 6,000 rpm and the peak torque of 73lb/ft doesn't appear until 3,500rpm. For best progress you must bear this in mind, and that of the approximate 1,000rpm drop in revolutions during upchanges. Therefore, to be in the torque after an upshift one has to wind the Suzuki to over 4,500rpm in the lower ratio. The results are pleasing but the real limit is only a little higher.

At 5,000 revs it begins to sound rather thrashy and the torque is dropping away. Revving to the 6,000rpm power peak, let alone the six-five red line seems pointless and a little cruel.

If I ruled the world, the first thing I'd do is stop Japanese manufacturers from designing their carburettor engines with a 'damped' engine deceleration upon closing the throttle. Most have it in larger or smaller amounts, the idea being to stop the revs falling too low, particularly in close-ratio boxes such as this, during up-shifts. Supposedly this makes for smoother gearchanges. It may do, if you take a full two or three seconds to move the lever 'tween one ratio and the next. For 99.9 per cent of drivers it is simply annoying. Coupled to the indifferent clutch in this machine, it is downright infuriating.

That high-revving engine saves the day, however. Rev it hard, briefly kick the clutch and snatch the next cog before the throttle damping knows what's hit it, and power away. It's more efficient and a good deal more enjoyable.

Power it may have in sufficient amounts but the lack of real stump-pulling torque is all too apparent on hills. The revs drop away rapidly and where the average diesel Fourtrak would delve into its reserves and keep plugging away in top, the Samurai needs 4th, sometimes 3rd gear to maintain progress,

even unladen; it is the only chink in the light-is-efficient armour.

The roadholding of any vehicle also benefits from lower readings on the weighbridge. The Samurai bears that out. The roll angles are a little higher than I expected, particularly for what is basically a stiffly sprung machine with the benefit of a front anti-roll bar.

The 205 tyres hold quite well on dry tarmac but are less sure of wet conditions and in conjunction with the vague steering make fast wet-road work something of a challenge without reward. No doubt still mindful of past bad press in the handling department, Suzuki's engineers seem to have gone a little over the top with the measure of understeer with which they have garnished the overall roadholding.

The long-wheelbase layout obviously creates less forward weight transfer than found with a SWB Samurai, but even by trailing into the corners, that understeer was impossible to neutralise; using large amounts of throttle produced much of the same.

Fail-safe in most cornering situations it may be, but for those odd occassions where it is desirable, even imperative that the line be tightened, I would feel rather vunerable. If I ruled the world, the second thing that I'd do would be to tune in a little lift-off oversteer into the Samurai's suspension. The brakes are excellent. They are powerful enough but moreover have feedback and are wonderfully progressive.

The ride quality, as you'd expect of a leaf-sprung lightweight machine, is hardly in the magic carpet league. The pitching which so badly affects the SWB version of this machine, and the SWB Fourtrak for that matter, is damped to some extent by the longer wheelbase, but it is still no match for a Land Rover

Ninety, or a Hilux pick-up, come to that. There is a deal of diagonal pitching on undulating corners, it isn't particularly self-correcting either, and in conjunction with a sympathetic gyroscopic effect from the live front axle, it makes the Samurai feel decidedly nervous in such situations.

Otherwise, the ride is quite well controlled. Potholes do not produce the almighty crashing which afflicts some vehicles of this weight, the damping seems reasonable, Japanese never achieve, nor I believe even aim for, the damping characteristics of European vehicles. The Suzuki is none the worse for it.

Feed-back over bumpy surfaces, via the steering wheel, can reach lively proportions. Despite a modest lock angle, dictated by the leaf springs, it has a curious, over-centre feel to it that I've not experienced on other live-axle machines and will tug this way and that if not kept in check over indifferent surfaces.

OFF THE ROAD

This vehicle in its many forms has always been good off the road. Unimogs may weigh 5 tons and have massive wheels, but as a general rule, small light vehicles will have the edge in the class with which we are concerned. They are more maneouvrable in any given situation by virtue of their lack of bulk, lighter vehicles have greater flotation in soft conditions and are easier to recover if they fail.

Those who love the Suzuki love it for those reasons. However, such machines lack the shear brute power of larger vehicles and therefore require different techniques. This one is no exception.

Once in low ratio, the Samurai feels well able to attack serious off-road terrain. Peak torque revs being relatively high means it won't pull along at idle in low-3rd like a V8 – indeed serious hillclimbing can be accomplished only in 1st-gear low box, which does leave you with a sense of vulnerability. Nevertheless, the Suzuki tackled everything we threw at it, and we spared it nothing in comparison with larger, more powerful machines.

The only downside of the small, high-revving engine off-road is

engine braking, which feels decidedly poor. In the mainly dry conditions of the off-road test, I took to gentle braking on some descents, which with the excellent braking feel that this vehicle has, is not the disaster-waiting-to-happen that it could be in other vehicles.

Away from steep inclines, the Suzuki will potter along quite happily at much lower revs than its torque curve suggests.

The suspension travel is better than most would expect. We have grown so used to the massive wheel travel available from Rover's coil springs, that we seem to think anything less is a recipe for recovery. As it is, the leaf springs on this vehicle are quite supple, again because they aren't burdened with much weight, and overall I would rate its axle articulation, front and rear combined, as being better than any of the front torsion bar, rear leaf-sprung machines I've encountered, including the old model Trooper, which was the best of its design.

This makes the Samurai's limitations in crossing severe terrain all the more apparent. The approach and departure angles are the real limit. At the front, the approach is limited by the rather vulnerable, exposed spring shackles. Although leaf springs are generally considered to assist the passing of a live axle by acting as skids, in this case they meet obstacles head-on, stopping the vehicle and causing potential mis-alignment of the front axle.

At the rear, it is a case of overhang. There is nothing particularly vulnerable, indeed the Suzuki's towbar

grounded on a couple of occasions without drama, the fuel tank is also well protected; it's just the physical aspect of that sizable overhang which halts the proceedings.

The ramp-angle is nothing special in itself but the Suzuki's narrow track saves the day, because on most unsurfaced roads, the obstacles can be tackled at a slight angle where wider vehicles would be forced to take them square-on. The relatively good suspension travel also makes this a viable proposition without immediately lifting diagonally opposed wheels.

Traction was virtually guaranteed in the mainly dry conditions of the test period. The M+S patterned Dunlop SP Qualifiers were at home in such conditions and other than a reluctance to climb from dry ruts, owing to lack of side tread lugs, they performed well. A brief foray a couple of days after the test proper, showed that they lacked real bite on a carpet of wet grass and forest floor debris and the Suzuki failed a short, sharp 40 degree climb.

The ride off road is predictably bouncy. Most of the shock seems to be transmitted through the lighter laden (at least at the loads we carried off-road) rear axle, although the front can become fairly lively and the steering kick-back reaches quite violent proportions. Slight deviations in line, however, are generally self correcting, and the steering rates better overall than some of the excessively light power-assisted systems I've experienced.

Protection for life away from the highway is reasonable. The steering

Far left: The interior has a reasonable layout, but is cramped. Driving positio is poor. Left: Away from steep inclines the Suzuki will potter along quite happily a much lower re than its torque curve suggest:

gear is out of harm's way, and the diffs being offset give a much greater clearance than the 205/70R15 tyres would lead you to believe. Fuel tank and gearbox have shields.

Part of the exhaust looks a little vunerable but being slightly offset in such a narrow vehicle, it is never far from the protective influence of one of the chassis legs.

At the front, a small towing eye is provided, the towbar at the rear will suffice but the rear bumper is not suitable for lifting and the front bullbar promises little more than trial and error.

ACCOMMODATION

The cab is hardy the most spacious place. Occupants sit almost shoulder to shoulder, and the doors are so close as to be intrusive.

Headroom is no problem although this is helped by the 'enforced' reclined driving position. Noise levels are quite high once above town speeds and on the motorway the Suzuki lets you know it's working hard. Road noise is well controlled although wind noise has a major role to play.

Oddments space within the cab is limited. No door bins, no centre cubby. Only a small passenger-side glove box which is almost filled by a small toolkit and owners' documentation.

The load bay in our example had not only a plastic load liner, à la most pick-up options lists, but a rubberised net mat to restrain light items of luggage from sliding around too much. A tubular frame guard was also fitted between load bed and front seats. Nice touch that.

The hard top is equipped with a series of over-centre sprung lever catches, and looks as if it could be removed quite quickly to convert the machine to a pick-up. In the same vein, the upper half of the rear door, the frameless glass section, can be unbolted. Showing it's soft-top origins, the cab roof panel can be removed in a similar manner, making for a very versatile vehicle.

CONCLUSION

For the most part, the lightweight-equals-efficiency adage seems to be proven. The fuel consumption of our test example didn't fully bear this out, but the need to rev it hard seems to have accounted for most of our disappointing 21mpg average, although I suspect a Defender 90 petrol would have difficulty bettering this.

There is little in the way of competition for this machine. A Defender 90, a SWB Fourtrak, or Trooper commercial are considerably more expensive. Other options include a Mitsubishi 1200 pick-up fitted with a hard-top, or even a similarly equipped Subaru pick-up. However, these are not true vans, having separate cab areas.

Suzuki appears to have done it again – niche carving is becoming a habit! Nobody is going to pretend that the Samurai is a match for any of the larger, more powerful models listed above. As an estate-maintenance vehicle or local use site runabout, it is ideally suited. Its simple design holds one more advantage: excellent value for money.

BASIC SPECIFICATION

SUZUKI SAMURAI LWB COMMERCIAL

Price £6,808 excluding VAT
Engine Four-cylinder, water-cooled petrol, all alloy, SOHC, eight valves **Capacity** 1,300cc, **Fuel system** twin-choke down-draught carburettor with automatic coldstart choke **Maximum output** 63bhp (47kw) at 6,000rpm **Maximum torque** 73lb/ft (102Nm) at 3,500rpm

TRANSMISSION
Five-speed manual main gearbox with synchromesh and two-speed constant mesh transfer case providing part-time four-wheel-drive

SUSPENSION
Live axles suspended on semi-elliptical leaf springs front and rear. Telescopic dampers, and anti-roll bar at front

STEERING
Recirculating ball and nut, unassisted. Turning radius 6 metres

BRAKES
Solid discs at front, drums at rear. Servo-assisted

WHEELS/TYRES
Pressed steel 5½J rims shod with 205/70 R15 tyres (Dunlop SP Qualifiers on test car)

DIMENSIONS
Length 13ft 2in (4,010mm) **Width** 5ft 0in (1,530mm) **Wheelbase** 7ft 10in (2,375mm) **Interior load bed length** 4ft 7in (1,420mm) **Width** 4ft 1in (1,260mm) **Between arches** 2ft 11in (900mm) **Height** 3ft 6in (1,080mm)

WEIGHTS
GVW 1,400kg (3,086 lb) **Payload** 430kg (948lb) **Kerb** 970kg (2,138lb) **Towing** (braked) 1,100kg

FUEL CONSUMPTION
Government figures **Urban** 32.8mpg **56mph** 33.6mpg **On test** 21mpg

In the last two issues I dealt with techniques taking advantage of a vehicle's inertia. With most 4x4s being on the heavy side, compared to other cars of similar carrying capacity, there is usually plenty of inertia to play with. Indeed, there is a common fallacy which holds that a 4x4 *needs* to be heavy to work properly – something about making the tyres bite.

Holders of this belief are therefore often perplexed by the performance of light 4x4s such as Suzukis. The conundrum is very simply resolved. It's a matter of weight divided by the area of the tread *ribs* on the ground.

Suppose we're on a site which is mainly wet clay, and by testing it we find that a load of 25lb is required to push a 1in-square stake into the ground a distance ½in.

This then means that to get a similar bite on this soil we want our vehicle weight spread over the tread ribs at a rate of 25lb per square inch. Much less than that means the tyres sit on the surface and spin; much more and they sink in too far.

It's easy to see now that it doesn't matter what weight the vehicle is, it's the area of tread rib on the ground in relation to that weight that counts. A 2,500lb vehicle needs 100 square inches on the ground; a 250lb vehicle needs 10, and so on.

The *total* area of tyre contact counts only where we're concerned about flotation, such as sand, snow or very soft mud.

Of course we're all aware that surface conditions change constantly off-road, and whereas in one place a high ground pressure may be required for traction, it's just as likely within a few yards to be the opposite.

Finding a happy compromise, making an average assessment of what we're likely to have to deal with on a given day's outing, is what it's mainly all about.

To a certain extent we are helped by the fact that wheels are round. As they sink in, more tread makes contact and spreads the load. Animals, with fixed areas of contact in their footprints, are at a disadvantage here – which is why horses and oxen,

Our monthly series on off-roading preparation, equipment and techniques
No 24: Mass — pros and cons

Nine times out of 10 the lighter vehicle has the advantage

not to mention humans, always make a much worse mess of dirt roads when wet.

All this will sound extremely elementary to many readers, but it's amazing how often this fallacy about the necessity for weight can be heard repeated.

Confusion often creeps in when vehicles of very different weights end up on the same tyres. Certainly, on a soil which suits the pressure applied by the heavier, the lighter will be at a disadvantage, and this is a situation which often arises.

The converse, a soft ground suiting the lighter, is more rare, with soft conditions usually leading rapidly into a bog.

There is also the factor of tyre casing stiffness, which is not to be glossed over. Even if the driver has lowered the tyre pressures to a suitable figure for his vehicle in the conditions, if a casing suits a vehicle of around 1½-2½ tons, a much lighter vehicle will not make them work. The answer

here is not to add weight, but to find a more suitable tyre.

For pure off-road work some improvement can be made by cutting away some of the tread ribs, or breaking them up into smaller lumps in the case of dumper tyres.

A good deal of a casing's stiffness is imparted by the tread. Radials are also a help, but the main problem lies in the fact that tyre makers seem to see the off-road market as being mostly in the heavy bracket.

There is a real gap for vehicles in the ½-1 ton class. Suzukis, at the top end of this group, are not well-catered for.

All the foregoing was meant to be a preamble to the main point, which is that nine times out of ten, a light vehicle is preferable. With tyres of a suitable rib area for the load, the light vehicle has an advantage in its lower inertia, most of the time.

Inertia, as we saw in the January issue, keeps a vehicle going in the same direction at the same speed until some force acts on it to change it, and the greater that

inertia the greater will be the force required.

Power steering takes the work out of turning for the driver, but the tyres still have to find something to push against.

Soft surfaces don't provide much resistance, and the lighter vehicle, given tyres of an equivalent loading, will have a better chance of turning. The same applies to braking and accelerating, or perhaps more importantly, moving away from a standstill.

Note that all this applies only to *changes* of velocity or direction. For a constant speed there is no difference between the two, but since driving off-road requires continuous changes of speed and direction, in the matter of which will perform better, the lighter has the advantage.

The exceptions are, as I've stated at other times, fording deep fast-flowing rivers, and forcing a way through undergrowth.

Otherwise, the implications for the serious off-roader are clear: go for the lightest vehicle you can get, commensurate with your requirements, in terms of carrying capacity and power – and keep it light! This means not hauling about with you any more gear than you actually need.

Going out for a day's fun equipped with every bit of tackle you own – ready for conditions ranging from tropical to arctic – may wow the onlookers, but it will also reduce the vehicle's ability to cope with what you do meet.

4x4

■ *This is the last in the Off-Road Wise story. Next month, Peter Phillpotts begins a six-part technical series on the subject of building or rebuilding vehicles.*

While every care is taken in the preparation of this series, neither the author, the editor nor the staff of 4x4 Magazine can be held responsible for any errors or omissions contained therein, or from any consequences arising. Readers are reminded that they are responsible for their own actions.

RHINO ROUND-UP

Diminutive and low powered, the SJ is clearly aimed at the fun market. Right: M P Davis's soft top, has non-standard General Grabber AT tyres

In the first of a regular series, readers sound off about their own production off roaders. James Taylor sifts through the mail and provides the background

THE FIRST time most of us got to see of the SJ-series Suzukis was at the 1982 Motor Show, when soft-top and three-door estate versions of the SJ410 were displayed on the importer's stand. There was a picture of a rhinoceros (intended to suggest ruggedness) on their spare wheel covers, and the rhino went on to become a symbol associated with the SJ range.

The SJ410 was a new breed of 4x4 as far as Britain was concerned; diminutive and low-powered, it made no pretensions to heavy-duty off-roader status, but was quite clearly intended as a fun buggy. As subsequent sales showed, it succeeded only too well, appealing both to those who wanted a chic and cheerful town runabout and to those who wanted an inexpensive off-roader for weekend amusement.

The 970cc, SJ410 models remained available until 1990. In mid-1984, they were improved by the addition of front disc brakes and better seats; in 1985 came a new grille; and from March 1987, the SJ410s sold in Britain had five-speed main gearboxes. Now licence-built by Santana in Spain, they wore Suzuki Santana badges, and the soft-top was marketed as a Santana Sport. The end of the 1980s saw some limited-edition SJ410s, distinguished by special cosmetic features.

Meanwhile, the bigger-engined SJ413 had been introduced in 1985. In 1988 (after widespread stories of

has down in Portreath, Cornwall. He and others think the brakes are very positive; to be fair, though, we didn't have any views of the early all-drum system, which might not be so good.

Nobody thought the bad press about the SJ's stability was justified: "I have found it to be just as stable as any other off-road vehicle I have driven," says Nic Blanchet. On the other hand, Jim Lythgoe sounds a note of caution, pointing out that the SJ doesn't handle like a hot hatch and that he wouldn't recommend one to an inexperienced driver.

The suspension came in for some pretty harsh criticism as well, although some of our correspondents did pull their punches, and it's clear that they liked their SJs enough to forgive quite a lot. "Bumpy", "uncompromising" and "harsh" were descriptions we received; "not as bad as a Series III Land Rover" was Mike Clarke's opinion. But you don't have to put up with it if you don't want to: 'Rhino Ray' from Beeding in West Sussex has plenty of praise for a coil-sprung conversion (using Ford Orion parts) fitted to his vehicle. We intend to find out more about that later.

Other on-road criticisms included high noise levels at speed on soft-top vehicles and a sad lack of interior space: "If you do manage to get everything in," says Rhino Ray, "it takes around five minutes to build up enough momentum to break the 70mph speed limit." Not that he ever would, of course...

Off the road

If it all sounds like bad news for the SJs on the road, it's very much the opposite once you get them off-road. "Generally," Nic Blanchet tells us, "any prospective buyer will find the SJ a tough and willing off-road companion, often capable of cheekily upstaging more exotic machinery." John Mitchell from Cirencester in Gloucestershire confirms that off-road, the SJ is "in its element", and Mike Clarke's first experience of one in the rough left him with the view that "the SJ was astounding, tackling many obstacles I thought would be impossible for any vehicle".

stability problems, particularly in the USA), it picked up wider tracks, low-profile tyres and softer suspension.

From 1990, production transferred to Spain and the SJ413 was renamed the Samurai. Soft-top (Sport) and three-door Estate versions remained available. They still are.

On the road

As a buyer, you shouldn't be discouraged by an SJ's lack of performance, by its harsh ride, or by its vague steering: according to our readers, all three features are standard! However, if the roadholding seems sloppy, the gearbox slack, or the brakes feeble, then the example you're looking at has problems.

It's pretty clear from the letters we received that a Suzuki SJ is all right for town work, but that it isn't so good on long journeys. Several owners said the SJs were nippy in town and great for urban pottering. The gearbox is a major factor in this; Jim Lythgoe from Teignmouth in Devon spoke for several others when he described it as "a pleasure to use".

However, on the open road "is where the vehicle fails terribly", says Barry Weeks, from Witney in Oxfordshire, about his girlfriend's SJ410. Long journeys are "noisy and uncomfortable", and "lack of power on the open road causes frustration". That absence of accelerative urge was echoed by several owners who wrote in, and it isn't confined to the 970cc models, either. Jim Lythgoe's SJ413 is "underpowered for a 1,300", but it will cruise at 65mph on the flat.

That seems to be about the right cruising speed for the smaller-engined vehicles, too. You can push an SJ410 up to 80mph (the importer claims 81mph for the current Samurai "but engine noise soon makes you feel guilty", says D G Pettit, from Culford in Suffolk.

Several of our correspondents criticised the steering as vague, and even the more committed Suzuki lovers agreed that it took some getting used to. Mike Clarke, of Shildon in County Durham, thought that it was very much improved when he added the optional freewheel hubs to his SJ413. If you can live with the steering, though, roadholding is "tight and positive" as Nic Blanchet says of the SJ413 he

BASIC SPECIFICATION

ENGINE
Four-cylinder, in-line, OHC, water-cooled petrol. **SJ410** 970cc, single carburettor. 45bhp at 5,500rpm and 54lb/ft at 3,000rpm **SJ413** 1,324cc, single carburettor. 63bhp at 6,000rpm and 74lb/ft at 3,500rpm

TRANSMISSION
Four/five-speed synchromesh main gearbox with remote-mounted two-speed transfer case; part-time four-wheel-drive. **SJ410** Four-speed main gearbox to March 1987; five-speed thereafter. **SJ413** Five-speed main gearbox

SUSPENSION
Front and rear live axles suspended on leaf springs. Front anti-roll bar on SJ413

BRAKES
Drum/drum (1982-1984); Disc/drum (1984 on). Servo assistance on Santana-built SJ410 and all SJ413

WHEELS/TYRES
5.5x15 rims. 195 SR 15 tyres (to 1988); 205/70R15 (from 1988)

DIMENSIONS
Length 3.440mm (135.4in) Width 1,530mm (60.2in) **Height** 1,675mm (65.9in) **Wheelbase** 2,030mm (79.9in) **Ground clearance** 225mm (8.85in)

WEIGHTS
Kerb 920kg (soft top), 940kg (estate) **Towing** 750kg (five-speed SJ410); 1,100kg (all other models)

FUEL CONSUMPTION
Government figures **SJ410 four-speed Urban** 27.2mpg **56mph** 33.2mpg **75mph** - N/A **SJ413 five-speed Urban** 31.7mpg **56mph** 35.7mpg **75mph** 33.6mpg

Bary Weeks speaks admiringly of the SJ's approach and departure angles and of its high ground clearance, and Rhino Ray points out that the SJ's light weight prevents it from sinking out of sight as soon as the soft stuff appears.

What was particularly noticeable from our mailbag was the high proportion of SJs which had introduced their owners or drivers to off-roading, and how those same people had since come to recognise the fun element in tooling around in mud and on grassy slopes. Typical was Miss K Barnes, who lives in Weymouth: "I find my little Suzuki able to keep up with all, even with a novice at the wheel. It seems to enjoy all that's thrown at it and to cope extremely well."

It isn't all accolades for the SJs off road, though. That light weight causes problems when tackling rocky ground, according to Nic Blanchet, and the only thing to do is to go more slowly or to exploit the vehicle's agility by driving around the obstacle. There also doesn't appear to be much doubt that the larger-engined SJ413 is more able than the 970cc SJ410.

You'll need 1st gear for steep ascents in an SJ410, which means the motor will be screaming by the time you reach the top; the SJ413 will often allow you to do the same in 2nd, without the urge to bite your nails or the need to wear ear defenders.

As a buyer, it makes sound sense to find out what sort of off-roading (if any) the vehicle you're looking at has done. If it's been used for reasonably gentle stuff, it should have survived intact. But if you think the vendor is a gung-ho off-roader, you'd be well advised to check for damage down below. There isn't much protection underneath a Suzuki, and diffs, axle casings, spring hangers and sump can all take a battering in the hands of an idiot (or, indeed, of someone who's been just plain unlucky).

What drops off or breaks?

Mostly, it's good news in this department. Many of our Suzuki-owning readers praised the robust-

ness of the mechanical elements, and some added that the little engines actually thrive on the high revs which they need to tackle steep slopes (in low gears) and motorways (in high gears).

"Nothing" was a frequent answer to the question of what had broken or fallen off the vehicle and, although a variety of problems had surfaced, there didn't seem to be a common thread which would point to a particular weakness.

D G Pettit, for example, was alone in experiencing a series of electrical failures, and Jim Lythgoe was the only one to pick out high oil consumption as a failing. However we did hear some cautionary tales. Several people underlined the need to use only lightweight (10W/40) engine oil, and those who were used to picking up pattern service items from their local branch of Halford's were none too impressed by the fact that Suzuki dealers seemed to have a monopoly on vital parts – and charged appropriately.

Undeniably, the SJs were not built to last as long as some of the bigger 4x4s, and their construction is relatively flimsy.

Many older examples suffer quite badly from very visible rust, which gets a hold in the body seams, around the door and bonnet hinges, and in the bumpers.

Well-used SJs acquire a whole repertoire of squeaks and rattles which weren't designed in. Sometimes, these come from items which have worked loose, so check whether you can eradicate the odd noises by judicious use of a screwdriver and a socket set, and then bargain hard. The problem might be more deep-seated, however. If you can't work out where the noises are coming from, are you sure you want to risk buying the vehicle?

If there's one weakness in the body, it's the soft top. The popper-type fasteners aren't all that robust, and several readers told us that it can take an unacceptable amount of time (and patience) to erect the soft top if the sunny day you started with suddenly turns to rain. Check the condition of both fasteners and top on a used example.

Summary

All the reports we received pointed to the same conclusions; the Suzuki SJs can be great fun as off-roaders, and great fun as town runabouts. But if you want an off-roader which will also transport you comfortably, quickly and quiety over long distances, then you really don't want an SJ.

Towing? Nobody even mentioned it as a possibility.

It's reassuring for intending buyers to know that SJs don't break, even though they are nowhere near as robustly constructed as some of the bigger off-roaders. Probably what saves them is the fact that they simply can't be driven into situations where they are likely to be overtaxed. An SJ will stop moving before it gets to the point where an over-enthusiastic driver will wreck something. SJs do rust, though, and that's something to watch out for on a used vehicle offered for sale.

Most of all, SJs are a hell of a lot of fun, and every one of our correspondents stressed this element in their make-up.

They make excellent off-roaders for people new to the sport: inexpensive, easy to drive, and much more capable than they look.

Owners seem readily able to forgive their many shortcomings, and it's not hard to see why the Rhino Club - set up by Suzuki (GB) for SJ owners - is so successful.

YOU'LL be lucky to get a tidy SJ, or one which hasn't covered an enormous mileage, for less than £3,000. Cheaper examples do exist, but rebuilding costs can easily exceed the difference between the cheap vehicle and a very much better one. Be careful.

If you want one of the bigger-engined SJ413 models, be prepared to spend a little more to get something respectable. About £4,000 should do it. Again, you will find cheaper ones, but make sure you know exactly what you're buying.

Bigger money buys more recent examples, with E-plates (1987/88) and later registrations. What you'll be buying here is SJs which haven't been used as much as cheaper ones, but there are worthwhile specification differences, too: you get five-speed boxes on post-1987 SJ410s and the revised suspension/tyre package on post-1988 models.

For comparison purposes, the current list prices for new vehicles are:

Santana Sport	£7,199
Santana Estate	£7,399

Also available (but not covered in this survey) are long-wheelbases and commercial variants of the SJ-series.

SUZUKI SAMURAI

How do you say "Jeep" in Japanese?

by RAY THURSBY
PHOTOS BY THE AUTHOR

True story: A few years ago, I took part in one of the better-known events organized by and for fanatical off-roaders. A variety of the host marque's products performed without a hitch, traversing terrain a sensible person wouldn't even consider walking over.

At run's end, however, among the specially prepared 4-bys that survived this test was…a bone-stock Suzuki Samurai, looking showroom-fresh after completing one of the roughest trials in organized off-roading.

So much, then, for the notion that a Samurai can't do much more than pick its way daintily across a beach while laden with surfboards and ice chests. It is, in fact, rugged enough to do just about everything and go just about anywhere one might reasonably expect, and a little more. And the price is certainly right.

At a buck below $6700, the entry-level 2wd Samurai JA is the cheapest way this side of used-car lots to get into the sport-ute market. An extra $1900 will get you into a 4wd JL, and there are numerous extra-cost goodies applicable to both that can make them more comfortable, utilitarian, or dressy, as you wish.

You should not be surprised to learn that minimal dollars buy you a pretty stark vehicle. Plain painted metal—be prepared to like white if you're looking at a JA, white, black, or aqua on a JL—abounds. Rubber floor mats, limited instrumentation (speedo, water temp and fuel-level gauges) and lots of empty switch locations are other reminders of a 4-digit sticker.

Be prepared to have a preference for *al fresco* motoring as well, unless you're willing to pay extra for a canvas top. And if you do go the cover-up route, be prepared to expend more than a little effort raising and lowering said lid, a bewildering maze of Velcro, zippers and snaps. Other near-vital options include radio and air conditioning, with chrome bumpers, mud flaps, and a combination altimeter/inclinometer waiting in the wings.

Mechanically, the Samurai duo share a sturdy ladder chassis, to which are bolted a welded shell, a live axle under each end, front-disc/rear-drum brakes, a 5-speed manual transmission, and a sohc 1.3-liter 4-cylinder engine. Opting for the JL adds a 2-speed transfer case, extra driveshaft and driven front axle with manually operated locking hubs.

With only 66 bhp underhood, the 2100-lb Samurai is not particularly speedy on the highway. Truth to tell, anything more than local driving means putting up with a noisy and none-too-smooth engine. The Samurai mill cries out—if you'll pardon the wordplay—for an increase in displacement, or at least some additional insulation between engine bay and passenger compartment.

Low power and minimal torque also demand that experienced off-road drivers alter their techniques. While some 4-bys can be coaxed over obstacles in low-low at idling speed, the Samurai engine needs to have its revs kept up to avoid getting bogged down. A neat trick, but possible with some practice.

That said, the minuscule motor does get the Samurai from point A to point B regardless of terrain, while delivering more than reasonable fuel economy. Our test truck matched the EPA's 28/29 mpg ratings in all-around use, using a little more fuel in 4wd driving, but a bit less than expected on the highway.

Around town, Samurai driver and passenger—there is no rear seat—will find the little Suzuki's ride to be merely firm; on the freeway, it can be downright rough, especially over damaged pavement or expansion strips.

Stiff suspension does not provide sports-car handling. The Samurai, short, narrow and high off the ground, rolls and understeers its way through turns, and gives its driver little feedback through the recirculating-ball steering box.

During off-road maneuvers none of these negative factors come into play. No vehicle will provide much comfort when crossing a rocky stream bed; the Samurai, like the Jeeps that inspired it, gets you through the rough stuff. Jounces and jolts are the rule rather than the exception here.

If the Samurai is unrefined, none too fast, not overly comfortable and Spartan to a fault, why does it continue to sell? Low price and reliability are major factors, of course, but the primary reason has to be that it is, warts and all, a fun machine: fun to look at, fun to be seen in, and capable of taking you to any number of out-of-the-way places in pursuit of pleasure.

SPECIFICATIONS

Base price, base model	$6699
Base price, premium model	$8599
Country of origin/assembly	Japan
Body/seats	2D/2
Layout	F/R, 4wd*
Wheelbase	79.9 in.
Track, f/r	51.2/51.6 in.
Length	135.0 in.
Width	60.6 in.
Height	64.6 in.
Minimum ground clearance	8.5 in.
Curb weight	2108 lb
Maximum towing capacity	1000 lb
Gross vehicle weight rating	2870 lb
Cargo capacity	33.9 cu ft
Fuel capacity	10.6 gal.
Fuel economy (EPA city/highway)	28/29 mpg
Base engine	1.3L 66-bhp sohc inline-4
Bore x stroke	74.0 x 75.5 mm
Displacement	1298 cc
Compression ratio	9.5:1
Horsepower, SAE net	66 bhp @ 6000 rpm
Torque	76 lb-ft @ 3500 rpm
Optional engine(s)	none
Transmission	5M
Final-drive ratio	3.73:1
Suspension, f/r	live/live
Brakes, f/r	disc/drum
Base tires	P205/70R-15
Steering type	recirculating ball
Turning circle	33.5 ft
Warranty, years/miles:	
Bumper-to-bumper	3/36,000
Powertrain	3/36,000
Rust-through	3/36,000

*indicates model described in specifications

When George and Adam Jenkins, familiar competitors at trials around the country, found their old Series IIA too heavy and lacking agility, a state–of–the–art lightweight trialler became the family project. Roger Crowhurst reports

I THOUGHT YOUNG Adam Jenkins' Suzuki SJ410 looked somewhat special when I first saw the 17-year-old tackling the slopes on a recent trial. No matter what he threw it at, the little suzuki always conquered, and in safety too. It seemed to have plenty of low-down power and was capable of controlled descents, even on the most treacherous downhill sections.

It looks good, too. It's surrounded by an exterior roll cage, is peppered with gismos inside and out, looks chunky and purposeful and is dedicated to the job for which it was conceived: trialling competitively and in safety in all types of terrain. The bright and multi-coloured paint job is quite excellent too, and is the result of a build-up of many coats carefully sprayed on by experts at dad George's own commercial vehicle body manufacturing plant, J S Keam.

From an early age, Adam — he passed his driving test in November — was taught to drive on the farm in an old Land Rover Series IIA by his father. As he became proficient he entered junior quad racing and was doing well, until the sport was banned in Britain after a series of highly publicised accidents.

Competitive motorsport is not new in the Jenkins family. Twenty-year-old brother Daniel was a keen Motocross rider, entering all the top competitions and achieving a high place in the British Motocross championships. His dozens of winner's cups and shields, on the bressamer above the inglenook fireplace in the family's 15th century beamed farmhouse, bear testament to his achievements. "Plus all the broken arms and legs doing it," quipped George.

Major surgery

Four years ago, Adam, who had been suffering poor health from Cystic Fibrosis (a mucus condition principally affecting the lungs and pancreas) and other ailments for some time, underwent major surgery with a heart and lung transplant. Before long he was up and at 'em again, and this time, because Adam had an unquenchable thirst for driving but was still years away from being able to take the test, it was off-roading that would occupy the Jenkinses' spare time.

George and Adam joined the All Wheel Drive Club and soon became familiar faces at trials venues all over the country. They were using dad's old Series IIA, taking it in turns to double-drive, but it wasn't long before Adam found handling the old girl's weight and lack of power-steering a problem with his now reduced strength.

What they needed was a lightweight, nimble

THE CONQUEROR

and capable off-roader that could be fitted with the most competitive equipment, yet not require a tremendous amount of muscle-power to be able to drive successfully. They found it in the form of a standard 1989 Suzuki SJ410 soft top at their local garage. So began what was to become an epic and total transformation.

They first decided to fit more aggressive tyres and change the off-sets on the standard eight-spoke steel wheels, by removing their centres, turning them inside out and re-welding. They then fitted 205x15 Trakker tyres, but decided after all that re-welded wheels might not be 100 per cent safe and they were junked. Mangels 7Jx15 chromed steel wheels and General Grabber 30x9.5x15 Mud Terrain tyres were the combination they finally decided on.

First problem: the new wheel/tyre combination wouldn't fit, as the vehicle body was too low. They fitted an Add-a-Leaf extra leaf spring all round which re-profiled the standard spring, bending it like a bow. This gave a 2-inch lift, but they needed more, so they added extra long spring shackles, which gave another inch.

Now they could get the wheels on, they gave it a brief road test. It was hopeless, because the original equipment shock absorbers were compressed to their limit. As they hit each bump, there was absolutely no movement underneath and the vehicle just jarred and rattled along. Extra-long travel Rugged Trail Nitro Cell shock absorbers solved the problem.

Meanwhile, Adam busied himself by researching magazines for information on building specials and getting hands-on experience by talking to other triallers and checking

top: On trial. Centre: The Mantec snorkel allows for serious wading. Above: The SJ410 sports 'Smitty Blit' 3in tube front bumper, extra tow points, auxiliary lamps and M6000 Warn winch

out their modifications. 'Rhino' Ray Edwards from Sussex was most helpful and before long had crafted them an external roll cage to go over the new MPM targa top.

Ray also fitted a 1,600cc standard Vitara carburettor engine (an early model as they give better low down torque), which George obtained at a good price from '4x4 Spares' in Swanley, and now they could sail past the original 410's maximum speed with ease. But they couldn't shut the bonnet because of the higher Vitara engine, so they swapped it with a higher profile secondhand SJ413 bonnet.

All that power was strangled by the tiny Suzuki exhaust system, so naturally they fitted a free-flow manifold and exhaust system, opening up the full potential of the conversion.

The vehicle was shaping up, but as father and son had only the basics of off-roading behind them and had never received any professional tuition, they decided to combine a holiday in Devon with a few days at David Bowyer's Off-Road Driving School, at Zeal Monochorum. They found the course most rewarding and in particular the emphasis on safety training, which was their main reason for attending.

Their next holiday took them to California, which they again combined with off-roading. While there they were invited to tour Warn's factory facility and headquarters, at Portland in Oregon, with International sales manager Tom Nelson.

"It was brilliant," said Adam. They had already fitted a Warn M3500 winch, but on return purchased a much tougher M6000. They let Adam drive a Ford Ranger V8 4x4 truck off-road during the visit, fitted with an XD9000 winch. They were soon to use the winch too, to self-recover from the amazingly deep washouts and ravines that their American hosts were directing them into. What did Adam think of that?

"Real off-roading — fantastic!" he said.

Rock lobster

Their American break, included a trip to Los Angeles and it was here that they met the American Suzuki Association, one of the USA's leading clubs, which took them on a once-in-a-lifetime off-road trip in Suzuki's in the San Bernadino mountains, 11,000 feet above sea level. They also supplied the Jenkinses with a very special set of 'Rock Lobster' gears for their SJ 410 transfer box. Once fitted, the low-ratio gearing is changed to 4.7:1 and Adam says steep downhills are no longer a problem. George reckons low ratio is now lower than that on his Land Rover Tdi.

Back home it was time to consider the advice of their new American friends. Those old axles would have to come off and be replaced by the beefier and wider 413 units. These also have the advantage of using stronger differentials. Next, they fitted a Lock Right automatic locking differential, for those awkward moments in the mud. That gearbox had to go, too, in favour of a five-speed 413 unit and they also fitted a 413 flywheel.

They brought back a tough Smitty-Bilt 3-inch tube front bumper from the States, fitted four Dixon Bate tow jaws, two Warn 100 watt driving lamps, four Dick Cepek 130 watt lamps on the front roof bar, a rear skid plate plus strengthening angle across the rear which George had made at work — "I think that's a potential weak point on the SJs," said George — and front and rear axle guards. They also moved the door-mounted spare wheel to a newly fabricated bracket in the interior, removing and discarding the bench seat and repainting the inside.

The almost totally re-built Suzuki was now looking the business. Could they do more? Indeed they could. A sports steering wheel, Cobra buckets (they fit straight in), four-point harnesses, a Terratrip 303 for Randonees, a fire extinguisher, 4ft high-lift jack, snatch block, tree strop, multiple shackles (doesn't it make your mouth water?), various ropes and a box full of off-roading goodies strapped to the floor. A Mantec snorkel kit was added for deep wading.

Surely they had equipped the vehicle with absolutely everything? No — they'd forgotten power steering, so it was off to the breaker's to source an Isuzu Trooper unit and pump. This required quite a lot of modification and careful welding, together with new braided hose.

As I turned to leave, the father and son trialling team of George and Adam Jenkins, I knew there was one question I shouldn't ask, but I felt I just had to. "Surely your vehicle is absolutely, totally, complete now. There just can't be anything left to add, can there?"

"Only the rear coil-spring conversion and disc brakes all round, next month," they said, almost in unison and with wide smiles of anticipation. Silly question, really …

Above top: Adam gets into the wet on trial. Centre: Extra angle was welded across the rear for safety and more tow points were fitted. Above: Adam finds the MPM targa top with separate tailgate and door ideal

Second thoughts

This month our real-world drivers dish the dirt with drink, drugs, under-age driving and ancient Belgian basket cases. There are times when we really worry about our readers

1980 Suzuki LJ80

Purchase mileage: 38,000
Current mileage: 44,000
Purchase price: £120
Purchase date: 1993
Owner: Jon-Paul Bowles
Occupation: GCSE student
Location: Barnham Broom, Norfolk

It's not often we hear from 14-year-old off-road drivers/part-time trainee car mechanics who have been driving 4x4s since they were eight years old. As we all know, you can't take to the road before your 17th birthday, so if a young car enthusiast wants to get behind the wheel before it's considered legal, then off-roading on private land is the ideal solution.

'JP', as he's known to family and friends, has been encouraged to drive along the way by his father Paul, who took his son with him to all his 4x4 meetings. JP would ride passenger and watch his father who has been driving a 1953 Chevy since 1976. 'I first bought JP a Fiat 126 because I wanted him to learn steering, clutch control and how to brake properly at an early age, and to get any recklessness out of his system before he takes to the open road' says Paul, who now considers his son to be a natural behind the wheel.

The Fiat's clutch and brake pedals were extended for JP and he would trundle around local farmland with dad in the passenger seat. Once his driving prowess improved, at the age of 11 JP was given a rear-wheel drive Skoda. 'It was a bit bigger than the Fiat and great off-road' enthuses Jon-Paul. But on one occasion he got a little too adventurous and too much oversteer found him in a muddy ditch.

Time for a change again as just driving about on the farm and through the fens wasn't terribly exciting for his son – dad decided to get a real off-roader. A friend who knew they were on the lookout for something found the LJ80 which was due for the scrapyard. It was in a bad state and the owner didn't want to fork out for a repair bill that was bigger than the Suzuki's value. Paul has always worked on his vehicles himself and decided it was time to get JP into the real world of owning a 4x4. A Lada Niva came up but it was rotten, literally rusting away. JP wanted a Land Rover, but it wasn't really practical for an 11-year-old, so the offer of the 800cc Suzuki at a

ridiculously small price was an opportunity too good to miss.

Although the LJ80's mechanicals were fine and the chassis was perfect, there was a lot of work to be done on it. With the help of his dad JP replaced the water pump, cylinder head, steering joints and brake system, which included new shoes and pipes. 'I'm a bit reckless when I drive in the fields' JP admits. For that reason they fitted a roll bar. The bodywork was in poor condition, with a fair amount of rust so, instead of replacing the panels, including the floorpan, the Bowles team cut out some metal sheets and welded them on to the bodywork and gave the whole thing a coat of dark green paint. The original soft-top was in tatters so Paul asked his friend Nick to make one especially and the replacement 'fits like a glove'.

All this work took about two years, and a large chunk of JP's earnings working as a cutlery polisher at the local golf club, to complete. But once all the hard work was over, the vastly-improved Suzuki was ready for use on and off the road. Paul drives it to 4x4 events at the Mid Norfolk Off Road Centre in Runhall and lets JP have a go in the mud in the lunch break. Paul thinks it's a shame that kids aren't allowed to take part in Trials events and, given the time and means, would like to run an event especially for younger competitors.

Despite JP being a natural at the driving game – 'his clutch control is terrific' – his dad still keeps a beady eye on what he's doing. Now that Bowles junior has grown to 5ft4in he can reach the pedals without any extensions, but he is a bit heavy with the

right foot and dad has to constantly tell him to make better use of it on the brake pedal. There is a system of signals that Paul uses to communicate with his son in the cab telling him when to put on the gas, to brake and whether to change up into second gear and back down again.

Jon-Paul is very impressed with the handling of the Suzuki. Although there's no power-steering he finds it light enough for his greenlaning and general playing about in the mud. 'It feels quite light and the front wheels are pretty thin so it's not heavy to haul about' he says. The 16in rims are tyred by an inherited pair of Lasas on the back and BFGoodrich on the front. The young aspiring Trialist thinks the traction is fine, but he would ideally like BFGs or Kelly Safaris all-round.

When it's on the road, the LJ80 manages about 28mpg – a figure most 4x4 owners would love to achieve, and its only real drawback, according to JP, is the lack of rear seats. He would like to drive his dad and his two brothers around with him. His brothers are both younger and drive a Panda 4x4 about under the ever-watchful eye of dad. They are perfectly happy with their lot at the moment. However, JP wants to progress again and the need for more space and 'grunt' means that he's looking for someone to swap a Lightweight for his LJ80. If he can't find one then the Suzuki will do fine, either that or a lot more cutlery polishing may buy him one when he's 17 and legally entitled to get himself a full driving licence.

'When I get my Lightweight I will put a V8 in it' he says enthusiastically. We wish him luck and look forward to another tale in a few years' time.

Likes: all-round off-road ability, handling, looks, suitability.
Dislikes: lack of seats.

SUZUKI SJ

The Suzuki SJ may be a lightweight 4x4, but it's a heavy-weight fashion accessory for the younger driver on a budget. And off-road, the nimble, slender SJ is a real giant-killer

May '82: all models, 1.0L 4x4 utility, 3dr, s/top, 45bhp, dual 4sp man, 2/4wd or 1.3L 64bhp 5sp man. 1.3L cat, 68bhp. Apr '90: LWB. Jul '93: discont.

Jan '87: SJ410, h/top and s/top. Jun '87: discont s/top. Mar '88: discont h/top.

Feb '87: SJ410 Santana/Sport, h/top, s/top opt. S/top with white hood. Both with body stripes, c/keyed bumpers, lamp guards, split/fold r/seats, carpets. Nov '88: 5sp std, h/top named 'Style', with removable roof, r/w/wipe. Apr '89: discont. Apr '90: discont both models.

Jan '85: SJ413 Samurai Sport 1.3L 68bhp cat eng, 5sp h/top only. Mar '88: with wider track, flared arches, c/keyed grille, body stripes, new gear ratios. Dec '89: s/top. Apr '90: LWB, fixed plastic h/top, r/w/wipe. Apr '92: unleaded, only in blue, 68bhp eng upgrade. Jul '93: discont LWB. Jan '94: discont s/top. Jan '95: discont all models.

Engine

The tiny 1.0L lean burn engine is an excellent little buzz box. Okay, it's not going to break any speed records, but it doesn't demand that much money is spent on it, just regular maintenance. Start the engine from cold and listen. A good engine will be silent, ticking over like a sewing machine. If you hear any noise, you can be sure it's been caused by negligence.

The engine runs fairly hot and the oil, when not changed, breaks down. This can lead to sludging, which blocks the restrictor (feeding the overhead camshaft). An engine with cam noise, more noticeable at high revs, should be avoided.

Many pattern oil filters contain an incorrectly set valve, which again stops the camshaft from getting the necessary oil feed. Suzuki dealers claim that, of the engines they've rebuilt, the cause can almost always be traced back to the oil and filter used. Check the exhaust for blue smoke when revving the engine. The bores can glaze up on high mileage engines.

The later 1.3L engine is an all-alloy affair with a hollow crank and camshaft – don't expect it to be as quiet as its predecessor. Some higher mileage vehicles (60,000+) may suffer from piston slap. This is noticeable only when the engine is started from cold.

Even with an engine this worn, you're unlikely to see blue smoke in the exhaust.

The carburettor is a complex affair. Many garages, unfamiliar with the unit, have difficulty tuning it to meet emission tests, so don't be surprised to find the present owner proudly displaying a new £600 carburettor.

The choke unit is notorious for sticking or being out of adjustment, and consequently the engine may prove difficult to start when hot and blow black smoke from the exhaust. In severe cases, you may get misfiring and flat spots when accelerating. But don't worry. A good tuner can usually sort out all the carb problems for under £100.

You'll notice that oil leaks haven't been mentioned. This is not to say that you shouldn't look for any, it's just that oil leaks are very rare in SJs.

Drivetrain

Oil leaks are also rarely to be found on either the early 4sp or later 5sp gearbox. A 4sp 'box should be tested for worn synchro-mesh, particularly in third gear, and the bearing on 5th gear (where applicable) can get a little noisy after 40-60,000 miles.

Neither 'box should cost more than £150 to overhaul. If the gear-change linkage feels a little sloppy, it's because the 25p securing pin at the base of the stick is worn.

Should you find excessive clutch pedal travel, the spot welds on the clutch lever arm may have broken. Again, the repair bill is light. Talking of clutches, make sure the rubber inspection bung is in place on the bellhousing, otherwise water and mud will soon get on the clutch – expensive.

The transfer box centre gasket, on post '87 vehicles, doesn't retain oil that well. Suzuki has now introduced a new gasket, with a different compound, to stem the flow. Transfer boxes should be checked in low range – they shouldn't jump out while accelerating or coasting.

UJs on 99% of propshafts are sealed for life. The few with grease nipples are known to seize, and should be renewed. As long as the splines have been greased, there should be little play. There shouldn't be any axle problems on a road-going vehicle. But an off-roader should be examined carefully for damage. Occasionally, you'll find dents in the diff housing.

Front driveshafts on the fully drum-braked early SJs may knock when cornering. This is usually due to worn splines caused by poor servicing, and may prove expensive to rectify. Gaiters on the front driveshafts should be checked for splits.

Chassis/suspension

You're unlikely to find anything bar the odd patch of surface rust when examining the chassis, but you should look out for accident damage to the rails. Pay particular attention to the front end. Be suspicious if the bonnet alignment is incorrect, showing that the wings have moved. Also look for signs of damage to crossmembers. Such damage, probably caused by off-road excursions, could lead to transmission vibration in some cases.

Check that the SJ sits squarely. It's rare to find a weak or broken spring, as the Suzuki is not an ideal towing vehicle and is rarely used as a hauler, but it's better to be safe than sorry. The dampers should be checked for leaks and corrosion, and examine their bushes for splits and wear.

Contrary to popular belief, the Suzuki's leaf-sprung suspension is not a bad design. Admittedly, the earlier vehicles have a slightly narrow track, but realistically you'd have to drive like a complete animal to put the SJ out of shape.

Steering/brakes

There's no PAS but, on such a light vehicle, you don't need it. The well-made steering box makes manoeuvring, even at low speeds, a delight. If you find an oil leak from the seal at the base of the box, it can only be repaired by a steering specialist. The seals are no longer available from Suzuki.

Over-light steering is probably caused by worn swivel seals. The swivels should be checked for corrosion and pitting, which can tear the seals. Any knocking on cornering may also be traced to the CV joints, housed within the swivels. If the SJ veers slightly, you should examine the steering damper for leaks or worn bushes. Any play in the box can be adjusted out, but first make sure the Pitman arm splines aren't worn.

Early vehicles were fitted with drum brakes. Those on the front tend to let in muck. Guards were later fitted to prevent this problem, and – where they're not fitted – it's worth investing in a set.

You'll occasionally come across an early SJ which pulls to one side on braking, even after the shoes have been adjusted. But, for some strange reason, you'll often find that swapping the drums from one side to the other will cure the balancing fault.

The later front disc brakes did much to cure the problems associated with the all-drum set-up. But the discs still need to be checked for rust and wear. A transmission handbrake was fitted to early vehicles, and this is easily damaged if applied while the vehicle's still in motion. A conventional handbrake was fitted to later SJs.

Body/interior

Unless your intended purchase has been badly neglected, corrosion problems are few. Pre-'87 vehicles are most susceptible to rust, due to their age. Examine the wheelarches, bottom of the doors and front valance. The windscreen surround on s/tops is also vulnerable. Bumpers will often appear spotty, but they're easily painted. Cheap replacements are available.

Soft-tops are easily damaged and water can literally flood in. It's worth lifting the carpets and mats to check for corrosion in the footwells. You'll be lucky to find an undamaged set of vinyl seats. They split in the middle of the backs and squabs, but replacement covers are cheap and easy to fit. Cloth seats can fray – the driver's is the most likely to be damaged. Again, replacement covers are relatively cheap. The front passenger seat is cleverly designed to slide forwards as well as tilt, a walk-through assembly which can wear in time. Grasp the passenger seat – if it moves, the frame must be repaired or renewed.

Examine the s/top, where fitted, for rotted stitching. Also examine the zips and Perspex windows.

You'll find that a s/top rarely survives for longer than five years. Fortunately, Suzuki offers a huge range of different colours at relatively inexpensive prices.

Verdict

The reliable 1.3L SJ is an ideal entry point to the 4x4 market. Though it's uncomfortable on longer journeys – and slow – you'll enjoy owning a baby Suzuki. If your budget is really very small, the 1.0L makes a great town runabout.

For: Popular and trendy, good for summer fun, inexpensive, handy off-road.

Against: Slow, noisy, harsh ride.

Prices

With such low prices, these vehicles tend to be bought by young owners eager for wind-in-the-hair motoring. Prices can vary according to the time of year – cheaper in winter, more expensive in summer.

Service history makes little difference on vehicles more than 5-7 years old.

Insurance

1988 1.3L Samurai (value £2200) £160 – Sun Alliance 01422 325816; £476 – Holdsure 01268 735522.

Prices quoted on 34-year-old, living in south-east with no convictions and FNCB. Subject to underwriters' criteria.

Performance figures

Eng/cyls	BHP	MPG	Fuel type
1.0L/4	45	31	4 star
1.3L /4	64-68	34	4 star/UL

Sample prices (approx for average mileage and good condition)

Model	87	88	89	90	91	92	93
SJ Santana	1900	2100	2400	–	–	–	–
SJ 413 Samurai	1900	2200	2500	2900	3300	3800	4500

V6 SUZUKI

Suzuki Lightning Conversion's Hot Samurai

BY PHIL HOWELL
PHOTOGRAPHY: PHIL HOWELL

No one disputes the trail ability of Suzuki Samurais anymore. The little 4x4s are small, light, and inexpensive — a perfect combination for the backcountry explorer on a budget. They also can be built to take on the most extreme trails, easily! Clubs such as Southern California's Gad Zuks! have proven that not only does the Samurai make a fantastic 4x4, but there are plenty of owners willing to push the four-wheeling envelope.

Alan Kempton, of Suzuki Lightning Conversions located in Tampa, Florida, has put together kits to convert your Suzuki into the ultimate backcountry or highway Samurai. These kits allow you to bolt a Chevrolet Vortec V-6 and a 200-4R automatic into your vehicle. No longer do you have to put up with a lack of horsepower in your Suzuki. In fact, your Samurai will go from the back of the pack to the front with the horsepower-to-weight ratio the V-6 affords.

We ran into Alan in Moab this year. He was driving this clean example of his work, which we thought you'd like to see. The Samurai started as a 1988 model that was completely stripped. Suzuki Lightning Conversions then installed a central port-injected, 200 horsepower 1996 Chevy Vortec V-6 and 200-4R automatic tranny. Alan claims that with the automatic, he doesn't need to install lower gears in the differentials or transfer case. We watched him on the trails and this seemed to be true, as he was able to go anywhere anyone else

did — with ease.

To clear the 33x14.00 15LT Super Swamper Boggers mounted on 15x8-inch Mangel alloy wheels, Alan used the stock springs in a spring over-configuration and Rancho RS 5000 shocks at each corner. This setup allows good trail performance and keeps the stock ride quality intact.

As we said in the beginning, the Samurai started out stripped. The interior was entirely redone by using Suzuki Lightning Conversion's interior kit, which includes leather seating and door panels, custom armrests, sound proofing and carpet. An SJ 410 folding windshield and removable half doors were installed.

A Smittybilt front bumper has a collection of KC lights bolted up, and a rack in the back holds two five-gallon gas cans. Dual batteries ensure there will be no starting problems in the outback and a 12-volt air pump keeps the tires inflated. The stunning custom paint was applied by Roy Tanner.

As you can see, Suzuki Lightning Conversions turns a stock Samurai into quite a 4x4. What's really amazing is the price — $5000.00 if you supply the vehicle, or $9000.00 if they do. Alan's unit is worth a bit more with all the extras, but he still claims a value of only $13,500.00! You can reach Alan at (800) 839-6150.